The

Road to Armageddon

The Life and Letters of
Lieutenant-Colonel Henry Cadogan, RWF
(1868–1914)

Henry Cadogan

Edited by
Colonel Henry Cadogan, RWF

bridge
books

The Road to Armageddon,
the Life and Letters of Lieutenant-Colonel Henry Cadogan, RWF, 1868–1914
First published in Wales in 2009
by
BRIDGE BOOKS
61 Park Avenue
Wrexham
LL12 7AW

A CIP entry for this book is available from the British Library

ISBN 978-1-84494-056-1

www.bridgebooks.co.uk

Printed and bound
by
Gutenberg Press Ltd
Malta

To the memory of

those indomitable officers and men of the
1st Battalion, Royal Welsh Fusiliers,
who lost their lives in the First Battle of Ypres, October 1914.

But also to Harry, Oliver and Matilda, and Max, Felix and Ned,
in the fervent hope that they will be spared a daunting
challenge of the kind faced by their great-great-grandfather.

Note: The Royal Welch Fusiliers used the archaic spelling 'Welch' in their regimental title until the late nineteenth century when it was changed to 'Welsh'. The official title reverted to the archaic spelling in the early 1920s. For this reason the regiment is shown as using the modern spelling for the period covered by this book, but the archaic spelling in references to people and events post 1920.

Contents

Maps

Acknowledgements

While using primary sources as far as possible, in ediiting these letters I have used the excellent books and articles listed in the Bibliography to set the letters in their historical context.

I am particularly grateful for the co-operation of Lieutenant-Colonel Peter Crocker and Mr Brian Owen, the previous and current curators of the Royal Welch Fusiliers Museum at Caernarfon, and to Mrs Anne Pedley, the Assistant Curator. Lieutenant-Colonel Richard Sinnett, the biographical sage of the Regiment, unfailingly and speedily answered my frequent queries.

I received great help from the staff of the National Archives at Kew, the British Library at Colindale, the Photographic Department of the Imperial War Museum, from Mr David Taylor of the National Maritime Museum, and from Mr Andrew Orgill, Senior Librarian at RMA Sandhurst. Also from the staff of the Liddell Hart Centre of King's College, London, and from Mr Richard Reeves, the Deputy Librarian of the New Forest Museum at Lyndhurst. Mr Michael Crumplin, FRCS, commented on medical matters. Major Edward Crofton, Regimental Adjutant Coldstream Guards, kindly introduced me to the staff of the respective Regimental Headquarters Grenadier and Scots Guards, who allowed me to browse through their records of 1914.

Initially, Professor Richard Holmes gave me a steer, the late Mr Roy Ramsbottom lent me many of his books, and I was encouraged both by Mr Roy Jackman, the Lyndhurst historian, and enthusiastically by Mr Franky Bostyn, curator of the Memorial Museum, Passchendaele 1917, at Zonnebeke, Belgium.

Mr John Beaumont read my manuscript at various stages and gave his very useful (and critical!) comments. Mr John Krijnen and Mr John Tyler have very generously allowed me to access their researched and edited copies of the 1914 Star Roll and RWF Casualty List from which it has been possible to produce what is hopefully a definitive list of the officers and men of the RWF who served in Belgium during October 1914.

I wish to thank, most sincerely, Colonel Philip Eyton-Jones for the enormous trouble he has taken to draw the accurate and clear maps. The map of the Black Mountain Expedition is based on one found by my late cousin, Captain Patrick Mackintosh-Grant, whose father was killed on the North-West Frontier while commanding the Guides. My thanks are due also to the many friends and regimental colleagues, particularly the late Sir Kyffin Williams, who have given me useful information and allowed me to publish family photographs. I am indebted to Mrs David Howard, Colonel Henry Platt's great great grand-daughter, for permission to print his photograph. I would like to thank Mr Alister Williams, my publisher, who has most carefully studied the various rolls and sources in order to produce as accurately as possible a roll of the 1st Battalion in October 1914. It has been a pleasure to work with him. Finally, I would particularly like to thank my wife, Daphne, for her constant support and encouragement over the four years it has taken to produce the book.

Henry Cadogan, 2009

The Cadogan Family Tree

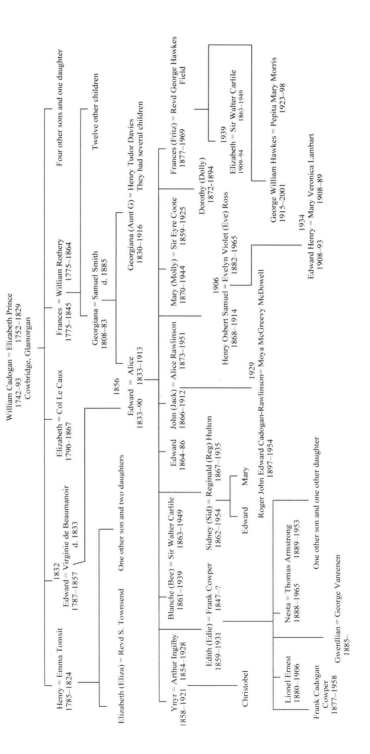

The Descendants of H. O. S. Cadogan

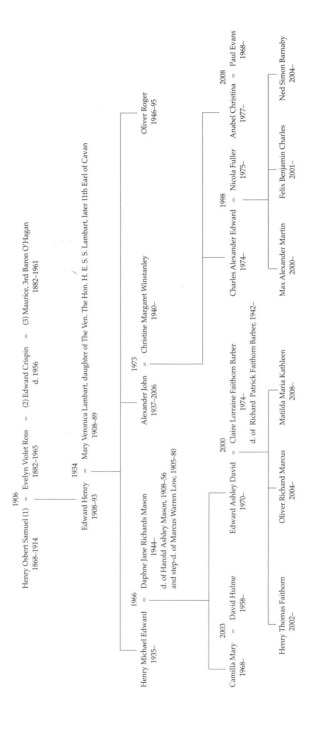

The Cadogan Family

Short biographical details of the members of the Cadogan family to whom most of the letters were addressed.

REVD EDWARD CADOGAN: Hal's father. Born 1833, the son of Colonel Edward Cadogan and his wife, Virginie de Beaumanoir. He spent part of his childhood in Paris. Educated at Harrow and Christ Church, Oxford (president of the Christchurch Boat Club). Ordained 1856. Married Alice Smith, his first cousin once removed. Curate at Stevenage. Vicar of Walton d'Eiville, Warwickshire. Diocesan Inspector of Schools. Rector of Wicken, Northamptonshire, 1873. Died 1890.

MRS ALICE CADOGAN (NÉE SMITH): Hal's mother and main correspondent. Born 1833. Died 1913.

YNYR INGLEBY (NÉE CADOGAN): Hal's eldest sister. She was born in 1858 and married Arthur Ingleby. They lived at Lawkland Hall near Settle, Yorkshire (now part of Lancashire). Mother of Christobel. She died in 1921.

Revd Edward Cadogan
Painting by Chevalier
Desanges.

Henry Osbert Samuel
Cadogan (Hal).

Alice, Mrs Edward Cadogan
Painting by Chevalier
Desanges.

Constance Alice Ynyr

Edith Eliza (Edie)

Blanche Anne (Bee)

Sidney Alice

Edward Mordaunt

John Herbert (Jack)

Alice Dorothea (Dolly)

Evelyn Mary (Molly)

Frances Georgina
(Fritz or Freedom)

EDITH COWPER (NÉE CADOGAN):, Hal's second eldest sister, known as Edie. Born in 1859, she married Frank Cowper but the marriage eventually broke up. Lived at Lisle Court, Isle of Wight. Mother of Frank, Lionel, Gladys, Gwenllian, Nesta, and three other children.

BLANCHE CARLILE (NÉE CADOGAN): Hal's third sister, known as Bee. Born in 1861, she married Walter Carlile (probably Hal's greatest friend). He served as member of parliament for North Buckinghamshire (1895–1906) and was created a baronet in 1928. They lived at Gayhurst House, a large Elizabethan mansion in Buckinghamshire. She died in 1939.

SIDNEY HULTON (NÉE CADOGAN): Hal's fourth sister, known as Sid. Born in 1862, she married Reginald Hulton and they travelled widely before settling down at Bryn-y-Frid, Tenby where she died in 1954.

EDWARD CADOGAN: Hal's eldest brother. Born in 1864, he died in 1886, from the effects of a boyhood attack of rheumatic fever.

JOHN CADOGAN: Hal's brother, John, known as Jack. Born in 1866, he married Alice Rawlinson. They lived at Duddon Hall, Cumberland. He lost the sight of an eye while training for the Royal Navy and never really settled down thereafter. He died in 1912 in Canada.

HENRY OSBERT SAMUEL CADOGAN: Known as Hal. The subject of this biography. Born 1868, killed in action, Belgium, 1914.

MARY COOTE (NÉE CADOGAN): Hal's sister, known as Molly. Born in 1870, she and Hal were close. She married Sir Eyre Coote (1857–1925) of West Park, Salisbury, a descendant of General Sir Eyre Coote (1726–83). They had no children. She presented her harp to the Royal Welsh Fusiliers in memory of Hal. She died in 1944.

DOROTHY CADOGAN: Hal's sister, known as Dolly. Tragically she drowned in February 1894 while sailing on the River Ouse with Walter Carlile.

FRANCES FIELD (NÉE CADOGAN): Hal's youngest sister, known sometimes as 'Freedom' or 'Fritz'. Born in 1877, she married the Revd George Field and lived at The Rectory, Milton Keynes, then in deepest Buckinghamshire countryside. They had two children, Elizabeth and George. She died in 1969.

Lieutenant-Colonel H. O. S. Cadogan, Dublin, 1912

Introduction

In an old tin campaigning box over 200 letters written by my grandfather, Henry Osbert Samuel Cadogan, lay in their envelopes scarcely opened for over one hundred years. It is only now that I have had time to study them in detail. Being the last person alive to remember many of those in the family and in the Regiment who are mentioned in this saga, including Eve, his widow, who died only in 1965, I thought I should waste no time. Many of the letters are of interest only to the family, but edited,[1] they weave the story of his career from school, through his time with the 4th (Militia) Battalion, Royal Welsh Fusiliers, in 1886 and 1887, his regular commission in 1888, until the death of his mother in 1913. By that date he was commanding the 1st Battalion and there is plenty of material from many sources to complete his story until his death on 30 October 1914 during the First Battle of Ypres. So fierce had been the battle and so few the survivors that, although my grandmother, strongly supported by the family, did her utmost to discover his fate, it was not until May 1915 that his death was confirmed. Fortunately she, and Mary, Hal's younger sister, kept many of the letters and newspaper cuttings of that terrible year. I have been privileged to have got to know my grandfather through his letters far better than even my father did; he, after all, was only six in 1914 when Hal was killed. My grandmother always referred to him as 'Hal', and so let him remain.

Most of the letters were written to his father, Edward, or to his mother, Alice, of whom he was the seventh child. But others were written to one of his nine siblings, or to one of the two brothers-in-law to whom he was closest; Walter Carlile (married to his third sister Blanche) or Reginald Hulton (married to his fourth sister, Sidney). It is sad that his father died in 1890, only two years after Hal was commissioned, because the letters he wrote to him contained more news of a military nature and were of greater general interest than those written to his mother. His mother did not keep Hal's letters after close family deaths. For that reason and because of his youthful idleness there are some gaps in the story.

Hal served much of his career in India and, because Victorian letters were franked at their delivery post office, it is easy to see that a letter from India never took more than three weeks to reach home – even when he was on active service with the Black Mountain Expedition, north of Nowshera on the river Indus in 1891. Carried by *dongah* (a small cart pulled by relays of galloping ponies) to the nearest railway, a letter was then taken to Bombay. From there, it travelled to Brindisi in southern Italy by ship, taking about two weeks via the Suez Canal. It then went by rail and cross-Channel ferry to England. Only once does Hal mention an interruption, which was when the monsoon washed away the road at the Kalsi bridge, south of Chakrata, in August 1903. Even then, mail got through by elephant.

In order that readers from outside of the family are not diverted from the central story I have pruned many of the family references. So now let a brief introduction to the family set the scene.

The Cadogan Family

The Cadogans are descended in male line from Cuhelyn, Prince of Fferlys and his son Elystan Glodrydd, a chieftain of Radnorshire who founded the fifth of the royal Tribes of Wales about the turn of the second millennium. The modern family line springs from Llewelyn, who was killed in 1099 in a border feud. Indeed, the male members of the family would all have been fighting men, defending their lands. This supposition is supported by a translation of the Celtic 'Cadwgan' into 'Battle-Keenness'. 'Cadwgan' was used as a baptismal name until the late eighteenth century, when it became anglicised. The family's remaining lands which lay '… between the upper waters of the Wye and the Severn' were lost by the end of the twelfth century, but would today lie in the county of Powys.

During a visit to Wales in 1187 the archbishop of Canterbury raised some 3,000 well-armed men towards a crusade. Among them was Maelgwm, Hal's ancestor, and his cousin, Einion; although whether they ever reached the Holy Land is not known.

There is little of interest to record in the following three hundred years. From time to time tombstones record the deaths in the area between the Llantony valley and Usk of '… Cadogan Gent'; many minor Welsh squires described themselves as such in that period. Then in 1548, Cadwgan ap William appears, living with his wife Catherine and their three sons, at Trostre Fach in Monmouthshire. Trostre passed from eldest son to eldest son until it was sold in 1670.

At the end of the sixteenth century, Henry, a younger son, needed a good dowry and this he achieved by marrying Catherine, great neice of Sir Thomas Stradling of St Donat's Castle in Glamorgan. Henry and Catherine had a son, William, born in Cardiff in 1600. After a period as a soldier of fortune William went to Ireland in 1633 as secretary to Thomas Wentworth, the ill-fated earl of Strafford, who had been appointed Lord Deputy by King Charles I. His great grandson, William, became the great Duke of Marlborough's chief of staff, quartermaster general, head of intelligence, and successor. He was created the first Earl Cadogan in 1718. Having only two daughters, he was succeeded as baron by his brother, and it was he who married the daughter of Sir Hans Sloane, a wealthy and fashionable Irish physician who was also lord of the manor of Chelsea, thereby establishing the fortune of that side of the family. Their son, Charles, was created Earl Cadogan of the new creation.

By the mid-eighteenth century, Hal's forbears were living in Cowbridge in the Vale of Glamorgan, where his great-grandparents lie with some other members of the family in the vault of Holy Cross Church. Hal's grandfather, Edward, born in Cowbridge in 1787, was very probably educated at Cowbridge Grammar School, before joining the East India Company. He became a lieutenant-colonel, and served as acting resident in Travancore and Cochin in the 1820s. In 1832, he married Virginie de Beaumanoir, the daughter of the governor of the nearby French colony of Pondicherry.

Virginie was the descendant of a celebrated French warrior. On 27 March 1351, during the Hundred Years War, there took place the *Combat des Trentes* between the French garrison of Josselin and the nearby English garrison of Ploémel.

> [It] became chivalry's finest military expression in contemporary eyes… It began with a challenge to single combat issued by Jean de Beaumanoir, a noble Breton on the French side, to his opponent, Bramborough. When their partisans clamoured to join in, a combat of thirty on each side was agreed upon. Terms were arranged, the site chosen, and after participants heard mass and exchanged courtesies, the fight commenced. With swords, bear-spears, daggers, and axes, they fought savagely until four on the French side and two on the English were slain and a recess was called. Bleeding and exhausted, Beaumanoir called for a drink, eliciting the era's most memorable reply: 'Drink thy blood, Beaumanoir, and thy thirst will pass!' Resuming, the combatants fought until the French side prevailed and every one of the survivors on either side was wounded. Bramborough and eight of his party were killed, the rest taken prisoner and held for ransom …

Les Trentes were 'celebrated in verse, painting, tapestry and in a memorial stone erected on the site [of the battle].[2] More than twenty years later Froissart[3] noticed a scarred survivor at the table of Charles V, where he was honored above all others. He told the … chronicler that he owed his great favour with the King to his having been one of the Thirty.'[4] In Brittany *Les Trentes* are still considered local heroes and the main street in Josselin is named after them.

Sadly, Edward and Virginie separated within eighteen months and Edward left both the Company and India, returning to England with his infant son, another Edward, who survived the journey home in the care of a French nurse.

Edward junior spent part of his childhood in Paris with his aunt Elizabeth, who was married to Colonel Le Caux, who had been ADC to Marshal Murat, and survived the retreat from Moscow in 1812. Edward then went to Harrow, followed by Christ Church, Oxford. There he became president of the Christchurch Boat Club and won the university pairs in three consecutive years. He won the Goblets [coxed pairs] at Henley in 1854, but was beaten in the final the following year. In 1856, aged twenty-three, he was ordained, and married Alice Smith, his first cousin, once removed, with whom he had spent part of his childhood. After four years as a curate at Stevenage, he was presented with the living of Walton d'Eiville in Warwickshire, where Hal was born in 1868. Edward also became the diocesan inspector of schools. The family moved to Wicken, in Northamptonshire in 1873 and it was there that Hal was brought up.

Wicken Rectory where Hal spent most of his childhood.

Hal's Early Life

By the 1860s, the developments of the Industrial Revolution would have had little effect on the household of a Victorian country clergyman. It is true that communications were much improved, with the country covered by a network of railways, and postage was cheap and efficient, but village life revolved around the seasons, no doubt the pub, and particularly the church. On his stipend, a vicar was able to bring up a large family in a comfortable vicarage, with indoor and outdoor servants. Hunting, accepted as a very proper occupation, took precedence over all but the most vital activities and involved much of the country population, for horses were an essential part of rural life. Edward and Alice, however, did not have money to waste, and Edward kept a tight control on the family budget. They were obviously excellent and very fortunate parents, for all their ten children survived to adulthood. They were friends of the local landed gentry, and their children were included in the parties of their landowning neighbours.

Born into this houseful of cheerful siblings,

Hal as a young child.

Revd Edward Cadogan, Hal's father.

Alice Cadogan, Hal's mother.

with servants, horses and dogs, Hal plainly revelled in the secure life of a happy family. He was a keen fisherman, rode, was an excellent shot (with both shotgun and rifle) and excelled at all games. As was customary, his sisters were all educated at home by governesses, sometimes German or French, while the boys boarded from the age of nine.

Hal's first school was at Stony Stratford, only some five miles from Wicken, and close to Milton Keynes (which was then a hamlet), where he joined his two older brothers, Edward and John. Judging by his letters, he enjoyed school although he appears to have been no more than an average scholar. His headmaster was W. F. Short (with whom his father had won the Goblets at Henley whilst at university) who reported that Hal at the age of ten, '… was fairly diligent, and bore a thoroughly good character as an honourable and gentlemanly boy'.

For boys of his background in the late Victorian era, career opportunities were limited. 'Trade' was not normally an option, but the church, law and certainly the armed forces were acceptable – ten per cent of army officers at that time were sons of the clergy. Hal seems to have decided on a military career at an early age for by 1882, when aged fourteen, he had followed his two brothers to the Royal Academy in Gosport. His eldest brother, Edward, went on to his father's old college at Oxford, where a promising rowing career, at least, was cut short by his early death; his heart had been weakened by a childhood illness and he died at Wicken in 1886. John's plan to join the Navy was ruined when he lost an eye in an accident. Thereafter he, too, spent some time at Christ Church, after which he seems never to have really settled into a career.

NOTES

1. The bulk of the surviving correspondence from Hal Cadogan was with his mother, and consequently only those written to other members of the family or friends carry the introductary line 'Dear …' in order to identify the individual concerned. All insignificant family and personal references, relating to minor illnesses or visits, have been deleted from the letters.

2. Known today as *La Pyramide (Obélisque des Trentes)*.

3. Jehan (John) Froissart wrote his *Chronicles* between 1356 and 1400. They are regarded as one of the most significant works of late medieval French literature, and are thought to have been brought to England by Sir John Arundell after the battle of Agincourt in 1415.

4. *A Distant Mirror*, Barbara W. Touchman; Macmillan 1979 p.131

Chapter 1

Gone for a Soldier
September 1883–September 1888

Hal's letters from The Royal Academy in Gosport are full of his sporting activities: football, cricket, and rugby. He became a precocious schoolboy rugby player, winning his 1st XV Colours at the age of fifteen. He was invited to play for Hampshire Schools at Blackheath but, due to a school muddle, was unable to take up the offer.

In January 1883 he wrote to his mother asking when the 'tennis ground' at home will be completed. Thereafter he seems to have written fairly regularly.

Royal Academy, Gosport, 17 September 1883

Dear Father,

I am preparing to go up for the test[1] at any time when I may be wanted to go, I have been moved up in nearly all my classes, and I have begun trigonometry. I suppose you have heard from Ted whether he has got any rabbit shooting yet in Scotland.

I am in the 1st XV now and so may have the cap put down in the bill and pay you by degrees. Only you see if I pay it all down out of my money it makes such a hole in it directly.

Old Burney[2] was very nice about Ted. He asked me whether he was going to see Doctor Andrew Clarke because he said he is a great friend of his.

There are several Chinese fellows here they are such nice fellows. When you write tell me where cousin Charlie[3] is now and I will ask them whether they know him or not. One of these is a captain in the Chinese Army and the others are all in the navy with long

Hal c.1884

pigtails (cues as they call them). They don't think there will be war with China and France, they say they think it will be all settled soon.

I suppose Mother and all the others are gone to the seaside give my love to anyone who is at home.

As I am going up for Woolwich I must go up for the Sandhurst test first as other fellows do, so that I can get off some of the subjects.

I must say good bye now I am writing under difficulties as everyone is shouting in the room.

> Royal Academy, Gosport, 12 November 1883

Thanks so much for your last letter. I ought to have written before but then I felt on Friday as if I could give myself a holiday after working all the week and playing a very hard game of football at the end of it.

You needn't think that because I talk so much about football that I don't work but I promise you I do, only one cannot talk about work and there is nothing to talk about so I talk about it.

We have won two more matches lately, [against] Marlborough and the Grammar School [Portsmouth].

I suppose that Ted is at home now – he will be very glad to hear that we beat the latter by three goals and six tries.

I am getting on at French and German. I do much better than I could before I came up into this Sandhurst class. I am doing trigonometry now that I am going up for Woolwich. It is dreadful stuff to pick up. I have got up to the sixth book of Euclid. Latin is my weak point I am afraid.

We were all photographed in the teams the other day. I have got my 1st XV photo, they are very good I think, better than last year.

Gosport Royal Academy 1st XV. Hal is seated on the far left, wearing his rugby 'Cap'.

We had a paper chase about two days ago I forgot to tell you, about six of us caught the hares up and they hid in a bush and we went on and lost them. Wasn't it a pity.

We had fireworks on the fifth of November and nearly all the school gave sixpence each and the masters gave some and we got some very good ones for it. The wet did not hurt us as we always have them in a sort of high roofed place we call the drilling yard. It is really a rackets court. They were really rather fine.

I am going on with drawing as usual but of course I don't do so much as I devote half my time to geometry which I need first of all.

Like many young men at that time, Hal failed the exam for entry both to Woolwich and Sandhurst. He may have passed 'The Preliminary', the first stage, which tested elementary skills, but the second, called 'The Further', came a year later and was a comprehensive survey of a candidate's knowledge and academic skills. It lasted for six hours a day for eight days.

Gosport, 16 July 1884

How dreadful it is about poor old John's eye. I am so sad about it. I can't bring myself to realise it. It seems to me that we have all been so happy all our lives that it can't last forever. When I come up for the exam will you let me go down to the *Worcester*[5] to see the dear old chap?

Bent has just come back he has had his eye cut open and a silver tube put down from it to his nose and this is in still. He has to have this taken out and cleaned every now and then. If you will let me go down and see him the day after the exams it might bring up his spirits a little. I keep thinking as I write this that I must be under some delusion, I have read your letter through about a dozen times.

Give my love to dear Jack, do let me go down and see Jack if possible the day after my exams that is the 11th. I shall feel quite wild until I have seen him.

I am so glad you did not keep this back till after the exams as I should have felt it all over again. I will do my best to pass.

 Please excuse my writing but I feel in no mood for writing tonight. I am first going to write to old Bee. She wrote to me in a very maternal way and I wondered at the style of it. I can see why now.

Don't show Aunt Georgie[6] this letter please. I know your way of handing round letters and Aunt Georgie would criticise this which has no more sense in it than a snail. How wretched this must be for poor little Father.

I will write to him and John soon only I don't feel like it now and if I wrote a letter like this I don't know what he would say. A thousand kisses and love to Jack.

As Sandhurst was no longer an option, Hal took the normal alternative route for aspiring regular military officers at that time, by joining the Militia and he became a second-lieutenant in the 4th (Militia) Battalion Royal Welsh Fusiliers, with whom he trained on their summer camp at Caernarfon.

4 Bn RWF, Carnarvon, 8 May 1886

Thanks so much for your letters which I ought to have answered long ago. I could not get my ticket at the government price, it turned out to be a mistake, not sending it, on the part of the Quartermaster.

Carnarvon is a lovely place as far as the country goes, but it is awfully dull. The officers here are an awfully nice set all through from the Colonel downward.

There were some theatricals given last night in the Guildhall here, by the adjutant and some friends of his, in aid of the lifeboat fund. They were wonderfully good. Afterwards we had a small dance for the people who were at the theatricals. It was very jolly.

I am going to Penrhyn tomorrow with young Hogg and Mostyn to spend the day. I am afraid my expenses will be more than father thinks. You see all these extras mount up, as last night [the entrance was] 10/6 each. I think we are going to have a steam launch at a about £50 between twenty four of us then I think there will be a ball at the end of the training at about £3.10 each and it is almost impossible to keep out of these things as everyone joins in, but of course I shall take care.

Give my love to everyone. I will write whenever I can, but directly one sits down to write somebody comes and says come out. I have two letters to you in the last two days half finished. Today most of the fellows are out.

During this summer training he was introduced to Colonel the Hon Savage Mostyn, then commanding 23rd Regimental District in Wrexham. He had lately completed his tour as the Commanding Officer of 1st Battalion, Royal Welsh Fusiliers.

At the end of the Battalion's training, his Commanding Officer, Lieutenant-Colonel Platt[7] wrote a glowing letter to Hal's father:

7 July 1886

I am pleased to think that your son will be with us one more training. He will be a loss to me. My opinion of him is most favourable. He will do well anywhere and he is a credit to his family and himself.

He recommended me an exceedingly nice and gentlemanly young man to the Regiment and I shall be glad if he can find me another as good.

I need not tell you that young men are impressionable and are apt to fall into the habits of those they associate with.

Colonel Henry Platt of Gorddinnog, CO 4th Bn Royal Welsh Fusiliers.

On of the earliest surviving letters written by Hal whilst serving with the 4th Bn, RWF, Caernarfon, 20 June 1887.

Therefore if he goes to a coach it is necessary to be careful in the choice of one.[8]

Hal decided to carry out a second year's summer training before going to a coach.

> 4th Bn, RWF, Carnarvon, 10 June 1887

My dear Father,

I must write and tell you how we are getting on. We got here all safely last Monday, and are camped up here above Carnarvon.[9] The first day or two we had were very wet but now the sun is so hot you would hardly know me for being so brown.

I have been let off parade this afternoon as I had to get up at 5 this morning to take my company to the rifle range[10] about 3 1/2 miles off and only got back at two. The range is on the shingley beach so you can imagine the heat of the sun.

We are going to have a field day here on the Jubilee Day and a feu-de-joie and some sports for the men.

I am sorry to say I have this bill from Hobson for the covert coat and the uniform, he takes off 15p.c..

One or two fellows who were here last year have not come out I am sorry to say but we have two new subs.

I am on the Sports Committee so I am to write out a programme.

I hope you are going to come up here. By the way will you ask them to send on the parcel it is a pair of trousers which I sent to be mended.

I am going to try and get some trout fishing up here. Young Hogg is going to get leave to fish at Penrhyn and I shall go with him. It will be rather good sport.

> 4th Bn RWF, Carnarvon, 20 June 1887

My dear Father,

I am very sorry not to have written before, but you have no idea of the difficulties of writing. I have been staying with the Colonel at Gorddinog since Saturday and your telegram was sent to me by post so I did not answer.

Tomorrow is our Jubilee Day and we are going to have a sort of sham fight, with the Naval Reserve, RWF Volunteers, and the Volunteer Artillery.

In the afternoon we are going to give sports to the men and this is one reason I have not written as there is so much to be done as I am on the Committee.

Everything is Jubilee[11] now up here. There is going to be a large bonfire on Snowdon, and Grt Ormes Head and the harbours are all going to be lighted up with coloured lights.

I suppose you won't be going up to London to see the procession you will have too much to do at Wicken.

We are going to two balls on this Wednesday and Thursday in Anglesea, a Mrs Massey[11] and the Anglesea Militia.

The weather here is something shocking, some of the men's faces are so much swollen with the sun that they cannot see out of their eyes and many of them are in the hospital. The only way to get cool is to get into the water.

All the hurdles and things have just been brought up so I must get out and see after their erection. I won't forget to write at the first occasion I have time.

From April 1887 Hal had attended a crammer in Camberley, run by Lieutenant-Colonel T. G. R. Mallock, and passed the Militia Comprehensive Exam held in March 1888, scoring 1,308 marks, about half-way down the list. In the *London Gazette* of 8 May 1888, the notice appeared: 'RWF – Lieut H. O. S. Cadogan from the 4th Bn to be second lieutenant in succession to Lieut A. P. G. Gough,[13] seconded.' He wrote joyfully to his mother:

> Limmers Hotel, George Street, Hanover Square, W. [10] May 1888
> I am coming home by the 5 train tomorrow (Thursday) could I be met, if not I will get over and leave luggage.
>
> I have seen Blanche today. You see I have got the *1st Batt RWF* [his emphasis]. I knew it the day before it came out in the papers. There were a lot of other fellows with their names down for it who passed above me and they are making a row about my getting in, but the interest, and also my belonging to the 4th Batt of the same Regt did it.
>
> I don't suppose I shall go to India until October.

The reference to interest is an excellent example of the practice at that period. It is described by Richard Holmes as '... that rich mixture of patronage, influence, family and regimental connection, the comradeship of campaign and arms of service, debts for past favours and sureties for future help ...'[14] It was being progressively restricted in Britain. In Hal's case, no doubt he was given a good chit from his time under Colonel Platt. He was probably also supported by Colonel Mostyn, whose opinion would have carried weight as a recent Commanding Officer of the 1st Battalion. Perhaps Sir Charles Mordaunt, his father's old friend from Oxford, also helped with a character reference. He had become a prominent QC and owned the living at Wicken.

Since 1881 all infantry regiments had two regular battalions, one based abroad and the other in Great Britain or Ireland. The home-service battalion was given the responsibility of keeping the overseas one up to strength. So, in 1888, in the case of the Royal Welsh Fusiliers, after training at the Regimental Depot at Wrexham, men were sent to the 2nd Battalion, then based in Galway in Ireland. Periodically, drafts would be sent to join the 1st Battalion, at that time stationed at Lucknow in India.

[2 RWF], Galway, 9 June 1888

My dear Father,

I got over here all right this morning. We had a capital passage over. I slept most of the time, the journey from Dublin here is about the worst of the lot, that is awful, about 4 hours through the most bleak uninteresting country. When I arrived here this morning I was simply besieged by car men wanting to drive me up. Lloyd and another fellow came up in the same train and boat as far as Dublin but they then went to the Curragh to their regiments. They stuck us for extra luggage wherever we went.

There are not many fellows here – only about nine and the barracks are foul, they have been condemned by government I believe. Their name is the 'Shambles' but you need not put it on your letters – only Galway.

[Grant-]Thorold keeps a horse here and he and several of the others have gone for a ride this afternoon.

I must take a little stroll around and see this place. Today the town is full of Irish peasants, hundreds of them, wearing red petticoats, shawls over their heads and no shoes or stockings on their feet. I suppose it is market day.

We had a capital dance at the Mallocks.

I got through the Levée all right.[15]

Galway, 9 June 1888

I got here as you will have heard without any adventure, and now that I am here I must tell you about everything.

The Band has been playing this morning for half and hour before Church. I did not have to attend church parade this morning but went to church and such a service too. It was a very nice church in size and construction but such a sermon and such a curate to read the lessons.

The fellows are very nice indeed. I like Ford the fellow who is going out to India with me very much indeed.

The barracks are horrible here. My room looks out on a magnificent salmon river about 60 yards broad in which you cannot see the bottom for salmon scarcely. What a place for you or Mary to sketch from my window, only very hard. The water seems to come from every direction through small channels about 8 yards wide and flows into the large stream. To fish in this stream you have to pay 15/- [75p] a day which is too much and then you only get $^1/_3$ of your fish.

I went down to call on the Connaught Rangers this afternoon with one of the fellows. There are only a few of them there at the Depot.

About four of our fellows have gone over to England for Ascot. Most of them go in a good deal for that sort of thing.

They have had about three weeks incessant rain here and this and yesterday afternoon are the first fine days they have had. I went for a walk round the town this afternoon, you could get such a folio of sketches of it, parts of the old walls with very old arches in places(this was an old Spanish colony). Then lovely old houses with carved stone doors and windows that were the ancient town houses of the Galway county inhabitants. I passed one curious old relic; on the front of one of these houses is a skull and cross bones carved in stone with a written monument above saying that 'James Lynch executed his son for the sake of justice at this spot as nobody else would do it'. The story is that this son fell in love with a lovely young lady and that they were engaged, when a friend of Lynch's came to stay, and the girl threw Lynch over and got engaged to the friend and this young Lynch killed his friend. Mr Lynch was boss of the town and everybody was very fond of him and his son so nobody would execute the son. The result was that old Lynch did it himself, hence 'Lynch Law'.

It is very sad to see great distilleries, great mills, and houses all in a state of ruin. The people are very much up against the soldiers, they set on to them when they can get them separate, and last night the adjutant was warned by the police who expected a row and asked him to send out a strong picquet through the town, so you see we have great expectations of fun.

The Irish houses are just what one has seen in pictures – half doors with fowls standing on them, pigs strolling in at the door, cows being led through to be milked at the back and women with bare feet and red petticoats and shawls over their heads instead of hats.

There are no places to play tennis in except at the Connaught Depot or private grounds out of the town. There is a large square levelled and everything, but the town council will not let *us* use it for tennis and so do nothing with it. It is grown over with long grass about 2 feet high and roughs lie about on it.

4 July 1888

Just a line to say how I am getting on here. I am on duty this week which is a beastly nuisance as I had arranged to go to a tennis party this afternoon and have just been told that I have to take a company up to put them under canvas at 5 o'clock, so I can't go.

I have just asked the Colonel[16] for leave until the draft goes out, and he says that he will guarantee my going home for one month and he does not think more, so that is a nuisance.

Will you send me a couple of bath towels and four ordinary ones – it will save my buying them, and there are so many things to buy. I shall be very glad when I get away from here not that I don't like the fellows, but I don't like the expense.

It is a marvellous sight to see the salmon lie here in the river. They lie so thick that you cannot see the bottom in places. Perhaps in a 6 foot square there are 25 salmon. But they only catch about 9 a day with the fly. They won't take this year.

I am going to a ball tomorrow night if I can get off duty, at the Militia.

Galway, 16 July 1888

Just a line in great haste to say that we sail in the *Euphrates* on Sept 7. I shall be home probably in about 10 days but cannot say yet for certain as we are doing musketry and depend entirely on the weather.

We played a cricket match today and won, against the county of Galway. I shall be quite sorry to leave here they are such a nice lot of fellows. I must wind up in great haste, with love to everyone.

Galway, 25 July 1888

You may possibly see me home this week but I cannot let you know for certain as we have not finished musketry and that depends on the weather, but I may get off on Friday night with luck and in that case I shall start on Friday. I will wire to you if I have not time to write.

We have been playing a good many cricket matches lately against County Galway.

I am going up the lake to fish with what they call a cross-line this afternoon it is great fun. You fish with another boat and about 12 flies on the same line.

Just off shooting to the range so good bye for the present.

Hal had his leave and returned to Galway.

Galway, 4 September 1888

My dear Father,

I have just arrived in this awful place. As usual it is raining and to add to the misery there is a horse and cattle show on this week and the streets are simply running muck heaps.

I had a nice journey across, quite calm, and met at Dublin Major Evans[17] who is going out with us. He is a very nice man indeed.

We are starting from here at 6 a.m. on Thursday to go down to Queenstown.

I had an interesting travelling companion from Rugby to Stafford, a man named Major Waller who was going round England to look for a site for the National Rifle Association and told me he had just sent his son on an expedition through Siam.

NOTES

1. Probably the preliminary test for entry to the Royal Military College, Sandhurst.
2. His headmaster at Gosport.
3. Hal's first cousin, Charlie Davies, was serving with the Chinese customs service.
4. His brother, John, lost the sight of an eye while undergoing his naval training.
5. HMTS *Worcester* had originally been HMS *Frederick William*, launched in 1860. Being obsolete, she was loaned by the Admiralty to the Board of the Thames Nautical College in 1877 where she served until 1939.
6. Georgiana, his Mother's elder sister, married to Henry Tudor Davies.
7. Lieutenant-Colonel Henry Platt, DL, CO 4th Bn, Royal Welsh Fusiliers, 1884–9. He lived at Gorddinog, Llanfairfechan.

8. This refers to the cramming schools which specialized in preparing young men for commissioning into the Army.

9. Probably on the Waunfawr road (A4085).

10. Probably near Fort Belan, a Napoleonic fort and dock near Llanwnda, Caernarfon.

11. Queen Victoria's Golden Jubilee, 1887.

12. The Massey family lived at Cornelyn Manor, Llangoed, Beaumaris. William Massey (a retired barrister), his wife, Margaret, and their two daughters, Edith and Gwendolen, were passionate hunting people and supporters of all field sports. The daughters were accomplished artists and some of their work is displayed in Oriel Ynys Môn. One of their sons, William Glynne, served as a captain in the Anglesea Militia and another as a captain in the Cheshire Volunteers.

13. Lieutenant A. P. G. Gough, Royal Welsh Fusiliers. See Biographies.

14. *Sahib*, Richard Holmes, p 189.

15. An assembly held by, in this case the Sovereign's representative, the Lord Lieutenant, at which men only where received.

16. Lieutenant-Colonel R. F. Williamson. See Biographies.

17. Major E. R. Evans, died of pneumonia on 5 April, at Palosi, Hazara, during the Black Mountain Expedition. See Biographies.

Chapter 2

A Subaltern's Life
September 1888– January 1891

On 7 September Second-Lieutenant Henry Cadogan sailed from Queenstown, (now *Cobh*) at Cork, with a draft of soldiers from the 2nd Battalion, Royal Welsh Fusiliers, bound for India to join the 1st Battalion. He was a well built, blue eyed young man of twenty, some six feet three inches tall, weighing about thirteen and a half stone. It was, of course, his first journey beyond his home shores.

[In HMS *Euphrates*] Atlantic Ocean, 10 September 1888

My dear Father,

We have just reached about a level with Lisbon. I must give you an account of our journey. We started on Friday night and had it pretty calm until Saturday night when a pretty fresh breeze got up and on Sunday very few people turned up to meals, I had been pretty sound all the time. I came into every meal, at least, which is saying a good deal.

It was very rough in the Bay but now the sea is like a mill pond and we sight innumerable steamers. We expect to reach Gib tomorrow night or Wednesday morning when I hope to send this letter to you. The heat today is intense, they are putting up awnings the whole length of the ship but still it is very oppressive.

We have 1400 troops on board and 250 of the crew besides about 100 officers and women and children. So we are packed pretty close – the men terribly so. At night their hammocks touch one another.

The most trying time on board is when they made you fall in, in the Bay, and all the men were ill all round you, and tubs placed for them along the decks.

This morning I saw two whales about a mile from the ship, and innumerable porpoises come round the ship. A few minutes ago a sort of hawk came across to us from Portugal and was so tired that it nearly settled on me as I stood by the side. It went to the ladders and the crew were after it in a moment but they could not get it.

They feed us very well on board. They give us soup or fish as entrée and joint, sweets and vegetables and dessert for dinner, and all other meals for two shillings per day. Wine is cheap and they do not pay duty on board, for instance Marsala is $1^{1}/2$d [less than .5p] a glass – not ruinous and very good too.

HMS Euphrates, an iron screw troopship launched in 1866 and sold in 1894. [National Maritime Museum]

You must excuse writing as I am sitting just above the screw and so there is a perpetual jolting and the ink dries on my pen all the time.

The *Euphrates* is a splendid vessel, quite a long walk to go from one end to the other. We are taking out a pack of hounds to India. The dogs have a very bad time I am afraid. They seldom get out and then only by special leave of the Captain.

I must stop my letter for the present. As we do not reach Gib for a day or two I will add to it any news.

Sep 11

Another lovely morning, the heat of the sun is quite surprising. Since I wrote yesterday we have sighted several points of Portugal; Torres Vedras, Cintra and St Vincent. We shall reach Gib this afternoon. We have just come off an emergency parade as they call it. We all have to fall in at a supposed fire or collision and the sailors get all the boats ready provisioned and untied ready to be let down. It is rather amusing only you get your toes terribly trodden on in the crush.

The colour of the water is most extraordinary here, it is a sort of blue you see in the chemists windows.

We had a merrier night last night. We had a piano on deck and sang and danced and had a good deal of fun. Only the ladies on board are rather terrible, they do nothing at all but sit in chairs and blob as we should call it at home, and such a set too. There are a lot of doctors and vets going out and these are their wives.

P.S. could not send this off at Gib as we passed it at night.

HMS *Euphrates*, Mediterranean, 12 September 1888

I must write you a line to say how we are getting on. I will not tell you about our cruise as far as Gib as I have told Father all about it. I intended to send his letter off at Gib but we passed at 8 o'clock and of course did not stop. For the last two days we have been going along the African coast about 2 miles from the shore. It is such a wild coast. This morning at 8 o'clock we passed so close to Algiers that you could see all the houses quite plainly and I thought of Sid and Reg and their stay there.[1]

I was on watch last night on deck from 12 p.m. till 4 a.m. While I was there I saw a perfect tropical storm a long way off towards the centre, you could see the lightning which was most vivid but could hear no thunder.

We shall reach Malta between 7 and 8 on Saturday morning and shall stay there until Sunday afternoon. The heat today is something terrible you can't do anything. You would scarcely know me I am so brown now, although we have awnings the whole length of the ship and flaps to them. I will end today and write again tomorrow when there is more to say.

Sept 14

Another baking hot day. Today we have all the punkahs in the saloon working so as I am writing this I am nearly blown away. We reach Malta in the morning and so at last I shall be able to post this to you.

This old vessel goes at a capital pace – 12 knots. We have passed every ship we have seen yet. We saw a lot of flying fish near the ship, at least we think they were flying fish.

Excuse this being a short letter but there is nothing to say. I will write longer when we have passed Malta where we shall stay till Sunday night.

I wonder if I left my big knife in my room? If I did, please send it to me.

HMS *Euphrates*, 19 September 1888

We have come and gone from Malta. I saw as much as I could of it in the short time I was there. The harbour is wonderful, a very narrow entrance with cliffs crowned with forts all around. First I went to see the 'armoury' where is kept all the old armour and weapons used by the Knights of St John against the Turks and also armour of the Turks used against Malta.

Also in the Government House the reception room is adorned with the most wonderful tapestry (French). After that I went and saw the monastery of Franciscan monks which is beautiful and below they keep all the old Friars dried standing in niches which is rather a ghastly sight. After this I went to see the Cathedral of St John which certainly surpassed anything I have ever seen. The enormous body of the place is entirely hung with tapestry (also French) while the panels are filled with pictures either originals of copies of great pictures. They have one by Michael Angelo, but off this large church lead innumerable small chapels all painted and covered with tapestry. One of these is divided off by gates and railings about 8 feet high and about 12 feet across made of solid silver. Another had the same of solid gold but these latter were taken by the French when they came to the island and the silver ones were only preserved by painting them black like iron. In the afternoon I went over the Civita-Vecchia and the Sanatorium which was the Palace of the Inquisition and you may still go into the dungeons and underground passages used and see the stone block where the peoples' heads were cut off.

I went down also into the cave were St Paul hid himself and also into the catacombs which are a sort of underground town with church, beds, burial places etc still remaining. They have blocked up the greater part of them as so many people were lost in the winding passages and never found.

The Maltese men are a fine lot to look at, the ideal pirate, dark, fine features, bony and savage looking. Wonderful divers, for sixpence [2.5p] they will dive right under the ship.

We have had a series of boiling days. It has quite knocked most of the fellows over, especially those who don't wear belts.[2] I have been quite fit all the time.

There are a lot of birds about the ship now. A peregrine falcon, and several flycatchers, very pretty with red breasts and blue striped heads.

We have passed Alexandria now although we cannot see land at all and shall reach Port Said tomorrow morning where we only stay a few hours. I hope to get ashore however to see what is to be seen. We have sweep stakes every day about the distance travelled. I won the big one yesterday 1/- [5p] entry and got

£2.10 [£2.50] for it which was not bad. I must end now but if I have time I will add to this tomorrow. In case I don't, love to all of you.

Later.

I am sorry I could not post this at Port Said. I put this letter ready to post and could not find it. However we shall pass Suez in about a couple of hours. We anchored in the canal last night and several steamers passed with the electric light to show the way.

The heat is very severe although there is a breeze, it is 82° in the shade of the awnings.

What a desolate waste of country there is on each side of the ship! Miles and miles of sand always.

Trooping between India and UK took place between 1 September and March the following year. Therefore Hal would have been on one of the first voyages of the season. Until about 1900, men who completed their service with the Colours in India had to wait at Deolali Camp for the next troop ship. Those arriving in April hung about until September for a passage home. They were away from their regiments and their friends and must have been desperately bored. Apart from the occasional route march there was nothing constructive for them to do. Frank Richards says: 'In some cases men who had been exemplary soldiers got into serious trouble and were awarded terms of imprisonment before they went home.' Hence the expression, still used by soldiers, 'He's gone doo-lally.'

Deolali Camp, Bombay, 6 October 1888

My dear Father,

At last I have got a few minutes to myself to write and tell you how I have got on for the last few days. I have been doing nothing but work all day getting men's kits ready and sending in certificates. Today we have got through most of the work and are getting a little to ourselves.

We got into Bombay on Wednesday morning but did not disembark till Thursday afternoon.

I procured a rather nice servant on the ship. They are generally an awful set of black sheep but this man seems to me a very good sort.

We started from Sassoon Dock[3] in two trains, we were in the second at 7.30, for this place Deolali. It is a ten hour journey and a most picturesque one on a moonlight night as you go right through the Ghats, sometimes round the edges of precipices. We got here at 5 in the morning, an awful hour as I had had no sleep like the other chaps, as I was made Orderly Officer of the train. Half way, half the train was detached as it was too heavy for the slope and I went in the other half.

It is a capital place as far as the temperature goes – about 90 to 95° during the day but very cold at night. Everything is so different to what one has come across before, the people, the trees, the birds and last but not least the reptiles. Vast spiders and things which jump and fly too are everywhere. Scorpions are also found in the crevices in your tent but they are rare. I have not seen one.

There are enormous sorts of white and yellow carrion crows which if you throw a piece of food into the air will catch it before it reaches the ground and this morning I saw a soldier carrying some food on his head on a tray, when one of these birds took it all and the soldier looked up as if the Devil had got him. I never saw such an expression.

There are some bison to be shot about 30 miles from here and a lot of small deer but it is no use going except with someone who understands it, and also they go for you if they see you, so you have to be pretty careful.

We start for Lucknow on Wednesday, today is Saturday, and we get up there on the 16th, five days by train. We stop for six hours and travel 18 in the day I am told.

I have had no time to go more than 100 yards or so from camp as yet but I am just off for a walk with two or three other fellows. They killed a cobra last night outside the camp.

You must excuse this short letter but I must get out for a bit and shall have all the more news to tell you in the next letter.

I got my guns through pretty cheap, for 20 rupees or so.

Tell mother that I am perfectly fit. I know she will be glad to hear it, and am very glad she thought of those flannel pyjamas.

Hal was not the first of the family to spend a large slice of his life in India. His grandfather had worked for the East India Company and in his time society was more relaxed. When he retired he was presented with a silver center-piece inscribed:

PRESENTED by the EUROPEAN COMMUNITIES of TRAVENCORE
AND COCHIN to Lt. Colonel E. Cadogan ACTING RESIDENT
in those provinces IN TOKEN OF their respect and esteem
FOR HIS CHARACTER PUBLIC AND PRIVATE 10 November 1834.

Although he had been given this by the European community, it would have been known and completely accepted that for some of that time he had been living with an Indian girl by whom he had had a son. This was common practice for the young bachelors of 'John Company'; The mortality rate of these young men and the dearth of European girls meant that a 'suitable' marriage was unlikely. From about 1830, however, the influence of Christian missionaries and the increasing number of British wives living in India who disapproved of this custom, meant that the races became more separate.

The 1st Battalion was stationed in Lucknow, a popular station, and both officers and men enjoyed serving there. There was plenty of polo, good black-buck and wild fowl shooting, and lots of cricket, football, boxing and even rowing. The social life of a young lieutenant, however, was pretty limited and revolved around the Mess and the Club. No Indians were invited to either.

Just outside Lucknow, La Martiniere College,[4] an excellent school run on public school lines for Europeans only at that time, had opened in 1845. But India was not a healthy place for Europeans, and as soon as they were old enough most children were sent 'home' to be educated. The educated Indians resented the distant and contemptible manner in which they were treated by the generality of English gentlemen which wounds their hearts and compels them to forget the blessings of British Rule[5] an attitude that had contributed to the 'Mutiny' or 'First War of Independence,' and which had exacerbated the mistrust between the two races.

Kipling describing Lucknow in the late nineteenth century wrote, 'There is no city except Bombay … more beautiful in her garish style than Lucknow … Kings have adorned her with fantastic buildings … She is the centre of all idleness, intrigue and luxury and shares with Delhi the claim to speak the only pure Urdu.'[6] Glamorous military uniforms, native costumes and tribal dress would have added to the colourful scene. Many of the glorious buildings of Lucknow remain and are being beautifully restored, while the Residency, site of the epic fight in the Mutiny, is maintained as a National Park.

The British Army at that time was going through one of its less dynamic periods, and it remained so until it was shaken by the Boer War. Even in 1902, when Kitchener arrived as Commander in Chief in India, he found regiments scattered higgledy-piggledy around the sub-continent. They were unprepared for a war with modern firearms, and their task was still to hold India against the Indians even fifty years after the Mutiny.[7]

The journey to Lucknow was by very slow train travelling by night and the passengers staying at rest camps by day. When Frank Richards,[8] later the author of '*Old Soldier Sahib*,' joined the 2nd Battalion in Meerut in 1902 he found the battalion about 1,000 strong, 700 of whom were cockneys or midlanders, and no more than 300 were Welshmen. The composition of the 1st Battalion in 1888 was probably much the same.

[1 RWF] Lucknow, 16 October 1888

My dear old Molly,[9]

At last I have time to write and tell you how I am getting on. We arrived here yesterday it is such a delicious place. I must tell you all about it. The cantonments are scattered all over the place and everyone lives in bungalows and each bungalow is separated by what we call a compound which is a garden full of shady trees to sit under. I am in a bungalow with three other fellows just opposite the Mess.

The fashionable season is just beginning in Lucknow and the people come swarming in from everywhere so bungalows are hard to get and lots have to live under canvas. Last night I went down to a sort of club where the band plays in the evening and everyone comes out and walks about. Tonight I am going out to another Club, The United Service,[10] on the river where the band also plays. It is four miles off so I must get someone to drive me down in their cart. Nearly all the fellows keep about 5 or 6 ponies and play polo and also traps. You ride everywhere here- up to parade, and Orderly Room. When we got to the station with the Draft (of soldiers) there were three ponies waiting for us to ride up to the lines on.

This is a very expensive place I expect. There are some races on soon and we are giving a dance. I believe all these clubs are so expensive, 80 Rs entrance to the Bagh Club. 90 to the Polo Club which everyone must join, and then monthly subscriptions also. Then we have to pay for our own bungalows and furnish them and everything.

The fellows are a very nice lot. There are only about 12 here now, but they are all coming in soon, then we shall be about 28 to Mess. We shall be worked very hard soon as during the cold season they have 8 or 12 regiments in for the manoeuvres.

There are heaps of English people here, I must begin my calls tomorrow. Everyone calls here between 12 and 2. It is an awful time in the day but that is the thing to do. You see we are 3 or 4 hours earlier than you are, out here. We parade at about 5.30 in the morning and get through everything by 9 nearly.

How are you all at home I wonder I wish we were not such a beastly long way off that we could have a peep at one another more often than we were likely to have.

Tell Father that his roll of cutlery has come in already. Before going on parade in the morning we have what is called *Choto-Haziri* and if I had had no spoons or knives I should have had to buy them.

Hal's annual allowance from his father was £105, which was increased by 1890 to £144 (or about £8,624 at today's rates). Pay varied according to length of service, the type of regiment and where it was stationed. In England, an infantry second lieutenant received 5/3d [27p] per day. As he was promoted an officer's pay rose, but not very fast; an infantry lieutenant colonel was paid only 18/- [90p] per day. There was a remarkable difference when it came to general officer rank; major-generals received £1,095 per annum, and full generals £3,923. Interestingly, staff officers and ADCs received allowances that more than doubled the pay for their rank.

In India, officers were paid in rupees – a rupee being worth about 1/8d [8p] in 1889. An infantry second lieutenant with less than three years' service stationed there was paid 202 rupees per month, or about £160 per year; considerably more than the £96 he received in UK.

In 1903, a committee that looked at officers' expenses found that initial clothing and equipment expenses for an infantry officer were £200, and for the cavalry £600–£1,000. Even then, nothing was done to pay officers a living wage.

These figures illustrate how essential it was for an army officer to have a private income in the late nineteenth century. A young officer in the artillery, engineers or infantry was required to have an annual allowance of between £60 and £100. He really needed much more to get by when he was stationed at home, or if he joined an 'expensive' infantry regiment like the Rifle Brigade or 60th. To belong to a cavalry regiment he required an allowance of at least £300–£400, and for some regiments even more in order to keep up with his fellow officers.

Lucknow, 4 November 1888

My dear Father,

Thanks very much for your letter, also for the trouble you have taken about the false accusation.[11] I am awfully obliged to you, dear old Dad for all this trouble, but it was the only way to go at it, and wait.

I am going to write to Fiennes by this mail as I have not done so yet. I was so glad to hear that you are going away from Wicken for a bit of leave, it will do you all the good in the world. I wonder how you got your harvest in at Wicken very much. I wish you had some of our weather, if you had you would have the harvest in in about 2 days. However, it is much cooler than it was, in fact we have coming on what is called the cold season. I wish Reg and Sid were up here this week as the races are on.

We are giving a ball and so is the Club here.

We had a cricket match yesterday against the 17th Lancers and beat them. I was to have played only I rubbed some skin off my foot the day before and it has festered a bit as things do up here they say. If you get a mosquito bite and you scratch it, it is bad for a week. One of our fellows did some most remarkable bowling, he bowled the Rajah Kutchbahar, The Prince of Teck, and the Earl of Ava [the son of the Marquis of Dufferin] in successive balls.[12]

One is bound to keep a pony here as the distances are so great, e.g. to parade at 6.30 in the morning, it is a mile off, and then when you are on duty you have to go quite 7 miles in the course of duty going round dinners. All the soldiers are in bungalows and you have to go round one half battalion in about half an hour. There are 8 bungalows and each about 300 yards off each other. Then the Club is 4 miles off and one goes there every other night before Mess for about an hour.

I will write all particulars on a separate sheet as they will not interest other eyes perhaps. It is funny as I look out now into the compound- the birds the animals, the trees, butterflies and insects are all so different to English ones. You see green parrots, golden orioles, yellow wagtails, swallow-tail butterflies, monkeys and so on.

I was dining with the 17th Lancers the other night and who do you think was there! A friend of Walter's named Miller who was at Blanche's wedding, he is in the 17th and has an immense amount of side on.[13] He is a very good polo player, however.

Lucknow, 2 December 1888

A very merry Xmas and a happy New Year to you. I am already looking forward to us all blobbing and eating too much in 5 years time and drinking dear old Troopling one's[14] health afterwards.

How funny it seems out here in the middle of the day, one goes about in a huge hat called a 'solar topee' like an enormous mushroom, and you having frosts and ice probably. However at night it is awfully cold, in fact it freezes and one has to be pretty careful about coats.

Tomorrow we begin the manoeuvres which will last three months, they march us out about 7 or 8 miles and bucket us about from 6.30 am. to 2pm. There are six infantry regiments here now counting natives and two cavalry regiments and four more coming in at the end of the month so we are pretty gay, but it makes an awful lot of work.

I had a letter from Sid this morning who is at Bombay she seems in high spirits and likes everything. I am glad she did not come a month or so earlier as I fancy she would not be so well at Bombay. My recollections of the place are not at all brilliant, as it was so hot one could not move hand or foot. I hope Pa's little trip [to Scotland] has done him good, he wanted a rest badly.

What fun you and Dolly[15] must have had settling Jack down in his rooms at Oxford.

I miss Dick sadly – out here if there is a thing that is a boon it is a dog and they are so hard to get (good). And one does not like to get hideous ones which are also hard to get. A fellow in the next bungalow to mine had two beautiful Dachshunds and a sad fate happened to one the other day it was bitten by a cobra in his compound and died of course.

By the way please remember the postage is 5d [2p] to India not 2^1/2d [1p] as they always charge me double out here, at least 5 annas for insufficiency of stamps. Besides there is a delay of the letter in the post about a week which I mind much more.

Old Sid sent me their proposed programme which seems as if they are going to have a very good time. They are going to Poona & Calcutta before they come here and they will be here in Feb for the 'Cup' which will be the gayest time in the year.

We had a photo done of the officers of the Regt the other day I will send you one as soon as they are ready. I am going to begin to collect photos soon but they are expensive and starting here is also severe.

I went over the Residency the other day. It is so interesting, you can see every mark where the bullets and cannon balls hit, as the walls are brick covered with plaster. How 900 men held 2 miles of ground against *280,000* is most extraordinary *for 7 months* [his emphasis].

I must end now with heaps of merry Xmases to every one, as the Mess bugle has gone.

The ruins of the Residency at Lucknow, photographed in 1858.
The building had changed very little by 1888.

To commence again. It is two days since I wrote the last. We have begun our manoeuvres and today were bucketed about for 3 hours without any rest. Tomorrow we have a huge field day, all the Regiments in Lucknow. I don't look forward to it.

I have just been having a terrific set to with my bearer who has brought me a bill for household expenses to the tune of 70 Rs for 1 month. That does not include Mess expenses of course but only oil, candles, blacking, fuel for warming water etc – these chaps are such awful swindlers when one does not know any thing about housekeeping. I wish you were out here to put me straight. By Jove, talk about India being such an economical place. I don't find it so at present. However if I get along alright for the next two months I shall be alright as these are the worst in the year. You see all these regiments which are coming in, dine with us bodily so that runs away with any spare pay one has over one's mess bill. However there are four or five of us about the same which makes it much more comfortable than the other Battalion.[16] And the remaining fellows are so nice, all of them.

What a difference there is between the men out here and the men at home. You see those boys at home without any chests or anything but here you see all the men with 6, 7 or 10 years service nearly all of them with the Burma medal, great square shouldered men with big mustachios, and faces as brown as a berry.

I am told the Regt. is only to be out here five years more I don't know if it is a fact or not but we came out in 1880 and although we are supposed to stay 16 years, most regiments stay about 13.

You must tell me who gets the ring, three-penny piece and thimble this year in the plum pudding.

Probably the reason Hal found the men in the 1st Battalion '… great square shouldered men …' was because many of them would have been older than those in the 2nd Battalion, and much older than the young soldiers in the draft with whom he had travelled out on HMS *Euphrates*. 'Short service' had been introduced in 1870; men now enlisted for twelve years, but spent three to seven years with the Colours and the remainder on the Reserve. Previously men had signed on for twenty-five years.[17]

Lucknow, 1 January 1889

My dear Father

Thanks very much for your jolly letter. I just got it a day or two before Xmas day so I was awfully pleased to get it. It is rather late to wish you a Happy New Year but I think I did so before.

I have been doing a good deal of shooting lately. A fortnight ago I went with a fellow snipe shooting and we got 18 couple of snipe of which I got 15 & 1/2 couple so I was rather pleased. Last week I went to try and shoot some black buck (antelopes) but could not get near enough to shoot them as unless you go a good way out they are very wild. I am in rare good condition what with the field days and shooting 'shikar'. I was weighed the other day and only weighed 12-10. What do you think of that, a stone lighter than when I was in England.

By Jove, there goes the Mess bugle so I must hurry over this letter or I shall not get it off by the mail. I wish you could see this country. This weather it is delicious – quite perfect. Except the animals, moths, maggots and things which eat all your boots clothes and things into holes if you leave them more than three days without having them brushed. They are so bad that a worm will eat a chair leg through in one day indoors.

I was going to write to Jack by this mail but I am afraid there is not time so I must write while I am about it and let it catch the next mail.

I have got a ripping little dog wirehaired like Dick but white with black and tan, he belonged to another of the fellows who gave him to me. He is a rare little watch dog and allows no one to come into my room except my bearer and he will not let him come near the bed when I am in bed. He is a rare little chap.

I am going to send you a portrait of my pony by a native here who copies awfully well but he has not finished it yet. At least he has put my '*syce*' [groom] in, which it would not be complete without.

I am picking up this lingo pretty well now at least I can make myself understood in a sort of a way. When I have time, in the hot weather I shall get a '*moonshie*' (native teacher). I must finish now or I shall be late for Mess.

P.S. It is a funny thing – a pal of mine in the Regt, Gwynne, lives at *Crickhowell* [his emphasis] in Wales.[18]

Lucknow, 1 January 1889

My dear Molly

Thanks muchly for your letter of a week or two back, also thanks for the cards from all of you I was so pleased to get them. I had a letter from old Blanche

Officers, 1st Battalion, Royal Welsh Fusiliers, Lucknow, 1889.
Back row: (L–R) Lt H. B. Ford; Capt H. J. Archdale; Lt R. S. Webber; Lt J. H. Gwynne; Lt A. F. Cooper; 2Lt H. O. S. Cadogan; Lt G. F. Bartelot; Capt & QM Gray; Lt Paymaster Evans Gordon (R. Berks Regt). Seated: (L–R) Capt C. H. Milford; Maj C. A. B. K. Leighton; Maj C. Norman; Capt & Adj R. H. W. Dunn; Lt-Col E. S. Creek; Maj E. R. Evans; Maj R. B. Mainwaring; Capt P. R. Mantell; Lt J. A. H. Walford. Front row: Lt H. Delmé-Radcliffe; 2Lt J. G. Braithwaite; Lt E. Layton; Lt W. C. Hall. [RWF Archives]

today wishing me a Happy New Year. It came rather timely didn't it. Thank the dear old Troopling one for her card and letter & say I was so awfully pleased to get it.

I have just stopped and begun again because my 'bearer' brought my last months expenses. Oh what a thing it is to housekeep for yourself.[19] I believe by the time I come home I shall be quite an experienced housekeeper. Tonight I am weeping and crying over the bills like little Pa does when the postage stamps have run out or Jack comes round to the back door with pots and pans.

Parades whirl on. Today we had a New Year's Day 'peacock' parade which means a ladies' parade in red, marching past etc. We had 10 Infantry Regts, 4 Cavalry Regts and 2 Artillery batts. So it was a pretty large parade. Tomorrow we have another large Field Day out in the country which lasts from about 9 till 2.30.

I wonder if there is going to be a Buckingham ball[20] this year. I wish I was going to be at home for it if there is. I hear in Blanche's letter you are quite gay rushing off to the Banbury Ball and then going up north for another.

You must tell the other children that I will write to them soon but there is no time for anything and I am afraid of missing the mail as it is.

I wish I could have sent you some little things from out here but the expense of sending things home is so great, as most of these native things are so heavy made of brass or wood you see.

It is awfully cold out here now at night. I suppose one feels it so much after being cooked during the middle of the day by the sun.

Tell Mother I am very glad of these flannel pyjamas and warm vests now.

Fancy you being frost bound it does sound funny. By the way I had a letter and some Xmas cards from the Mallocks on Xmas day. They all seem to be very fit and awfully gay at Camberley.

It seems so funny to me to think I have only been out here two months and a half. It seems such ages I suppose the month's journey makes it feel so, it is such an awful long way.

I must stop old girl as I have another letter to write and want to catch the mail. By the way, I spent Xmas night with some very nice people, the Colonel's sister who is married to a Capt. Williams who was wounded in the Black Mt. Expedition[21] and is here.

Lucknow, 8 January 1889

I have not written to you for some time so now I have a little spare time I will write. There is very little news to tell, the same old Field Days go on, only more so as the Commander-in-Chief[22] is here. We provided a Guard of Honour when he arrived and I carried the Regtl Colour and the Goat stood in front at the Railway Station.

Yesterday we had a meet of our hounds[23] for the Chief and lots of people were out including the Chief, his daughter and niece and two or three of his Staff. I went out too and we had a capital day, killed two jackals and had a good run after which the jack escaped. Lots of people had falls but no one was hurt.

My pony is a ripper. He was with the hounds all the time till we left off and

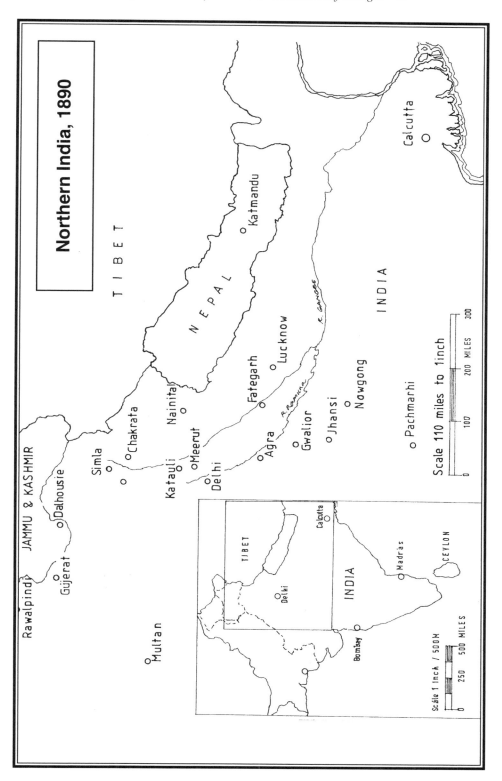

Northern India, 1890

went over everything and never attempted to come down. He is like a cat, if he comes to a mud wall too high for him, he jumps on top and then down again.

The Chief comes up to our barracks tonight to see some Christy Minstrels got up by our men. Tomorrow there is a dance at the Club, they are every fortnight and subscription dances so I don't think I shall go. As I am dining out I have a good excuse for staying away from the dance and saving rupees.

I have not heard one word from Sid lately, I have written two or three times but I think they must be having such a good time with the Charringtons that they have no time for anything. I believe they want to come up here for the races next month but unless they write to me to get rooms soon they will not be able to get them as nearly all the rooms are already taken.

I have written to Jack and also to young Hogg by this mail so I consider I have done my duty.

There is another draft coming in tomorrow from England. They come by the *Crocodile*,[24] by Jove I am glad I am not coming with them as it does take such a time to settle down.

I have found that I turned over two leaves instead of one when I began this letter and it is too long to begin over again so you must excuse the way it is written. My friend here in the Regt[25] is going home next year as he has served five years out here altogether and was in the Burma War where he was shot through the knee and he's to be invalided home from here. He is going home to the Depot at Wrexham. I shall be sorry to lose him.

We have quite a menagerie in our Compound; horses, ponies, goats, a black buck, two monkeys, two or three dogs and a mongoose (a thing like a large Ferret only clean and very tame which kills snakes, cobras or anything).

Lucknow, 3 February 1889

Thank you very much for your letter which I got last week. What fun your dance must have been, you must have had such chunks of people.

We had a large fancy dress ball here three days ago at the Club, the dresses were very good at least a good many of them. I went in uniform as a fancy dress is an awfully expensive thing out here and you are bound to get a really good one if you do.

This is the Lucknow race week, they begin on Tuesday and we are already very gay. Any amount of people have come in and more are coming every day. The sweeps were drawn last night and a friend of mine drew Blitz, the favourite, and if it wins he will get 7000 Rs. The sweep was 10 Rs and at the last moment there was one ticket left so he took it to make the thing square, wasn't it a bit of luck.

Our manoeuvres have at last come to an end I am glad to say, and two or three of the Regts have gone away to their stations.

A Kashmir man has been here the last few days. He has such lovely things, Kashmir shawls, and curtains rugs and all kind of things. One longs to buy everything but Kashmir shawls are so awfully expensive – 150 to 300 or 400. They are most exquisitely worked in silk.

Fancy your having frost and snow, here it has been very like an English spring. Although the leaves are never off the trees, the new leaves come on while the old ones are dropping off. We have had a good deal of rain lately with thunder storms. By Jove it does come down when it rains, in a few minutes every ditch is running like a torrent. All bridges have to be very strongly built. You see bridges over little dry ditches built like London Bridge.

I have not been shooting lately, the weather has been bad and I have had a great deal to do. I have not heard from Sid for some time but they are not coming here this year, they are going on to Japan and China and coming to North India on their way home. So that they may do it all well, I think they are quite right as it is very fatiguing work travelling much in this country and climate.

Lucknow, 10 March 1889

I have not written to you for an age, there is very little to say certainly.

I had a letter from old Sid the other day she is down in the Nilgerry Hills or somewhere near there. She says she has gone there to see some very fine old Hindu temples. She says she finds it very hot and also says they intend moving on to Ceylon soon. Talking about heat it is getting very hot here, the wind is like a hot draught out of an oven. The roses in our compound are marvellous, Marshal Neils and Gloire de Dijon are the best I think. You have only to keep them well watered and the roses will break the branches down unless they are looked after.

Last Sunday I went for a walk with a Major Dyce who is Adjutant General here, he manages the gardens at Dilkusha.[26] We went all over the gardens, they are about 10 acres 1and laid out in thousands of the most beautiful roses and every kind of hot house flower almost that you see in England. There are kitchen gardens too, which reminded me very much of England – quite green.

Dilkusha, the hunting lodge of the Nawabs of Oudh, Lucknow. This very English-looking palladian house, built in about 1800 in the style of Vanbrugh's Seaton Delaval Hall in Northumberland, was located close to the RWF barracks.

The whole place has to be continually watered which is done by little canals from wells and from twenty to thirty bullocks drawing water in a huge skin at the end of a long rope.

The above is the sort of thing going on in my compound now. The two bullocks walk up and down a slant. The slant goes into the ground where I have continued the dotted line, only the slants are much greater really. The well is between the two pillars and the place at the back is a sort of reservoir where the water makes of sort of stand, otherwise if it ran by degrees down the little channels it would always dry up.

I wish I could send you home some of these roses, but that is unfortunately impossible. By Jove how people would prize them early in March.

Our polo team has left for Waeballah. They went three days ago and so have left us all their duty to do which comes rather severe as there are so few left. The 17th Lancers from here won their tournament the other day. The fellow Miller, Walter's friend, played very well indeed for them. He is not a pleasant chap but a beautiful polo player.

We are to have the new Viceroy[27] here for a few days soon. I believe they are going to stay at Simla as his daughters feel the heat too much. I am glad to say I am going to the hills for a bit this hot weather. I don't know where, but I have been a bit seedy with anaemia the doctor calls it, and he has arranged with the Colonel for me so that is a very great score. There was a report the other day that the whole Regiment was to go up to Rhaniket which is in the hills but alas it was only a report. You see the Regt. has never been to a hill station since they came from the worst climates in Burma so the health of the men is not very good. We are getting quite deserted again, everyone is going out of Lucknow to Simla and Naini Tal and such places.

I have taken to playing tennis here every day at the Bagh but I don't like the courts like the England grass. They are like concrete, only sort of mud baked by the heat of the sun and turned into what they call sun dried brick.

Our Colonel[28] has just come back from sick leave, he has been very seedy indeed with liver for sometime. They were afraid he was going to have typhoid, I expect he will either go home or to Australia. His wife has some children at home and so wants to go home, he wants to go and see his brother in Australia. It is a pity, he is a very nice man off parade and out of barracks, but on parade he is most awfully unpopular from Majors to Subalterns, Sergeant Major to drummer boys. He is a Staff College man for one thing and therefore does not know his drill and has impracticable theories about everything which he has tried until they do not succeed.

Tell the dear old Troopling One [the family cook] that I am using her ink pot and have never used any other since I have been out here. It is very useful to me.

I have had a little lucerne grass planted in the garden for the ponies during the hot weather you can hardly get grass at all and what there is is all dry roots so a little nice food is a capital thing every day.

I have just heard from Eley, he is in the 14th Hussars quartered at Brighton and seems to be enjoying himself with 5 horses.

I see a very good portrait of Lord Penhryn in the *Graphic* or *Illustrated*, I forget which it was, only it was very like him.

I looked for the Ghost Story by Frank[29] in *McMillan* which we take in and found in the Mess. As luck would have it someone had taken away the October & November nos although they have no business to remove them from the Mess at all. I was very disappointed, although nothing that Frank did could interest one much.

Four of our fellows went shooting the other day and got *329* duck in three days. That is pretty quick work.

I can't write any more, it is too blobbing, the heat I mean, although it is 6 pm. Everything is now a sort of buzz of crickets and tree frogs and reptiles.

Lucknow, 17 April 1889

The weather is getting awfully hot. You can't do anything now between 8 in the morning and 5 in the evening. The men are not allowed out of barrack rooms between these hours.

We got up a sing song last night in the open air. We had a square piece walled off outside the theatre. It took tremendously, 120, nearly all soldiers, 72 in 3 anna tickets. So we had about 300 or more soldiers. It was a great success.

We have started what are called paper chases. They always have them in the cold weather. One of our Captains manages the whole thing and has regular steeple chase jumps put up over a distance of about 3 or 4 miles and paper is laid down to mark the course.[30] Everyone goes in for them. It is the finest thing in the world to see fellows going down like ninepins over these jumps as there are about thirty or more out and all keep together until they fall. At the end of the season they have a Cup over a course. It is a splendid thing to keep you going as the country is very rough and you get a rare good shaking up.

There are very few of us here now and two more go away today. My friend Gwynne went tiger shooting the other day and brought back a tiger I am glad to say, but it is a very expensive game to play at.

I am on our Mess Committee now. You would laugh to see me ordering the dinners and checking the linen and plate and things. I rather like it as it gives one something to do writing the Mess invitations.

By the way I want you to send me out my two boxes of compasses. One little fat box with two instruments, and the other a long flat one with rulers in. I can't do without and if they are not sent to me I shall have to get new ones from Calcutta. If you can send them you might ask Mary to put in some of my songs, as they would not be much more expensive. In fact it is almost as expensive to send a small parcel as a larger one.

I have just found out that the mail goes out at 12 today. Up till now there has been a mail train from Calcutta which allowed the mail to go out till 8 tonight but they have stopped it.

I am so glad that dear old Jack is getting on so at his rowing. It will be splendid if he follows Father's example at Oxford in the 'eight'.[31]

Lucknow, 17 April 1889

My dear Father

Thanks very much for your letter. I suppose this will reach you somewhere about your birthday so I must wish you 'very many happy returns of the day'.

I cannot write a long letter today as I was taken by surprise as we can normally post letters for the mail up to 8 pm but they have stopped the fast train and so they have to go by 12 am.

I will soon get photoed but at present it is so hot one never can get out at midday and then we always wear white uniform. You have no idea of the heat. The men are not allowed to leave barracks between 8 am and 5pm.

I am beginning to learn Hindi or rather Urdu which is the other dialect. It is rather awkward to master the letters as they are written backwards and so is all the writing.

This way —

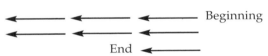

Beginning

End

and there are two or three forms of each letter according as it is at the beginning, middle or end of a word. Hindi is the second language but the higher standard. I can speak enough to make my *syce* or coolies understand what I want. It is very easy as there are so few words and the verbs are all so regular.

I must wind up old Dad now. By Jove how Jack is getting on with the rowing. We shall have him a second Cadogan … rowing at Henley and all sorts of things.

29 April 1889

My dear old Father

I wrote you a very short letter the other day so think that I ought to write again. I have got a *moonshi* (teacher) at last and am going for the Lower Standard the first week in July. He charges Rs 20 a month and Rs 50 on passing, it is not a loss even on passing as they give one Rs 70 or 80 on passing, So that about pays one back.

One has to take up a little of both the lingoes. Hindi & Urdu. Urdu is Persian, very like Sanskrit. Hindu and Urdu are the same almost in conversation but entirely different in character of letter. Urdu is written backwards and Hindi the usual way for instance.

جادوگر *Urdu*

n a g o d ca

कदोगन *Hindi.*

ca d o ga n

My name *not quite correct I believe.*

I have a tremendous lot of work to do now as one fellow is sick. I have got two companies to look after. I am also on our Mess Committee and have all invites to write and answer. This morning I had to check all the cooking utensils of the Mess and weed out all the bad ones.

Today we have what is called a paper chase. We have them weekly. Everyone in the garrison who rides pays 1 Rupee each day he rides and a steeple chase course for ponies of about 3 to 4 miles is made in the country and we have a sort of race. Last week on my pony out of 26 ponies my pony brought me in fourth which was pretty good. All except 5 ponies refused the first jump which was rather stiff.

I heard from Caryl Fiennes two or three days ago. I am very glad he has settled down to some work at last. I hope that he will get through his exam.

I suppose soon you will be looking to the grass coming. By Jove it seems more than a year since I came out to this country, but one has seen such a lot of new things. I am always meaning to try and make some sketches of places near, for instance the Residency, Dilkusha and the old Brick Bridge, but there is no time whatever.

The heat is so great that last night driving from the Club in the dark we had our hats off and from the heat of the wind you felt as if you were going to have sun stroke.

I wish you had some of our fruits, splendid melons 2d., bananas, lychees like plovers eggs, mangoes.

I have come in again and as the mail goes at 12 noon tomorrow and I go to barracks at 6 in the morning and do not come down till about 2 o'clock, unless I send it off now it will not go by this mail.

Lucknow, 19 May 1889

We got a very sad piece of news yesterday. One of our Majors, Major Knyvett Leighton[32] died yesterday morning at Naini Tal. He was my Captain and such an awfully good chap. He went away from here, about a month ago, rather seedy, but he looked as hard as leather. When he got up to the Hills he had dysentery which must have weakened him very much, then he got this intermittent fever on the top of it and the last thing we heard was that he was much better, that was two days before his death. His wife was out here with him, which is a good thing and his sister was staying with them.

There is very little to say, only continual work, more than in the cold weather. We had an anniversary Gymkhana here a few days ago, postillion race – fellows riding one and leading another, side saddle race men up, *doolie*[33] race – two fellows carrying a pole, and another sitting on the top, the man on the top to come in right side up.

One of our fellows Gough,[34] who is ADC to the General here has gone on two months leave to Japan, so I gave him a letter for Sid. He is a very amusing chap & also I thought it would be useful to Sid when she comes here next cold weather.

I am getting on with the lingo in fine style but it wants a great deal of energy to stick to it with a beastly native teaching you. They are such despicable brutes at least that class of them.

Will you send me a list of peoples' birthdays or ask someone to. You see before I always knew, as about a week or so someone used to say "it is so and so's birthday next week" but now I am quite at sea as I have to write a month beforehand.

Very best love to all there is no news at all ~~Your affecto Mother~~ not at all absent minded!!!!!!

Try again. I keep thinking of the Hindi grammar, 'I am the Mother of this boy's father', 'this boy is my sister's son.' Etc. etc.

Lucknow, 23 May 1889

My dear Father

Some rain has fallen at last but only a storm. The weather has been absolutely baking here for a long time and 98° in the bungalow. A storm has been threatening here for the last few days and today, being a holiday, I got up at 6am to have a gallop round the race course with some other fellows there. We drove on down to the Club, had a swim in the bath and breakfast and were going to start when first came a sand storm and then down came the rain. So we had to stop there for an hour or two, now it is cool as an English spring morning.

We have got a big march past Brigade Parade tomorrow (Queen's Birthday) and I am going to be galloper (ADC) to our Colonel who is Brigadier. We have so few officers. The Colonel – Brigadier, Adjutant – Brigade Major, Gwynne – Adjutant, one Major in command, I, galloper, and only four Subalterns left for the Battn.

We shall not have a long day of it I expect only just a March Past and then to Barracks.

I am getting on famously with the Hindustani, I shall only be able to keep it up so as to pass the Lower Standard, as there is much too much to do in the cold weather. The days are much shorter and parades in the middle of the day.

This is a very bad cholera year out here, one never hears as much about it as you do at home probably. Only the other day a doctor was sent out from here about 15 miles and died and they say the people are dying in thousands. In Lucknow the people grumble because there is no cholera and they say that the gods send cholera to clear away the over population and that the English are doing away with it so that the people starve.

Such a funny thing happened last night at the Mahomet Bagh (a sort of outdoor club). They are digging up the cricket ground and they dug up three pots of cowries. I suppose about 20,000. 64 go to an anna. They are used as money by the poor natives and must have been buried there about 150 years. There is an enormous amount of money buried here only they can't lay their hands on the right spot. The stories one hears of money being found are just like story book stories. A soldier in the Mutiny buried 30,000 gold manhwes under a tree about a quarter of a mile from here, when he was wounded and when dying wrote to his brother and told him he had marked the tree by 11 nails. The brother came out, got leave to dig, found the nails but the money was gone, and a coolie who had a hut under the tree has since been a very rich man, although of course he does not say he found it.

Lucknow, 8 June 1889

My dear old Molly

I have not written to you for such a long time that I am quite ashamed of myself but really the weather is so hot that one is quite a 'bloblet'. It goes up to 98° in the Bungalow and in some to over 100. As I write one has to get a tremendous lot of ink on the pen and then write like anything for about one line then the ink dries up into a block on the pen.

I have been learning this lingo for sometime now and am going up for an examination in about three weeks. Thank you very much for sending out the songs and the compass only unfortunately they are no use as they are not the right ones.

Our 'paper chase cup' comes off this week only I can't ride in it because I am too heavy. I only weigh about 12.6 now. I think that is about Jack's weight.

The heat is so great now that one has to have men pouring water on the carriages in the coachouses about every hour to prevent them cracking. It is too hot now even to have parades. We just go out at 5.30 am and then get dismissed. The monsoon will be on in about a week now and then it will be quite cold because it rains for about three months or so without stopping.

There are all sorts of rumours about our being moved next year from Lucknow. Some people say we are going to a place called Rhaniket in the hills near here. There is nothing to do there and you are at the top of a hill with *khuds* [hollows or ravines] on all sides. Others say we are not going to move till March [next] year and then [we] are going to *Peshawar* [his emphasis]. Others say we are going to Poona. I don't mind either of the last as they are good places. I would rather go to Peshawar as it is on the frontier and there is always a certain amount of excitement there.

I suppose you are in the middle of the hay season at home now. I wish we had some of your hay to dry for you. We would do it in *three hours here*. [his emphasis]

Lucknow, 17 August 1889

It seems quite ages since I wrote to you but I have been very busy. There are mountains of people to write to and we are so hard up for officers here. I am managing the whole Mess under instruction as to the ordering wines etc. You have no idea what a housekeeper and caterer I am.

I am now doing a Mounted Infantry Course with 30 men of the Regt. It is a three months course and we are attached to the 17th Lancers. I like the work – it is rather amusing and a change. Besides in my opinion it is a bit of an opening as on service there are not many fellows with certificates and they will give me one on passing the course.

We have our Monsoon Races on this week but unfortunately it has been rather wet each day and so not so well attended as most years.

I am awfully glad that you had a good hay season. It is a great thing. I wish we could get good grass out here. Of course just now it is very green and long but not fit to eat for ponies as there is a lot of poisonous stuff in it. At other times of the year it is nourishing but 'you know how Charlie and Joe weed'. Well that is how your grass cutters in this country get your ponies' grass.

Sid sent me some very nice silk handkerchiefs from Japan the other day by one of our fellows who was travelling there on two months leave. They have gone on a trip to Siberia. Sounds odd! Doesn't it.

It is cooling down wonderfully now although next month is usually a scorcher as the monsoon is over and the sun comes out again.

There are a lot of people here now, just for this time all the big swells are here for the races.

I am glad they are getting up a regatta at Gayhurst. It will wake the place up a bit and will be a very pretty sight down at the river. Tell Pa I want a letter from him. He has not written to me for 5 months.

Dilkusha,[35] 24 September 1889

The hot weather is nearly over now, at least the nights and mornings are quite cold which is a great thing.

I have not finished my course of Mounted Infantry yet and shall be very sorry when it is over as it does one such a lot of good riding about every morning from about 6am till 8.30. I am sorry to say that it will be over in another fortnight as the men are all getting quite proficient cavalrymen.

The Monsoons are nearly at an end. It rains in showers now and the leave season will be at an end next month and our Band will be back which will be jolly as it is a nuisance to miss the Band during the lowest time in the year. By the way we have a <u>Welch Harper</u> coming out to us this cold weather so we shall have instituted again what we have trying to get for a long time. He always used to play at Mess in ancient Welch clothes and a long white beard. He will be rather hot in this country with his beard I expect.

Our Colonel[36] comes back again on the first Oct. He has been away sick for some time. He suffers very much from liver. We thought that he would not have lived when he went away, but apparently he is alright again.

They have changed the mail day. Instead of starting out from here on Sunday it goes out on Wednesday which is not easy as the first days in the week are our busy days.

We have a Major coming out soon and one or two new subalterns I expect as we have several vacancies.

I must write a letter to old Jack, I suppose that by this time he will be back at the House. He must be getting a very fine rower by the things that they won at Gayhurst because they don't seem to have been crews to be despised.

Dilkusha, 3 December 1889

My dear Father,

A Merry Xmas and a Happy New Year to you and many of them. By Jove how funny it seems that two Xmases have passed since I was at home.

I think Blanche intends to stay here a bit while Walter goes off and gets some big game shooting. I have been on my back for more than a fortnight with a strained groin. It is nearly alright and will be quite so in about a week.

They have begun another of these camps of exercise here but not with as many troops and not to last as long, as last year. However I hear there were five regiments on parade this morning not counting two cavalry regiments and three batteries of guns.

It is a nuisance being laid up as I am as fit as a flea and was going through a gymnastic course which does one all the good in the world.

There does not seem any expectation of our moving from here yet. I dare say not until the cold weather after next. They are keeping us here a wonderful long time. I should like to move. This place is all very well for fellows who are fond of society but I would much rather go somewhere where one could get some shooting instead of polo, it doesn't cost as much and everyone can do that.

Dilkusha, 3 December 1889

As this is the mail for Xmas I must not put off writing lest I should be late in wishing you all a very Happy Xmas and New Year. I hope before the fourth comes I shall be at home again on leave for even now it seems a very long time since I was at home.

I believe Blanche and Walter come up here in a week or two before Xmas, then Walter goes on to shoot somewhere and Blanche is to stay. I wish I was in a position to put her up but I dare say she will make some friends here who will ask her to stay with them.

Sid and Reg are coming up next month and will stay for the Civil Service Cup week. I heard from Reg at Singapore the other day. I should think they are nearly tired of travelling.

Our camp of Exercise is only going to last a month this year instead of two and a half. I am rather sorry for it makes one very fit, marching about all over the country.

I was so awfully surprised to see young Loder (Eustace) elected for Brighton. I did not know he was taken that way, he always seemed to be such a quiet sort of chap. He is very young for a great place like Brighton. I am awfully glad that brute Sir Robert Peel[37] got ousted. It serves him well.

His mother did not keep the letters he wrote after the deaths of his father or siblings, so there is a gap in Hal's correspondence between 31 March and

The young blades at Gayhurst, about 1885. L–R: Charles Hulton; Walter Carlile; Reg Hulton; John Cadogan; Edward Cadogan. Two years younger than John, Hal, aged 17, would have still been at school

12 July. However, he kept the last letter his father wrote to him before his death on 16 April 1890. Sadly none of his mother's letters survive.

Wicken Rectory, 8 January 1890

My very dear boy,
I was sorely disappointed when Bee's letter came to find it so full of sorry news! With your usual pluck and consideration for others, you kept us in the belief that you were quite fit and only laid by with a slight sprain, while you seem to have been ill all the while.

First to business. At the end of last September you wrote me a letter clearly defining your position, and saying that you could live fairly comfortably on £12 a month. I wrote back to say I had lodged £50 at Cox's and that your wishes should be further attended to. I thought that was quite plain – you suggested what you could do upon, and I adopted your suggestion. This seemed to me quite clear, but one is apt to forget that the time wh[ich] elapses between a letter written from India and answered from here and received out there, takes so many weeks causes some confusion of ideas. At all events I will give you the £12 a month, and intended to go to town next week to deposit another £50. It will be done and the balance at the end of May.

I earnestly wish you could get active service, or change of air and scene. But active service is the best thing for anyone especially a soldier. I am afraid you won't get it. All looks like peace – though it is somewhat of the white wash order.

Mother will give you all the news. There is no need dear fellow to get others to witness some of your troubles and difficulties. I quite trust you – and always have. I don't think you can ever remember my asking you a question a second time – at school, at Portsmouth, at Carnarvon, or in Ireland, and I hoped that my prompt answers in September, that I would act up to your own suggestion, would have proved the same.

Little 'Dick' still looks out for you I strongly believe. John is at home and is John still – masses of new boots, and all the last new thing, but always nevertheless in rags and tatters, and Burr slaving after him.

You will have soon the Hultons with you to replace Bee and Walter.

I am very stupid and can't think of anything to say, except that I hope this will make you easier in your mind.

Dilkusha, 10 February 1890

Dear Dolly,

You must excuse rather a short and hurried letter but I am so awfully busy.

We have had such chunks of gaiety, four days races and one ball and one theatrical in a week and two more balls and other things coming up directly. Sid is looking very fit and still says she feels 'out to here'. We all had lunch in my bungalow today and afterwards had in about six merchants, silvermen and Kashmiris. How you would love to see the things, they are so exquisite.

 We have got about five weddings coming off in the station and two already over, isn't it funny? Let me see there are Mr Cox, Captain Dunn, Captain Renton, Mr Gwynne, Captain Haggard and Major Duthy.

I am hoping to get away for my shooting soon which will be very nice. I have been so long in the station and all the gaiety in the world does not make up for that.

There goes the bugle for Mess. I must stop, old girl, with heaps of love to Burr and Fritz and everyone.

Dilkusha, 10 February 1890

I have not written to you for ages and I feel quite ashamed of myself but the sisters I know are writing and they always write such capital letters.

Sid is looking better than I have seen her since she has been married, she has lost all that sallow look she had for such a long time. Blanche, dear old girl, is looking well but has not been able to get about much all the time she has been here. She has missed all the best of the fun. We have had such a week of gaiety, four days of racing and then a fancy dress ball. This week on Thursday we have another ball given by the civilians, and the Lieutenant Governor gives one on the 5 March.

Today Sid and Reg lunched with me in my bungalow, and afterwards we had chunks of Kashmiri merchants in for Sid to see their things. Then Blanche and Mrs Mainwaring came in and Sid and Reg went 'globe-trotting' and I went with Blanche and Mrs Mainwaring to see the polo. Last night there were some very amusing theatricals and everyone went, such a lot of people.

I am going to be photo'd this week and I will send some home as soon as they are ready.

Blanche stays until Walter comes up at the end of February, I hope he will stay for the St David's Day's dinner and then they go straight home I think on the 7 March. I don't know when Sid and Reg go, they are such wanderers.

Mr Gwynne my friend is going to be married, I don't know if I'm sorry or glad, he's such an eccentric fellow one never knows what he will do next. Fred Hulton has been down here for the races, such a nice fellow. He is I think the nicest of the lot, he has lots of fun in him, which the others lack and he's such a talker. Everyone sits and listens.

I hope to get a couple of months' leave this year and if so I think they'll be soon, 15 April to 15 June, in which case I shall go shooting up in the hills, I think that is sound. It is better to go to the hills than stay in the plains.

I am fit. Indeed now, never was fitter in my life.

We have the English cricketers here, two were staying in our mess, De Little and Hornsbury [sic], very nice fellows.[38] Hornbury used to stay at the Peels' and play cricket. Isn't it funny how people meet one round and round.

The following letter would have been the last letter Hal's father would have received from him before he died at Wicken on 16 April.

Dilkusha, 17 March 1890

My Dear Father,

I have just got back to Lucknow after seeing Blanche safely to Bombay and meeting Reg and Sid at Mount Abu in Rajpootana, where we tried our best to circumvent the game but without success.

It's getting much warmer here now, we shall soon have our punka up again. I dare say by this time you will see we have got orders to go to Peshawar next cold weather. It will be a very long march if we march it, three months and a half, but I daresay we shall break it somewhere for a camp of exercise and train the last part of the journey.

Colonel Creek has left us from ill-health and Colonel Williamson from the other battalion is coming out to command us.[39]

The girls both looked very well when I last saw them. Blanche had quite a colour after being seedy so long up here, poor old thing.

I suppose you will see Blanche and Walter before you get this letter. I have sent you photos of myself by Sid, there are three different ones so that you can have what you want.

I hope to get two months' leave from 15 April to 15 June, in which case I shall go and hide myself up in the hills if I can and get some shooting.

I have sent by Sid some skins which you can have made up for a carriage rug if you like. They are skins from Bokhara called Sumburi I think, an Afghan horse dealer gave them to me. I believe they are rare skins. I also sent a carved wood box which Mother might like as a tea box or something.[40] Blanche got some beautiful things here but they mount up so and are very expensive. Twenty or 30 rupees go nowhere and that means £2.

I am going to a fencing class now with two or three more of our fellows. It occupies one's time in the morning for two or three days a week. But the worst of it is that one can't keep it up, they only take you through the primary book parts of fencing and I'm not sure (as far as usefulness goes) that a little knowledge is not worse than none at all. However, I daresay it quickens one's eye for the sword.

We shall be reduced in numbers directly. All the hill people are off on Saturday and my Captain, Major Griffith,[41] goes in command so I suppose I shall have command of a company again this hot weather. By Jove, I'm looking forward to the time when I shall be able to follow Sid and Reg and the rest. I felt awfully inclined to come away with Blanche when I left her at Bombay. When I come it will be from Peshawar.

Dilkusha, 31 March 1890

It is quite time I wrote to you, I have not written for so long. I suppose you know that we are to march to Peshawar next October or November. The march will take us three and a half months if we march the whole way but our Colonel is going to try and get us marched half and train the other half. We are all pleased because I believe it is a very good station and up near the boundary.

I'm going to get the first leave I believe. I was afraid until this morning that I should have to go on the second in which case I should not have gone at all as it rains the whole time and you can only go and stay at a place like Naini Tal or similar. I told the Colonel so and he has sent in my leave for the first.

I went out shooting yesterday and got with one other fellow 35 brace of quail before 8 a.m. in the morning. It is such nice clean shooting, you … [remain] much cleaner than in England after partridges.

I suppose you have seen in the papers the extent of influenza out here – any amount of natives are dying of it, they call it fever. One or two soldiers died of it and it is now going around the station.

The hot weather is quite in upon us again now and the men and invalids have gone off to the sanatoriums in the hills, and we have all the doors and windows shut up all day until 5 p.m.

I've been going through a fencing and gymnasium class three days a week and that keeps me very fit indeed.

General Sir Charles Gough[42] leaves us today and the new man comes out, Æneas Perkins by name.[43] They tell me he is worse than the last.

I am much annoyed at my bearer going, I expect he does not want to go to Peshawar and so takes his first opportunity for going away, they are brutes. Directly they want to go, they get ill or their father or mother dies over and over again.

As his father had died, his mother had to move out of Wicken Rectory. She and her small household moved to Woodlands, Alveston, near Stratford-on-Avon. This was near the parish where she and Hal's father had started their married life. From now on she had to be more careful with her money, which is reflected in the letters between her and Hal.

Dilkusha, 12 July 1890

When did you send off your parcel to me as I'm getting a little nervous about it, I think it's quite time it arrived. It's so sweet of you to think of sending me out his links, I shall treasure them very much.

Fancy the two 'Ultons off again, what two people they are. They will never

Gayhurst, the home of Hal's sister, Blanche, and her husband, Walter Carlile, probably Hal's greatest friend. After Hal's father died, this house became the focal point for the Cadogan family.

settle down I don't believe. They ought to go out to this East African Company. That would suit them down to the ground.

I do wonder when you will be moving into your new home, how busy you and Molly and Dolly will be moving everything, it will be such a business. I wish I were at home to help you.

It still rains daily in torrents, there's not been such a monsoon for years they say. I am afraid we shall some more hot weather when it is over and that is the only thing against it. However, I hope to be away in the hills again, I think I am going for a course of military signalling. If I go that will last me from 1 September until we start on the march.

I am trying to sell one of my ponies but everyone is away and I can't get a good offer. It's such a nuisance.

Dilkusha, 12 July 1890

My Dear Dolly,

What a jolly time you must have had in Scotland with Arthur and Ynyr. That journey to Staffa must have been lovely. Everything is now far greener [here] than England. It rains always but the only thing we fear at least it may stop, then it's horrid and everything is damp and wet.

We start on our three month walk to Peshawar on 1 November, 1,000 miles. I wonder what you people would think of a walk like that in England?

I have such a lovely butterfly, I bought it down from the hills as a cocoon. It came out of a thicket and two nights ago it came out and is about 9 inches long and about five inches broad and such a lovely colour. I shall send it home if I can. All the bird skins which I brought down have been eaten by white ants.

Dilkusha, 29 July 1890

Many thanks for your letter from Gayhurst. How strange it seems that you are now in the new house, it will be much better when one is settled down there as this moving must be great trouble and anxiety to you.

In your letter you say you've written to the lawyer to leave the money where it is. I don't want that, I want you to do whatever you want with it. I mean in about another month or so I must have some more. So please pay into Cox's when I write another £50 from that and then afterwards we can see how things are, and you will be more settled down then. Any interest of course you must use with the other.

So many thanks for the cheque into Cox's. I got the abstract from Cox's about two months ago and I can't understand how I never thanked you for it, it was very unkind of me.

We are not to march after all to Peshawar, there is to be a huge military camp of exercise at Akroa, near Attock and Nowshera, 60,000 to 80,000 men and we are to be trained there. I am sorry but perhaps it will be cheaper, as the transport of our things on the march is so expensive.

The bugle for Mess has just gone so I must dress and will finish tomorrow.

I find this morning that I shall hardly have a moment to finish this letter and I am on duty and am shooting in the rifle team tomorrow and am just off to practise.

I do so wonder when I shall get home to see you. All I hope in another two years is to be at home. I don't think much before as there are four or five to go home before my time comes. Yes, Ford does give me a vacancy, so does Colonel Creek, so does Major Knox who is going directly. I believe also when it comes to the second lieutenants being promoted I get promoted before Grant-Thorold.

Dilkusha, 12 August 1890

So many thanks for your letter, it must have been terrible work parting from the dear old place but it's over now and you'll be busy now setting Woodlands to rights.

I do not think I am going to the hills after all, they have not applied for any subaltern from this district, but I am working it up so that I may go in for a class[44] at the earliest opportunity.

We have had the most extraordinary floods here *on record* [his emphasis], all the railways round here have been washed away. The Ganges is about 15 miles wide between here and Cawnpore. I am sorry to say there has been enormous loss of life down there.

We do not march after all to Peshawar because we are to join in an immense camp at Fort Attock of the Punjab Frontier Force. About 40,000 to 60,000 men there will be I believe. We train to Rawalpindi and march 100 miles to Attock. I suppose the camp will last us a month or so, then I expect we shall march to Peshawar.

I am going to sell two ponies but cannot sell Tilly of whom I expect you have heard. I have only been keeping the others on until the cold weather because then one will not lose too much money on them.

I am going to *try* to get into the Bengal Cavalry if I can, but that does not mean that I shall leave the Regiment for another year. The only thing is that I am afraid I have not time, one ought to have 15 months at least and I have only nine to do it in and one has to be in before one's 23 years old, and as you know I was 22 last May. In the Bengal Cavalry there are numbers of fellows in my position, whereas in the Infantry most of the regiments are composed of the very refuse of all the British Infantry regiments. Remember, none of the above is settled in any way.

Seri [near Kasauli], 28 August 1890

You see I am back in Seri and that I am not going up for my musketry course after all. I have been made 'Superintendent of Army Signalling Hazara Field Force'. A very fine title, isn't it, but not lucrative. Peters, who held it before, has been recalled to his regiment. He drew some 300 rupees extra for it but the Government when he went, thought it an excellent opportunity to cut down expenditure so they cut the pay to nil with just the same amount of work. The General, however, says he will do his best to get me the pay.

There was a great Cuttack dance here last night given by the united 4th Sikhs and the 28th P.I. [Punjab Infantry] It is an extraordinary dance, about 50 or 60 men made a circle round a camp fire with drawn swords and then flourishing their swords and shouting, they did the most extraordinary figures. After about an hour they would stop and then one or two or three would come out and whirling their swords round so fast you could only see a sort of glitter. They danced or came on their knees or lay flat on the ground. They went on at it for about three hours, almost mad with excitement. There were only two men wounded, one cut in the arm and one in the leg, but they said this was wonderful.

People are very quiet now and come in to see all the strange sights. You see them in groups watching the bayonet exercise and the physical drill, as if it was some strange dance.

We are all in wooden huts here now, so very comfortable. I have had a telegraph wire laid onto my hut so that I can send messages when I want to. I want to go to Peshawar for a few days' leave as I have not been out of uniform for more than six months, and that gets a bit stale after a time.

I could not write last mail as I was moving about taking over this signalling equipment and have very little time to write much this mail as I am not settled down yet.

United Service Club, Simla, 18 September 1890

My Dear Old Blanche,

Here I am in Simla for a few days, it is such lovely weather, simply perfect, and Simla is full of people. The inter-regimental tournament is going on now (football) and we have a team in. The Royal Scots Fusiliers played the Gordon Highland[er]s and the Royal Scots Fusiliers won by four goals to two.

I am quite fit again, in fact I think fitter than I have been for months. I walked about 10 miles yesterday calling at Viceregal Lodge, on the Adjutant General and C-in-C's house, Snowdon.

I am staying here at the Club, it is so deliciously comfortable. Just fitted up like a very nice English club with Brussels carpets and billiards tables and everything.

There are such lovely things in the bazaar here, quite the pick of things in India I think.

I am going to a large fancy dress ball at the Viceroy's tomorrow night. It will be a very fine sight as Simla is so full.

Kasauli, 5 October 1890

Many thanks for your two letters. I am so glad you seem to like the neighbours at Woodlands and the people are nice. It sounds very nice for the girls.

For the next two weeks you must be content with rather short letters from me as I am simply full of work and have not half an hour a day to myself.

I doubt if I shall go to the manoeuvres at Attock as our class here does not end until 13 November and the Attock manoeuvres begin on the 15th. I am rather keen as my signalling will come in useful directly. A lot of the signallers are out on their manoeuvres and some have just signalled from a mountain called the Camel's Hump to say they have been sent up there and it is too dark to get up or down again. They are about 11,000 feet up and have no food or warm things, not even great coats. They will have to stay there till tomorrow.

The album has just come from you, I shall prize it so I have not time to say much about it as I am off to signals again.

An advance party of two officers and seventy six NCOs and men left Lucknow for Peshawar by rail on 27 October. The Battalion left on 8 November by rail, reaching Rawalpindi on 12 November and marched to Khysabad on the Indus. For the exercises it was in the southern, or defending, force commanded by Major-General W. K. Elles, CB, in 2nd Infantry Brigade. On completion of the exercise, the Battalion resumed its march to Peshawar, arriving on 9 December.

Camp Attock, 16 November 1890

At last I have five minutes to write to you. Since I wrote last I joined my Regiment at Rawalpindi and we marched here, four marches in very good weather, and had four very nice days. But for the last five days it has not ceased to rain day or night and everything is wet and slushy, and so much so that the manoeuvres have been stopped for the present until the rain stops. I have a sort of billet here and am bossing the signalling for the 2nd Infantry Brigade. Although it brings in no rupees I hope it may lead to something afterwards.

The Commander-in-Chief is here and all sorts of people, so there are very great manoeuvres. There are a lot of Australians over to see them carried out.

We march on to Peshawar on 4 December, I believe, and they say it's a very nice station now and very healthy.

The old fort of Attock is about a mile from here on the other side. It must have been very strong at one time and would make some very pretty sketches had one the time and the weather, not to speak of the ability.

I had a letter from Reg the other day headed 'Indian Ocean' so they are well on their way and they are very well. What a pity they didn't stay and settle down.

I have a photo of the signalling class to send you when I get to Peshawar but

I can't send it off until then. It may amuse you.

Peshawar, 24 December 1890

Here we are at last in Peshawar after about a month and a half in camp at Attock. We marched about 120 miles from Rawalpindi.

It is awfully late to wish you a Merry Christmas, little Mother, but although I wrote once to you and hoped to write again for Christmas I couldn't manage it.

The cold is tremendous up here now, we are in a circle of hills although in the plains. The tops of the hills are all covered with snow. The mouth of the Khyber Pass is only about nine miles from here and one can see it quite plainly. I have not been up there yet. Immored is at the mouth this end and one is not allowed to pass it as the Khyber tribes are quite lawless. The things that come through are quite beautiful, one longs to buy Turkamen and Persian carpets and Siberian sable and ermine, so cheap (considering what it is). The bungalows are funny up here. They are built of mud, roof and all on account of the earthquakes they have here.[45]

I am doing Galloper to Colonel Williamson up here on Brigade parades. They have a pack of hounds up here and the huntsmen and whips ride in pink, it looks quite familiar, and reminds us of old times but we hunt jackals and not foxes.

Do you see in the Army List that I made promotion. [Grant-]Thorold is above me but I go above him on account of that business in the 2nd Battalion.

We have had about seven days' torrents of rain without stopping.

The globetrotters even come up here – we had an American to dinner last night who is here with his wife.

NOTES

1. His fourth sister, Sidney, married Reginald Hulton.
2. i.e. quilted backs to their uniforms, which, at that time, were thought to give protection against the sun.
3. Siegfried Sassoon's family had had trading interests in Bombay.
4. Founded, with a bequest by Claud Martin (see Biographies) it did not admit Indian children until 1935. The boys are still housed in the enormous 'folly' that Martin had built and he is buried in the vault beneath it. There is now also a girls school. The editor was lucky enough to be shown round the boys school by Mr Nasir Abid, an old boy, in 2008.
5. Indian Office Library, H725, 393.
6. *Kim*, chapter VI.
7. *Kitchener*, John Pollock, Robinsons, 1998.
8. See Biographies.
9. Hal's sister, Mary. Nearest to him in age, she was probably his favourite sister.
10. The 'Club' eventually moved to Claud Martin's elegant town house which is now a government building.
11. Hal was confused with an impostor who was thrown, drunk, out of a London theatre. There was much correspondence between the magistrates, the Metropolitan Police, and the War Office. It even went as far as the Commander-in-Chief, the Duke of Cambridge.

12. The expression 'hat trick' came into use around 1877, when the taking of three wickets in successive balls was rewarded with the presentation of a hat. It seems to have spread only gradually through the cricketing world – and even more slowly into other sports like football. As Hal would almost certainly have used the expression had he known it, it very probably was not in common usage in India in 1888.

13. 'An immense amount of side on' meant that he was a tremendous snob!

14. The family cook.

15. His sister Dorothy, then aged sixteen.

16. See comments on pay on page 38 and how the allowances in India made it easier for a less well-off officer to keep up.

17. The introduction of 'Short Service' resulted in improved recruiting and a higher quality of volunteers joining up – not all from the lowest strata of slum dwellers. They included some young men who wanted a few years adventure before settling down at home. Recruiting difficulties sometimes caused the War Office to lower the physical standards of recruits; more and more men came from the big, increasingly industrialised cities whither the population had moved following the agricultural depression of the 1870s. By 1890 young men were significantly shorter and less well developed than those of 40 years before, but the intake of 1890 was better educated than their fathers. Nevertheless it was said that Jack Frost was still the best recruiting sergeant and many joined to escape poverty and for the food. Various contemporary reports show that between 70% and 90% joined to avoid unemployment. [*Old Soldier Sahib*, p222.]

18. Lieutenant J. H. Gwynne. The fact that Hal remarks on this is an indication of how few officers in the regiment lived in Wales at that time.

19. King's Regulations in 1900 said that the cost of food in an officers mess should not exceed 4/- (20p) per day, but this regulation was frequently exceeded. Added to this, maintaining the Mess, providing servants liveries and buying newspapers and stationery was paid for in officers' monthly mess bills.

20. Mary would have been eighteen – the dancing age! This could have been a remark in *Pride and Prejudice*, written some seventy-five years earlier.

21. The expedition of 1888.

22. General Sir Frederick Roberts (Bobs) VC, GCB. Later Field Marshal Lord Roberts of Kandahar.

23. After approaching friendly masters of foxhounds in England, ten couple of foxhounds reached the battalion at Chakrata in 1882 in time for the officers to hunt jackal during the march to their next posting, near Calcutta. The battalion finished its daily march by 9 a.m., and this left the afternoons and evenings free for sport and amusements, so plenty of jumping and fun was had two or three days a week. Hunting began at 3 p.m. and went on till dark. *Regimental Records of the Royal Welch Fusiliers*, Vol II.

24. Sister ship of HMS *Euphrates*.

25. Lieutenant J. H. Gwynne.

26. Dilkusha, on the outskirts of Lucknow was the former hunting lodge of the Nawabs of Oudh. The military garrison lay around it, and still does.

27. The Earl of Elgin.

28. Lieutenant-Colonel E. S. Creek.

29. Frank Cowper, married to Hal's second sister Edith.

30. Weekly paper chases were organized by Major H. T. Lyle. The first two or three jumps were made particularly stiff in order to thin out the field which usually consisted of 40–50 riders.

31. Hal's father may have rowed in the Oxford eight but did not win a 'Blue'. However, he was in the Christchurch eight, and won the 'Goblets' (pairs rowing), at Henley in 1854.

32. See Biographies.

33. A covered litter carried by two or four men. See picture on page 71.

34. Lieutenant A. P. G. Gough.

35. Dilkusha was the area of Lucknow in which the battalion was based.

35. Lieutenant-Colonel E. S. Creek.

36. Rt Hon Sir Robert Peel, GCB (3rd Baronet, 1822–95), eldest son of the Conservative politician Sir Robert Peel. Politician, he stood as a Liberal candidate for Brighton in the 1889 by-election in support of Irish Home Rule. He was defeated and his political career came to an end.

37. See photograph p32.

38. E. C. H. Hornby (born 1863, played for Lancashire) and E. R. de Little (born 1868, educated Geelong Grammar School, played for Cambridge in 1889). Members of an amateur English touring team, including the great Lord Hawke, and captained by G. F. Vernon.

39. Lieutenant-Colonel Creek and Lieutenant-Colonel Williamson swapped battalions with approval of the Horse Guards '… provided the public be put to no expense by the arrangement ...' Hal would have known Lieutenant-Colonel Williamson from his three months with the 2nd Battalion in Galway.

40. Still in possession of the editor.

41. Probably Major J. H. K. Griffith – see Biographies.

42. Lieutenant-General Sir Charles Gough, VC, KCB, GOC Oudh District.

43. Major-General Æ Perkins, CB, Late Royal Engineers.

44. Probably one of the courses to be passed before a subaltern could be promoted to captain. These included 'garrison' (administration), musketry and signalling.

45. What a pity they did not continue to build like that. Many lives would have been saved in subsequent earthquakes.

Chapter 3

Black Mountain Expedition
January–November 1891

In January 1891 it was decided to send an expedition under the command of General Elles to punish the Hazanzai and Akazai, two Black Mountain tribes, who, principally under the leadership of Hassan Ali, were 'disturbing the peace' and had fired on a column sent to examine the state of the roads constructed in 1888. The main advance was to be made up the Indus Valley, as it would lead straight to the centre of population. There the ground was more open, and a safer approach than one from the eastern side of the Black Mountain.

The concentration of the Expeditionary Force was made at Darband, about sixteen miles north of Attock, on the Indus, and at Oghi, about twenty miles to the north east of Derband. The force consisted of three brigades:

1 Brigade under (local) Brigadier-General R. F. Williamson (CO 1 RWF).

2 Brigade under Brigadier-General A. G. Hammond, VC, DSO (late The Guides). 1 RWF, commanded by Major Norman, formed part of this brigade.

3 Brigade under Brigadier-General Sir W. S. A. Lockhart, KCB, CSI. (remained in reserve).

Peshawar, 13 January 1891

Again, an awfully hurried line as we are working from 8 in the morning to late in the afternoon, and night manoeuvres are going on, in fact we are having no easy time of it. We are detailed, I am glad to see, at last for the *Black Mountain Expedition* [his emphasis] which starts on the 27th February so with any luck I shall have a medal when I come back to you and enough money to pay a passage, I hope. We are awfully pleased about it. Little Williamson worked it for us, he has got the command of a whole column himself. The 21st Royal Scots Fusiliers are very jealous of us and so are the 5th Fusiliers at Nowshera, for the doctors examined the Regiment and said they had never seen such a fit regiment as we are now.

I am managing the whole signalling of the station of Peshawar. That is six regiments and some artillery – quite a swell only it brings in no rupees.

However, one always looks to something in the future.

You need not be in the least nervous about this Black Mountain expedition as there will probably only be a few shots fired and then we will stay up there for about six months to show the people we can occupy the country if we like.

Peshawar, 24 January 1891

My Dear Molly,

It's such ages since I wrote to you, dear old girl, I've had such masses of work that I don't know where to find time to do anything. I dare say you have seen by the papers that we are in orders to start for the Black Mountain expedition on 1 March or thereabout. So that when I come home I shall be quite a veteran with medals and things. Our Colonel has command of a whole column going up, not ours. He has been made temporary Brigadier-General. We are all awfully excited about it. They say it will last from three to six months, so that we may have some money. Only 600 men of the Regiment are going so there will be about 400 left behind and a great many officers. I hope I shan't be among them.

This is such a cold place in the winter, there are hills all around us about 12 miles off and they are all covered over with snow so when it blows it's awfully biting. We hunt here but just now both my ponies are laid up so that I can't. I ran a stake into poor Tilly's foot the other day but he's getting better.

P.S. Many thanks for the ripping socks, they are splendid.

Peshawar, 24 January 1891

So many thanks for your letters. I am still so pressed for time that I hardly have time to turn round. Our inspection is on now and finishes on Tuesday so we're full of work.

I daresay you have seen in the paper that the regiment is off to the Black Mountain expedition next month on the 16th I hear (this minute the Colonel has come in and announced it). We are all wondering who will be left behind as somebody will have to. Thank goodness we have one or two officers sick so that they will be left behind probably. Our Colonel is in command of one of the columns going up but not us though.

The cold is tremendous here; the mountains round being covered with snow, more than they've had for years people say.

I went out hunting with the hounds the other day and staked poor Tilly, the pony I brought from Lucknow, in the foot. He was very bad, his foot in a poultice and things but he is getting better. However, as my other pony has a bad back I am reduced to walking except when somebody lends me a pony to hack.

What a tremendous cold winter you must have had in old England, but I see in the papers that a thaw has set in.

Only about a year more and I shall be home again to see all your dear faces. Happy New Year to all.

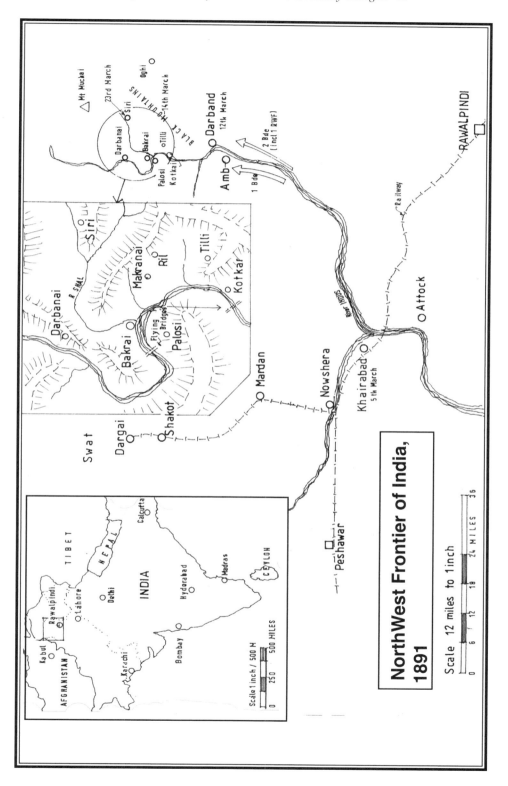

NorthWest Frontier of India, 1891

Scale 12 miles to 1inch

Peshawar, 16 February 1891

The expedition has been put off for 10 days as the roads are blocked with snow so instead of starting today we start on the 25th. The weather is beginning to warm up again here, it is quite extraordinary how suddenly it gets hot. Three days ago one didn't think about a big hat in the middle of the day, but now one has to wear one. All our kits are packed up and ready for the stores so that we are left with only the field service kits. Colonel Williamson does not go up with the Regiment, he has another column of four and a half battalions which goes up the river. We go to a place called Derband, thence to Tilly, thence up into the mountains, so we shall have the cold time of it I expect. I hope we don't come down again soon as it will be quite expensive instead of saving, and also we shall be marching in the hot weather which up here would be awful.

P.S. You must not be anxious if you don't hear from me often from the Black Mountains for we shall only have with us the things on our back and so it will be difficult.

Khairabad, 2 March 1891

Here we are on the line of march, we have reached here, a place where we were encamped for the big manoeuvres. We had three days of torrents of rain in camp at one place and we were up to our knees in mud but the weather is beautiful now. We are encamped on the river at the junction of the Kabul and Indus rivers. Tomorrow we march on to Attock, a short march of about nine miles. We can see the Black Mountains from here, about five marches off, but quite close, only there are three rivers to be forded.

The clergyman from Peshawar came down again today, he's taking a series of photos to send to the *Graphic* of the Regiment on the march to active service.[1] He took a group of the officers today, so you will see it when it comes out.

About the money, little Mother, when did you send it to Cox's last time, as you sent a letter telling me that you had placed some money there, but Cox's did not credit me with it? It is all right as you need not have put it in. However, I should be obliged if you would place it there this month as I don't think I have any balance with them

I am in great luck as I have a company on this expedition. Captain Lyle is going to be ADC to Colonel Williamson, so that it just comes to me. The men are full of spirits, even after their marches they play football all the afternoon and rush about all day. There are 300 of the Khyber Rifles going down with us, they are very fine men enlisted from Afghanistan and Afridis and all sorts, no discipline but rare plucky fellows and fine men. They come and play football with our men.

The day after tomorrow we have to ford a river up to our waists and take all our transport through so that will be a big business and a lot of trouble.

You must address your letters H.O.S.C., R.W.F., Hazara Field Force, India.

1 Brigade was ordered to move up the left bank of the Indus on Kanar, while 2 Brigade moved along the western slopes of the Black Mountain on Tilli. On 9 March the Royal Welsh contingent (20 officers and 612 NCOs and

Indian bearers carrying doolies, probably containing sick soldiers, follow behind a regiment on the line of march.

men), the Guides Infantry and the Khyber Rifles arrived at the camp at Derband, making the Hazara Field Force complete. Due to bad weather there was a delay, so the advance began at 8 am on the 12th. 2 Brigade reached Tilli on the 14th. A bridge of boats, brought up from Attock, was erected at Kotkai.

> Hazara Field Force, Derband, 12 March 1891
>
> Just a line in pencil to let you know how I am getting on. Here we have reached the Front and have been here for three days. All our kits are packed up and we march up into the hills tomorrow and there will be a fight tomorrow but not much, only our Artillery will shell the enemy while our other column under Colonel Williamson marches up the side of the river. We shall have no tents or anything and as it's raining cats and dogs it will be pleasant for there is no getting into barns or houses here.
>
> I met Archie Garden, he is in the Guides here and Sandy Garden[2] is about six miles up with the 32nd Pioneers. The enemy have been firing at our camps all the morning. They began by firing at three officers who were talking near the river but missed them.
>
> I am not doing signalling, the Colonel will not let me go away from the Regiment but I've got command of a company which is a good business as if there is any fighting it means a good deal.

During the next few days, heavy rain and thunder storms interfered with the road-mending parties, who were also frequently sniped at. General Elles visited Tilli on 15th from Kotkai, and seeing the difficulties of supply, decided to alter his plans by leaving detachments at Tilli, Ril, and Makranai, and by bringing 2 Brigade down into the Indus Valley to concentrate with 1 Brigade, the river column, at Palosi. Thereafter his plan was for 1 Brigade to operate on the right bank of the Indus and 2 Brigade on the left.

On 17 March there was a continuous storm of wind, hail and sleet all day, which again stopped the working parties. Extra rum and meat was issued.

17 March 1891

Excuse this letter but we have no tents, only waterproof sheets over us and it's been pouring with rain for the last 12 hours and will rain for 24 more I should think. The cold is tremendous as we are only about 100 feet from the where the snows are lying.

I was to have gone out foraging with my company but the rain is too heavy to do anything. I'm afraid if this goes on any more there will be lots of men sick with fever and ague and things.

There was a skirmish yesterday about three miles from here, we heard a lot of firing and it sounded like a pretty stiff action. But it turned out that some of the people fired on a covering party of our native troops whereupon they fired about 500 rounds at every native they could see, I believe without any damage to anyone. Colonel Williamson's column below has had some fighting with only two men wounded and Colonel Williamson himself was nearly shot, a bullet passed quite close to him and hit one of his Sepoys in the thigh.

I've just sent for my rum and it's the only thing that keeps one warm as you can't get any food cooked as the fires won't light and there are no tinned meats except each of us brought up a little in our kits.

My hands are too cold to write any more but I will do so as far as I can again and I write this just to show you I am well.

The weather cleared on 20 March and the advance on Ril and Siri was successful. Siri was burned on 24 March and the next day 2 Brigade left Tilli,

A 'beestie' or waterman provided water on the line of march.

reaching Palosi at about 3pm, crossing the Indus by the flying bridge at Kotkai.[3] It was a very trying, hot march of about eleven miles. The enemy was seen in some force in the valley to the north, and in the hills about Baio, a village some 3½ miles south west of Palosi.

On 25th, the column the column paraded at 6.30 a.m. in preparation for and advance on Darbanai. It crossed the Indus by boats and a flying bridge at Bakrai, and the enemy at once began to oppose them.

Tucked into a copy of the Koran (see Hal's letter of 29 March) which is still held by the family, was a letter to Captain & Quartermaster Gray[4] from C. E. Willes,[5] a fellow subaltern of Hal's, which describes admirably the events of the 21 March.

> Tilli, Saturday [21 March 1891]
>
> Dear Gray,
> I am sending a knife, a trophy of the Black Mountains, found among the rocks up here. I wish you would have it put with my kit … My servant is lurking about at Darband [sic] somewhere so you could give it to him and tell him to put it with my other things and 'bob cubidar'.
>
> We have begun our war up here and last night just after we had got to bed, there was a devil of a volley all round. We were nearly all sleeping on the roof of a house and of course they were potting at our tents. Of course we all had to turn out and they kept it up for about two hours. We had two very slightly wounded, and we have heard that we killed 4, but of course it was dark and hard to see and we don't know really if we killed any more. The right half Battn have just gone on with some other regiments (900 in all) to take Rill and tomorrow they are going on to Siri.
>
> News has just come that we took Rill and our loss was one Khyber wounded, enemy's loss not known. There has been a lot of firing, and now we can hear them in the distance shelling some village or other.

On 26th, General Hammond tried to negotiate with the enemy, to persuade them to turn on the water supply. He had no success. So, with an artillery battery in support from the north-east of Darbanai, the Khyber Rifles wound up the hill to reach the water supply which they succeeded in turning on. The 2/5th Gurkhas rushed Darbanai while the Royal Welsh and the 11th Bengal Infantry had a running fight as far as the village of Surmul. An enemy force of some 600 confronted them, but the Royal Welsh carried the neck in front of Surmul and the Khyber Rifles carried the heights on the right. Lieutenant C. H. M. Doughty was severely wounded in the knee, and Private A. Godfrey was mortally wounded. The enemy casualties were estimated at eighty. General Hammond in his despatch wrote '… that no troops could have behaved more steadily or shown more eagerness than the Royal Welsh Fusiliers and the 2/5th Gurkhas.'

The flying bridge across the Indus at Bakrai. Based upon a sketch by the eminent war correspondent Melton Prior of the Illustrated London News.

Two days later, a force of 400 men was sent on a reconnaissance to find a good alignment for the road. Hal described this in his next letter.

Hazara Field Force, Derband, 29 March 1891

Here I am at leisure to write to you. It is Easter Sunday and we have had a Service this morning. There are two companies of ours here and two companies of native infantry, on detachment. We came back here two days ago after the biggest fight we have had yet. We killed 80 of the enemy, drove them down across the river and burnt a village. We had no-one killed but six or seven wounded. Two days before that we had another fight and killed 40. One of our officers, Mr Doughty,[6] was wounded in the knee, however we have heard since he has gone down that he is not as bad as we thought, the bullet having gone up past the joint into the leg.

We had a big reconnaissance yesterday, 100 men of our own, 100 of the 11 Bengali Infantry, 100 Gurkhas and 100 Khyber Rifles. I was in command of ours. We climbed along the Shal River for about seven miles about 5,000 feet up where no Europeans had ever been. We were not attacked, only the natives threw huge rocks down from the heights above us. No-one was hit however.

They say the Yakmud of Swat is marching against us with 20,000 more men in which case we shall have a bigger business. We shot two men the other day from the picket. One was only wounded, shot through both his knees and he told us they had about 20,000 men here. Our people have ordered up the reserve brigade from Rawalpindi and our column, the hill column, is the only one that has been doing any fighting. They fired at us from the hills above last night but only a few shots, they are very brave fellows but no combination [sic] and their arms are bad. We have not got any of their arms yet as the Gurkhas and Khyberies get them all or they rush on after the fight regardless of discipline. I've got one knife from a dead man, and a handwritten Koran.[7] I hope we shan't have to stay long here as if it is awfully hot – we are some 800 feet lower than the column, although they are only about mile off.

So many thanks for the knitted things, when they come they will be so useful because although I am here now I might be sent off tomorrow up into the snows with a great coat and blanket and then they would be very useful. The worst things here are the bugs, lice and fleas in thousands. You see we have no tents and have to occupy the villages, and Mark Reed's house at Wicken would be a palace to this. Dung heaps inside the houses and one sleeps on them on the top because it is warm, etc. The men are very well indeed and we are all as brown as berries.

Please thank Mary and Dolly for their letters and tell them that I have so little time to myself and I have to write lying down on the ground so that one writes as little as possible.

I am just going to have a tub in the stream here, the first for weeks. So, goodbye little Mother, much love to all.

The next day, 30 March, another reconnaissance was made by some 250 men, including 150 Royal Welsh, under Major Mainwaring. A larger force left Darbanai, and patrolled towards the village of Sabé, which they burned, with some other small villages before returning. Thereafter life became a rather monotonous round of road-making, village-burning, and repairing water supplies. A gymkhana and concerts were held as diversions for the soldiers.

On 8 April, all troops were moved to the left bank of the Indus, with the exception of 37th Dogras who remained to hold the western end of the bridge of boats at Kotkai.

Hazara Field Force, Darband, 2 May 1891

Just a line to tell you I am quite fit as I have not written to you for two or three mails. We are still sitting at this place Derband. We made a little expedition to burn two villages and destroy all the wheat crops about seven miles from here. We crossed the Indus on a raft, with some men swimming on inflated skins brought from the other side. We caught about 200 sheep and goats but after bringing one load of sheep the raft broke up and it was with the greatest difficulty we brought the men across and had to leave all the remaining sheep and cattle behind.

I went up to Siri, the Headquarters Camp of General Elles, to take some men to the sports, but it rained in torrents the whole time. So much that all the bridges were broken down and the rivers so swollen that we could not get away for two days over our leave, and had to ford the rivers up to our waists.

So many thanks little Mother for all your birthday letters, I'd quite forgotten my own birthday until your letters arrived. Your parcel has not come yet, I expect if it was sent to Peshawar they will keep it there a little time longer and then send it up if we're to stay up here. At present we're quite uncertain as this war in Miranzai is much bigger than they expected, and they have let alone here several tribes they meant to have attacked originally because of it and the Manipore business. They are doing well there. They attacked a stockade and killed 200 Manipores with the bayonet. Our loss was four officers wounded and seven men, one man killed. In Miranzai they have killed 500 or 600 altogether so they are nearly sick of it now and I expect will give in shortly.

They have stopped all men whose term of service is up this year from going home next trooping season. No reason is given, but it may be that the Amir of Afghanistan is very ill and they expect war on his death.

What funny people politicians are, we are amused to see that Parliament had wired out to ask what steps had been taken by the Indian Government to avert the impending famine in the Black Mountain. The place is full of crops and we are here to try and tame the people by destroying their crops and villages until they give in.

The weather in the Indus Valley was now beginning to get hot, and as the inhabitants seemed submissive enough, most of the river posts were abandoned, the bridge of boats dismantled, and, on 7 May, Battalion Headquarters marched to Siri. The remainder followed two days later.

Hazara Field Force, Camp Siri, 11 May 1891
So many thanks for all your letters. Here we are in a new camp out of the heat of Darbanai. It got quite unbearable for British troops so we are up here within about 700 feet of the snow, in fact I was up there with a party of men to get fir trees for shelter and the men snowballed. Does it not seem funny, here it is almost unbearable in the middle of the day and up above one a few hundred feet quite cold! Even here, about three weeks ago when we made an expedition there was snow here.

The flowers here are quite extraordinary, there are thousands of different sizes. Clematis on the trees and peonies, Christmas roses, strawberries and a blue poppy, this is the only place in the world where it's found. I shall try and send you home some roots and bulbs if I can manage to do so but although one gets the mail daily they will not send parcels away for one.

Operations are over here now and the Hassanzais are allowed to come back to their villages. The Akazais are all coming in and when the last Jigar comes in I don't know if we are to stay or go down, anyhow we stay until the end of the month as our tents are to be sent up to us for the first time in three months. I've ordered from a photographer who is up here with the column some photos of the country and the fight places, they are rather expensive so that I'm only getting about 20, but they will be very nice to have, a sort of reminiscence of the country. From the top of the hill one gets the most glorious views of the unexplored tracks of the Hindukush, Afghanistan, Afriristan, Dadystan, and so on, some in perpetual snow.

I had a long talk with a native officer of the Guides, an Afghan, who told me the people were quite white and sat on chairs like Europeans. I believe they are supposed to be descendants of the Greeks who came with Alexander over these parts. They don't like Mahomedans but were very pleased to see the only white man who ever went there. I believe I should like to go up there very much.

That was a very poor picture of the Black Mountains you saw in the *Graphic*, it was taken by a rotten staff officer from a blue book sketch I believe. I think the photographer Burke is sending some. If so they are sure to be good.

What a pity it was we had General Elles in command of our expedition. We should have had a really large affair, the biggest for years and then there would have been DSOs and all sorts of things flying about.

We are all much amused by the English account of Grant and his 80 men against 4,000 Manoparis. [sic] I believe the number was 800 and no doubt it was a plucky thing but when none of his men were killed and only eight of the enemy you may judge what sort of fighting it was.[8]

I can't write on another sheet or this will be overweight so with love to all.

Hazara Field Force, 5 June 1891

Many thanks for your letter of last mail. We are to stay up here with two native regiments and a mountain battery of Artillery for all the hot weather, so that is a good business. It would have been awfully hot marching up to Peshawar and it is very unhealthy up there. 10 of the 5th Fusiliers have already died in the last month from enteric fever.[9] Our newest arrived subaltern has got it here but his is the only case here. He only joined about four months ago. He is quite out of danger I'm glad to hear and they say his was quite an English case, not like the Indian enteric.

You wanted to know what the people are like up here. Well they are Mussulmans, even the Hindustani fanatics. These latter do no work but are fed from India by the Mohammedans, mostly from Patna. They are large men, very good fighters, with a black beard like a Yankee on the end of the chin. They only use, or usually use, a blunderbuss with a barrel thus

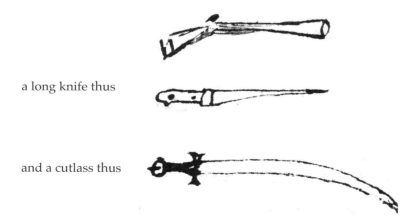

a long knife thus

and a cutlass thus

They are the remnants of a native regiment that in the mutiny was quartered at Hoti Mardan and after 500 Sepoys were shot at Peshawar for mutiny this regiment got frightened and bolted towards the Torbela Pass. They were caught there by Nicholson[10] and three guns, and out of 700 of them 490 were killed and the remainder got into the hills. These are the descendants, increased by modern malcontents and others. There are about 800 of them now. The Hassanzais and Azakais are much the same although they are not such keen fighters and never come to close quarters if they can help it. They grow beards and some of them that we have met have been in British service but these acted as guides for us and have now left for India. One man fought for us in the Bailey Guard at the Residency at Lucknow in the Mutiny. Another who has been fighting against us was in the Naizam's army in Hyderabad. They have all been allowed to come back to their homes except Hashim Alli and his connections. He was the late king or chief of the tribes.

A native Sepoy of the Guides saw a man one day when they were making a reconnaissance and shouted to him. He then went to his officer and said there is a brother of mine there, may I go and shoot him? So the officer said 'no'. Whereupon the man asked if he might go and talk to him, so he was given leave and he went and talked to him for a long time.

Some natives here use a tremendous long gun called a Jizail. It is about eight foot long and they fire it with a match. They shoot stone bullets too, made out of stuff like marble only softer and these are very nasty things to be hit with as they break up into powder after striking.

RWF officers on the Hazara Field Force. Back row (L–R): Surg-Capt Pinches, AMS;
2Lt W. F. Smith; Lt H. O. S. Cadogan; Capt F. Morris; 2Lt C. E. Willes; Lt C. M. Dobell;
Capt F. A. Cooper; Capt & Adj W. R. H. Beresford; 2Lt C. A. K. Johnson.
Front row: Capt H. T. Lyle, DSO; Lt W. C. Hale; Maj C. Norman; Col R. F. Williamson, CB;
Maj Evans Gordon, Royal Berkshire Regt (Regimental Paymaster).

A little amateur washing.

I have got a sword and some knives off some dead chaps in a fight we had at a place called Sansul. It was about the best fight we had although nothing was said about it. It was two days after the fight where Mr Doughty was wounded and was not mentioned as we had no business to have fought according to the boss General. The village was a Chakerzai village and although the Chakerzais were fighting against us all the time the General would not allow us to go against them. They are a big tribe and he has shown a good deal of nervousness all the time. These men cut off our water supply so General Hammond determined to punish them. So we attacked them and we killed 120 of them. One of our men was killed, at least he died of his wounds since and also a Gurkha and two Khyber Rifles were wounded.

You asked me in your letter what you could send me. If you have a few yellow-back novels, I mean the shilling kind, they don't cost much to send and you don't know how acceptable they are here where it so hard to find a book. We are all very nervous about our kit left in Peshawar because the white ants are so bad there and if they once get into a box it's all up with everything whether woollen, cloth, leather or anything else.

As the submission of the Hazanzai and Akazai was complete, on 11 June the main body of the Hazara Field Force started to return to India, leaving the Royal Welsh, among other supporting units, to occupy the Black Mountain and Oghi until the British terms were fully complied with. The Black Mountain was held until the late autumn, when a settlement was finally made, and the British force withdrew, leaving 200 Border Police to preserve order. The battalion returned to Peshawar, arriving there on 9 November. Flintcastle and Elliot-Lockhart in their report on the Malakand Campaign of 1879 wrote: '... the recent victories ... have achieved little bynod demonstrating the muscle of the Raj … The frontier remains a source of perpetual joy to the soldier, but to the politician a problem still to be solved.' With hindsight, men like Sir Robert Warburton (Assistant Commissioner in Peshawar, 1879–1896), who were able with patience and courtesy to gain the trust of the locals, had a much more beneficial effect. These 'politicals' were usually not very popular with the regular officers.[11]

Hazara Field Force, 20 June 1891

The expedition is over and we are among the regiments left up to garrison the country until Hashim Ali is given up. However, I expect it means annexation.

I am going away to Chandla Galli to do a musketry class in less than a month I believe. I am very sorry as I am saving a little money here and of course at a class it is more expensive than being down at Peshawar. It is a two months' course and is an excellent thing to get through as one must do it before one gets further promotion.

We are now on the top of a mountain called Minal, over 9,000 feet high and outside the Mess we have a border of edelweiss, the flowers that grow on the Alps at 8,000 feet and over and that people set such value by. I enclose a spray. I have shot a magnificent eagle, 8ft 6 across from wing to wing. I am sending it to England to be stuffed and shall go to no expense about it, but shall write and ask Walter if he would like to set it up for a lamp or fire screen. It would be no use to you little one as it is huge and would only be in the way.

What a fuss they are making about that chap Grant. Everyone up here is much amused as although the fellow was plucky enough the whole thing was such a farce. I hope they will hang the whole of the Manipuri brutes. By the way, please don't address me Lieutenant but Esquire. Only official letters are addressed Lieutenant.

I am getting about £40 a year more pay so that you can cut me for £15 or so. I have not said `all` as I don't know how I am going to get home if I don't have something in hand and I must get home if I can.

Hazara Field Force, Derband, 12 July 1891

I have not written to you for two mails now, but I have been very busy and have had a lot of other letters to write. I am putting through a signalling class here and that entails about six hours work every day. We have moved into a new camp here and it is so much nicer, no dust, only it's a little higher so a little further from the water.

So, Sid and Reg have got home again, I've heard nothing from them since Australia although I wrote to San Francisco, and two letters to the Metropole. I daresay Sid is full of bustle what with Ascot and getting fitted out again.

We had a call yesterday from Jhahin Khan, the new King of Hazara. We made him sit down against a tree with his servants and photo'd him. He's a good sort of chap only very weak-minded and I fancy directly we leave the country Hashim Ali will cut his throat. The people are quite quiet now, except for a few men who loaf about in the hope of cutting off a few stragglers, but they don't represent any people.

Fancy Molly playing the harp.[12] I am so glad, it is such a pretty instrument for a lady. What a band you must have at Woodlands. I do hope in the Spring I may be able to get home to see you all for a year, it would be delightful.

Camp Minal, 26 July 1891

I did not write last mail as I was very busy and there was no news of any importance.

The weather has changed here, after having no rain for weeks and months we have had about four days' perpetual rain and thunder. It's very funny, the thunder goes on below and then comes on above us and yesterday lasted all day without any check.

We have just heard of the death of Mrs Griffith, one of our regimental ladies, at Muri. It was very sudden and luckily her husband was with her on a few days leave.

We have just come off Church Parade. It will seem funny when we go back to some place where there is a church, as for five months we have prayed in the open, with rifles and ammunition and everything.

About a week ago we heard that Mr Hashim Alli was going to attack us with 19,000 Kokystanis and others but he never came. I fancy they have had too much bad handling to try us again, unless we go further into the hills.

I have got the *Daily Graphics* you sent me and am much obliged for them. We are pretty well off for papers here, as we all get the *Weekly Illustrated* and three *Budgets*, and three *Gazettes*, and *Weekly Times*, *Field*, etc.

A Cadogan family concert party. L–R: Dorothy; Mary; –?– ; Frances. Photographed c.1890. Mary later presented this harp to the RWF in memory of her brother Hal.

Camp Minal, 9 August 1891

So many thanks for your letter of the last mail. I am so sorry I forgot to put the edelweiss in the letter but I forgot all about it. I will put some in this afternoon if I can find any but I have not noticed any lately. I rather think the flowers have died off. Most of the flowers that follow the snow have done so and the place is quite green now that the monsoon is going on. It rains daily and we have the most tremendous thunder storms. Last night a huge tree about 200 feet high was struck and fell. It fell the only way it could possibly do so without falling on a tent, it was quite a miracle.

What a piece of news about Walter.[13] I had a letter from Blanche by the same mail as you wrote by telling me about it. I am so glad, he is just the sort of fellow for it. I have been writing to him this mail chaffing him and saying, 'I heard he was going to succeed Captain Verney as radical candidate.'

They are making a great road along the top here from Chittabut to Pabul Gully and the natives are to keep it in order if we go down. At least that is the order, but whether they will do so is doubtful.

I suppose I shall hear next week who won the Regatta at Gayhurst. I hope Walter's boat won it.

We have made a tennis court up here and play quoits, tennis and stump cricket with natives down the khud so as to fetch the balls if they go over. I have been very busy lately with my signalling class, they are getting along finely, and won't last much longer.

RWF officers' fishing party in Shal Nullah, Hazara Field Force, 1891.
L–R: Lt H. O. S. Cadogan; Lt C. M. Dobell; 2Lt R. A. Berners; Lt W. C. Hall.

As I sit here I can see right down the valley of the Indus, the way we marched in. On the other side when the clouds lift you can see the Hindoo Kush mountains and tracts of country, Kafiristan and beyond Gilgit, places never yet explored. They say the Kaffirs are descendants of Alexander's Greeks. They are white, hate Mohammedans and sit on chairs. These people are certainly Jews or descended from Jews, great crooked noses like a crow with shaggy eyebrows, regular Shylocks.

Siri, HFF, 12 Sep 1891

Many thanks for your letter and also the money at Cox's. I wish, little one, I could do without it because it must be such a drag on you, if only I could get the adjutancy of the regiment it would be everything but they only give it to such senior subalterns and generally to a captain. It is rather hard that I have the billet I have now and do not get any pay for it. I had a letter from Captain Hamilton who is inspector of signalling in India and he said he thought I was entitled to it and that he thought if I pressed the point I was bound to get it. So I shall do my best. It would make a difference of £10 a month while it goes on.

What a gay time the girls are having with regattas and tournaments and things, what a change to the old neighbourhood it must be.

We have been very busy practising shooting for the Honour and Glory match for the whole of India. I am shooting in the team, and the match comes off on Tuesday so we're rather excited about it.

The Hashims are still fairly quiet, but they stole three mules from Minal the other night and last night we heard four or five shots fired in the camp and it turns out this morning that three men came into the bazaar and bagged three blankets and the sentries heard them running away and fired at them but did not get anyone. I fancy a good many of them are entirely destitute and don't care what they do to get a little food or the money to buy it with. I do want to get home and have a good talk with you about everything, it is very hard to put things down on paper. I do wonder if I shall be able to come home next Spring, it would be very nice to see you all again

Siri, HFF, 18 September 1891

Many thanks for your letter of 27 August. What a bad time the farmers must be having with all that rain.

I am afraid you will not see the return of the Royal Welsh Fusiliers until the year 1897 or thereabouts I fancy. The Regiment will be nearly 17 years out this time.

Three or four fellows from here have left for Gilgit. That is the place where the Russians are exploring and building railways.[14] I fancy that is the way they will try and get in some time or other, but the Indian Government is fairly awake I think. I fancy these fellows who have gone up from here are to build forts and explore the country. Captain Bradshaw who is second in command of the Kashmiri Army says he will try and get me a billet up there. That would be a great business if it comes off. They are to start building a large fort at Attock, by the Indus Bridge, next month and in the latest news, have sanctioned 3 million Rupees for defences at 'Pindi', so it all looks like business.

We are having a great thunderstorm while I am writing, the first rain for a month now. It will cool the air as it has been very hot lately and there has been a good deal of fever about. I am afraid it will stymie our little picnic this afternoon to meet the Minal fellows, a pity because it is our one piece of gaiety in the week. Every Sunday we have tea together half way between. Our team did not go near winning the musketry match I wrote to you about.

Camp Siri, 12 October 1891

I am sorry I had no time to write last week but I was up at Minal when the mail went and the last day we had a long march to the highest peak in the Black Mountains, Muchai, 9,861 feet, about five miles off. I am quite fit again. When I was at Minal last week we had about three inches of hail which shows how cold it was and I was up there again yesterday and the snow was still lying on the ground.

I think the Regiment goes down in about a week, but don't know for certain. I expect to stay up with the Force until the native troops go down.

There is a good deal of cholera at Peshawar so that our men are just as well up here. I am told that all the troops except our men have it at Peshawar – the Royal Scots Fusiliers, the 5th Fusiliers, and the Battery, are out in the cholera camp for it.

The people here are still very peaceful but I fancy it is only until we are out of this and then they will be the same as ever. They're trying to get them to enlist as border militia but they have only got 40 out of 200 men required which shows they're not kindly disposed.

Our shooting team was 50th out of 178 teams who sent in their scores from all parts of India.

Camp Siri, 25 October 1891

The Regiment has moved from Minal to Oghi, that is at the foot of the hills on the Indian side so that looks hopeful. The worst of it is that cholera has again broken out in Peshawar.

The Chief[14] arrives in Abottabad in a day or two on his way up to Kashmir. I doubt if he will come here, General Hammond goes down to meet him.

They are enlisting all these people who have been fighting against us in the militia, they have now got 100 of them and are going to get 100 more so that everything is looking pretty peaceful.

I don't expect I shall get away to go down with the Regiment for I have a lot of work handing over stock to the arsenal at Rawalpindi. I am going down to Oghi tomorrow to take over some stock there I think, but I shall be up again in a day or two.

I do hope within a month you will get a letter from me at Peshawar, I am so sick of this place and one wants a change I think, after being within five miles of the same spot for nine months.

Camp Siri, 1 November 1891

Many thanks for your letter from Woodlands again. I am very busy and quite well. The Regiment has left for Peshawar at last and I shall join them towards the end of the month I think, but I am awfully full of work now. You must not address me 'Assistant Superintendent of Signals' – it is only an honorary title for the sake of business and not a permanent one at all.

We played a great cricket match at Oghi against the Regiment there and beat them by about 90 runs.

I shall not be very long behind them as I shall go by train

Nearly all these tents which cost 71,000 Rupees are down and are being carried down to Oghi by coolies. The Gurkhas move out from here on 13 November and the 4th Sikhs on the 15th, I suppose I shall move down on the 15th. So do not be surprised if you hear nothing from me in the next fortnight. I will write if I possibly can. The General is away just now, he has gone to Abottabad to meet the Chief[16] who is there on inspection and going up to Kashmir through Montserat.

We're going to have some fireworks on 5 November if we can. There are lots of rockets and I have some red signalling lights and we're trying to make a balloon in which we mean to put a dynamite bomb and explode it in the air.

1RWF returned to Peshawar on 9 November, leaving Hal and his signallers to follow later.

Camp Siri, 22 November 1891

Here we are still at Siri but only one more week so we are the only ones with the Gurkhas and Sappers and Pioneers in the Black Mountains now. I am very busy still settling up everything and getting ready for the move down. We move into Oghi on 30 November and out on 1 December. I shall go by tonga [dongah] to Peshawar, reach there on the 4th probably and then when the troops have reached 'Pindi [Rawalpindi] I shall return there to hand into the arsenal, and then all will be finished I hope.

I heard from Peshawar today and they seem to be very full up there this year. There is a little cholera and all the soldiers are kept in the lines but that is nearly over. The native regiments had it very bad indeed, and that was the reason the Regiment was railed up to Peshawar to avoid the regiments marching out who had it.

Yes, I met Captain Montgomery during the expedition. He is a fat, good natured sort of chap. He was mentioned in despatches but he never saw a shot fired. All the heads of departments get mentioned, even the treasure chest officer. However that is only fair if they do their work properly.

NOTES

1. See photograph p. 78.
2. These were two of Hal's cousins.
3. See illustration p. 74.
4. Typhoid.
5. Captain & Quarter Master W. Gray, 1RWF.
6. See Biographies.
7. Later Lieutenant-Colonel C. H. M. Doughty-Wylie, VC, CB, CMG. See Biographies.
8. Koran still in possession of the editor.
9. In April 1891, Lieutenant Charles James William Grant (1861–1932), 12th Madras Light Infantry, volunteered to lead a small force of eighty Punjabi and Gurkha soldiers to rescue British and Indian troops and administrators who were trapped in the state of Manipur on the north-east frontier of India. He fought a fierce action at Palel against some 800 Manipuri troops and went on to capture the fort at Thobal which he held until relieved. Despite Hal's playing down of the action, Grant was awarded the Victoria Cross.
10. Brigadier-General John Nicholson, a thirty-six year old who was mortally wounded leading the Punjab contingent in the assault on Delhi in the Indian Mutiny in 1858. His soldiers loved him for his fearlessness, a reputation he had won in the Afghan and Sikh wars.
11. See L. James, *Raj*, p407.
12. See photograph. After Hal was killed in 1914, Mary Coote presented her harp to the Royal Welsh Fusiliers in his memory. It remained part of the 1st Battalion's possessions, retuned at huge expense after every move, and was played in the officers' mess at the St David's Day Dinner and at Dinner Nights. It was sold in the 1980s being beyond economic repair.
13. Walter Carlile was adopted as the Conservative candidate for North Buckinghamshire. See Biographies.
14. From the mid 1880s, the British and Indian intelligence services had become increasingly obsessed with the progress of Russian railway construction who saw it in a strategic light. This railway got as far as Andijan, quite a long way north of Gilgit, in 1899 and then stopped. Nothing more was built until 1906. There is still no railway in Gilgit. The real aim of the Russian offensive was the control of Constantinople, thereby giving them access to the Mediterranean..
15. General Roberts, VC.

Chapter 4

Young Soldier Sahib
December 1891–March 1899

Hal finally rejoined the Battalion at its station at Peshawar, a few miles from the Afghan border.

Peshawar, 18 December 1891

I have not written to you for about three mails but I have been travelling about most of the time. We came down from the Black Mountain on the 3rd and met some friends in Abbottabad which is the nearest place for civilisation to those wild parts and stayed there for three days which passed a mail, I then came into Peshawar to get some clothes, which took two or three days, and then went into 'Pindi to settle up with the signalling kit which took a day or two, past another mail. I have now got back here and am settling down again and like it better than I did before we went away.

We have a new Colonel now, Colonel Norman,[1] and he is not very popular being very strict; very much the reverse of Colonel Williamson but he is a sound sort of man.

There's going to be a great week here at Christmas. The 5th Fusiliers are coming up and we're going to play them at all kinds of games. I've been very busy getting up a tug of war team and being the second heaviest man in the battalion (the first only beating me by one pound) I am expected to pull in the team.

I have never wished you all a Merry Christmas, I wish I were at home to share it with you all. I do hope to come home for the next one but if I only get six months I shan't come as I can't afford it. A year is all right but they are rather shy of giving it in this battalion now.

I hope I shall get my company by the time the battalion comes home, I suppose in about six years' time. I have a Mr Hayes-Saddler dining with me tonight, an awfully amusing man, he makes one cry with laughter. The brute has just finished his rubber of whist and is talking and I can scarcely write. He is very French and talks with a very French accent and belongs to the Royal Scots Fusiliers.

I heard from Blanche the other day and also from Sid. They all seem very fit and Sid and Reg appear to be going to the West Indies from what I can learn from them. What travellers they both are. Walter seems to be full of his electioneering now and I hope he will succeed.

Peshawar, 17 January 1892

Many thanks for your letter of today. What a terrible winter you seem to be having again, one can hardly realise it here where although it is very cold for India yet of course there is never any more frost that justifies the remark of frost.

I forget if I thanked you for your dear little pocket calendar you sent me, it came on Christmas Eve just in time for Christmas.

What a sad thing it is about the Prince, and especially sad for the poor Princess May of Teck.[2] Only about a fortnight from his wedding I believe it was.

It's such a nice season here, we had the first rain today for months and months which was pleasant as the roads were getting very dusty.

We were giving a big ball on the 10 February but it has been postponed owing to the death of the Prince. I suppose it will come off the first week in March.

Another step in the Regiment, I hear I am now half way up the list of subalterns in the Regiment so that if it goes on at the same rate I might get my company in four years or even less. That means I should get it before the Regiment comes home. By Jove it is something to look forward to. I do hope I may be at home by next Christmas but I'm not at all sure of it.

Peshawar, 22 February 1892

Many thanks for your letter. No doubt you are quite right about Molly, I daresay that Walter and Blanche are mistaken about him,[3] for it does not follow that because he races he necessarily gambles although it is generally the case. I believe that he does not as a matter of fact as he is a particular friend of a Mr Willes in my regiment and he says he knows he is rather a devil-may-care sort of chap but he likes him very much and says he does not gamble.

Now about myself, I have some news to tell you. A Captain Lock has applied for the Depot adjutancy and has got it so that I shall not. Therefore with Molly's marriage coming off and one thing and another … I have made up my mind to come home and I got leave this morning. I have applied to get home on board a troop ship sailing on 6 April. I may not be able to get home on this as there is always a rush for them, but if I don't I shall come either by second class P&O or else by a ditcher. I mean to come. If I can sell my ponies they will pay my journey all right.

Peshawar, 8 March 1892

No doubt Mol told you in the last letter I wrote that I intended to come home this summer, I am trying to get a trooper but if I don't succeed I shall get home somehow. As yet I have not sold the ponies but it is a bad time of year to do it as everyone is going off to the hills so I am rather low in spirits about it. I suppose it will turn out all right though. I hope so.

I have got influenza or something, I am so weak I feel as if I can hardly do anything. However, I suppose it will go off in a day or two.

There is an assault at arms today and tomorrow and I am running the tug of war, not pulling myself this time. The men are quite keen enough without me.

Peshawar, 14 March 1892

I suppose I shall be starting home in about three weeks from now, but I am rather despondent at not having sold my ponies. Not one yet, and I am told that probably I shall be unable to get a trooper. Could you put some money into Cox's for me, I shall come home as economically as I can but it will not do to trust entirely to the ponies as I might be sold altogether over them. If I can't sell them I shall lend them to fellows here and ask them to sell them when they can, which will be all right at the end of the hot weather, but the present is bad for selling as everyone is away in the hills or home. I wonder if I am right in coming home, you see I thought I might not get home at all until the Regiment comes in another four or five years and that seems such an endless time does it not?

Molly's engagement put the final decision on it and I hope you don't mind but I do want to see you all again.

Our dance went off very well and the 5th Fusiliers gave a fancy dress ball soon after. The 21st Fusiliers are giving one on the day after tomorrow, and that would be good too as they mean to cut out the other two.

Peshawar, 28 March1892

Just a line to say I am all right and am leaving here on Wednesday the 30th for Bombay and sail the 6 April so will arrive at home about 4 or 5 May. I have sold three ponies at 400, 300 and 250 having given 200, 170 and 200 respectively. A profit of 430 Rupees, and two of them I only had for two months.

I think I am certain of my trooper, I'm pretty junior but of course I'm not certain. These ponies pay off all the debts here and more besides so that is all square.

Hal was on leave in England for eleven months between May 1892 and March 1893, during which his sister Mary was married to Sir Eyre Coote in Alveston Church on 24 November 1892.

At Sea off Gibraltar, 22 February 1893

I'm writing this now although we don't get into Port Said for another six days, but the weather is getting fresh again although the wind is with us and if the ship rolls as she rolled coming across the Bay I don't see how there is any possibility of writing. There are only about a dozen or so passengers with us and mostly ladies except a Colonel Mainwaring[4] and a Major Edwards[5] who used to be in the 23rd and is going out to shoot in Kashmir and in fact is coming up to Nowshera to see the fellows again.

It blew great guns in the Bay, in fact we never saw any passengers for four days except Edwards and Colonel Mainwaring, but the ladies are all up now and are very nice indeed. We passed Gib this morning at about 5.30 and could just see it …. We don't stop anywhere until we get to Port Said and then not at all until we get to Karachi.

Dear old Walter saw me off from Liverpool and I believe it would not have taken much persuasion to have made him come as far as Port Said too.

We have the awnings up now for although there is a smart breeze the sun is quite hot. I wish I could send you a little of it in a letter, it does one so much good.

On 22 November 1892, the battalion moved only some thirty miles by rail to Nowshera on the Swat river to relieve the 2nd Bn, Royal Northumberland Fusiliers.

Nowshera, 4 April 1893

So many thanks for your letter, I am so pleased you have been having a pleasant time in Scotland. It will do you good – you have not been away for so long.

Now I am to tell you about the sort of place this is. It is a tiny little station, only about half a mile each way with 13th Bengali Infantry here and also the 37th Dogras, both rather slow but we make lots to do for if we did not there would be nothing to do. For instance, we are having a horse and dog show on Tuesday week which will be fun and we get up paper chases out in the country. It's beginning to warm up properly now, today it is nice but there was rain yesterday.

Most of the fellows will be going away, but it is much more healthy here than in Peshawar. Our men are picking up nicely again since they've been here. Poor chaps, they had such an awful go of Peshawar fever,[6] out of 500 men in Peshawar 63 died and nearly all the others were either in or attending hospital. Even now you could walk along the line and pick out nearly every man who was in Peshawar during the hot weather. It is curiously like cholera, the only difference being that instead of getting cold as with cholera, a man gets hot and it is not so deadly.

I missed last mail as I was over in Hoti Maidan shooting off the Guides team for the Chief's Cup.

My old pony Tilly is very fit and I've got one I bought off a baggage driver for £5. I wish you could get one at that price in England. I think he will turn out well, at any rate it's not a serious price to pay for a pony.

We have the inspector of nuisance, I mean Gymnasia, coming today so we all have to go and play before him with the foils and single stick.

Nowshera, 23 April 1893

I did not write to you last mail as I have been rather jostled for time lately. I'm putting my company through musketry now which takes up a lot of time.

The hot weather is upon us again and most of the fellows have gone on leave and a good many of the men too. It's a very dull little place, this, and duller because the two native regiments are very uninteresting and do nothing at all. We play a bit of polo and shoot a bit and have a gymkhana and a horse show to break the monotony. It is said that our next station is to be either

Lumballa or Jhansi. I hope Lumballa. Although Jhansi is a good sporting station, you are split up into three or four detachments and have to do sort of police work for Central India.

Very many thanks for the money little Mother, I got the intimation from Cox's all right about it.

I do hope you had a good time in Scotland with Ynyr, she always is such a ripping hostess to stay with.

I'm hoping to go up for a Garrison Class[7] and have been working for it a good deal. It's an excellent thing to pass and get rid of.

All the ladies are leaving for the hills like migrating birds, we have no Regimental ladies here at all now.

I'm afraid we will lose a lot of men in the hot weather, for after the last hot weather in Peshawar when we lost about 70 men, our men were inspected by a special surgeon, and he said that there were 200 men who would never be fit to serve in the hot weather in the plains again. Even now there are over 100 men in hospital. Up to the present it seems a very healthy little place, very dry.

Nowshera, 21 May 1893

I can't understand how you never received my letters. I wrote to you from Port Said, from Karachi and as soon as I arrived in Nowshera to you at Woodlands. I hope you will have got them before this for it is very provoking for you.

Here, needless to say, it is very warm but unseasonably cool as it was 106 on the veranda but the nights were fairly cool and the mornings gently cool.

The reliefs have come out and we are to move to Jhansi, 900 miles from here and near Bombay. We shall be split up into three cantonments, Jhansi, Nowgong and Sipri. Very hot places, but there is very good shooting to be got and at Nowgong, many tigers, so I may get some skins yet. We are all going over to Hoti Maidan next Thursday to play polo with the Guides. We go at about 5 a.m. and stay all day there and come back at night after dinner as it is too hot to go there in the middle of the day.

These Pathans stole four rifles the other night from one of the barrack rooms, and no trace of the thieves yet and I don't suppose there will be any.

The Pathans were very good at spiriting rifles out of British military camps. This was a continuing problem; Frank Richards wrote in *Old Soldier Sahib* of the recovery of some nine rifles seven months after they had disappeared from 2nd Bn, Royal Welsh Fusiliers' camp at Meerut in 1904. The rifles had been stolen one night from a tent by some Pathans. Seven months later, at the mouth of the Khyber Pass, a family of Pathans with a bullock-cart were being questioned by the police, before being allowed to enter. Their cart, which was half full of stuff bought during their visit to the plains, was searched in the customary way. Among the hoard was a closed coffin. One of the Pathans told the police that the coffin contained the corpse of his grandmother, and that he and his uncles and cousins were carrying out her last dying wish: she had asked particularly that she should be buried where she was born. The lid of the coffin was unscrewed and sure enough the corpse of an old dame was there all right ... Nothing was found in the first search, so the officer in charge made his own. He bundled everything out of the cart including the coffin. It struck him that the old dame weighed a good deal more dead 'than what she must have weighed alive. He pulled her out and began tapping the bottom of the coffin. It sounded wrong. He now turned the coffin upside-down and knocked the bottom in, and there, in the false bottom, were the nine rifles that had been stolen from the RWF at Meerut. They still had the regimental initials and their own numbers on the small brass plates on the stocks.'

Nowshera, 4 June 1893

What sort of a time have you been having with Blanche in town! I wonder how Molly looked at the Drawing Room.[8]

It's wonderfully cool here for a wonder, quite an exceptional year. It was awfully hot for a short time, very nearly a record, and then there was a thunderstorm lasting about three days and followed about every other night by sandstorms and now it's quite cool. Although one has punkas one really does not want them as it's only 86 inside and 108 outside. There are very few of us down here now, only six all told, so there is a good deal of work to do but it helps to pass the time which otherwise would hang a bit. I am hoping I may get a Garrison Class this year but I'm not certain.

What a brilliant time there has been at the opening of the Imperial Institute. Fancy their making so much of that fat pig Kapathala[9] at home, no-one thinks anything of him out here at all.

As you know we are going to Jhansi next cold weather, it will be a good march, about 1,000 miles and is only 30 hours from Bombay. That looks very much as if we are on our way home in another three years. There will be no polo I expect but excellent shooting of all kinds.

Nowshera, 19 June 1893

Excuse a hasty note. Many thanks for your last letter. I wonder how you liked 'Eyre Court'?[10] I think it is charming. What a good time you and Dolly must have had in town seeing the Imperial Institute (Exhibition), it must have been a very fine sight.

It's awfully hot here now, about 98 degrees perpetually and I'm sorry to say we're losing some men. I think a lot of constitutions were undermined at Peshawar last year. We have lost five, and two dying today. Also poor Paget of the Rifle Brigade is dead yesterday, and Lovett of my Regiment is very ill with enteric.

Give my best love to all. I am correcting about 100 signalling papers so that I have no time to write more.

Hal was, after all, sent on a Garrison course.

Strawberry Bank Hotel, Dalhousie, 5 September 1893

Many thanks for your last letter. Fancy you're letting Woodlands. I hope you will find your tenant satisfactory.

I am going to write you a very short letter today I'm afraid as I am so busy I haven't time for anything scarcely.

It rains here constantly worst luck as it's bad for the outside work which is the greater part of the work nowadays.

We march from Nowshera on 2 November for Agra I hear so that will not give me much time to prepare things when I go down from here. I did hope to get 10 days leave, but can't do it if we start so soon.

I nearly got a bear here the other night, they come down to the crops at night and I have slept out once or twice to get them. The night before last I sat up and one came into the Indian corn and I could hear it eating but I couldn't see. I went into the corn to try and get it but it heard me before I got up to it and it got away. I hope to get a skin before I go down, however. I know of a cave where they live and am going there when I can get a day off to myself, there is so little time for anything but work.

Dalhousie, 8 October 1893

Many thanks for your last letter from Gayhurst. Poor little Mother, how cruelly fate is treating you in money matters.[11] I do hope these Australian banks will be all safe again, I should think they are sure to; people think it is only a temporary matter. I will do whatever I can and I'm sure you know I will, but this is a beastly expensive place and makes an awful hole at once into one's allowance. At the next station I think I am going to Sipri which I think will be economical but the march is very expensive. You see they don't allow us anything extra, and all the Mess is on the move all the time, and then the Government doesn't allow anyone anything for carrying baggage. One must have a bullock cart to carry baggage which comes to about 70 Rupees a month at once.[11] I am not telling you this to worry you or to let you think that I am in the least hard up but to show you what a drag all these things are on one.

Our exam comes off this week and next and then off back to Nowshera to start on 4 November. I will give you a list on a separate sheet of some of the principle places when they come out. I have a list now of the places but it does not give the dates so it's no use to you.[12]

I got such a beautiful little dog two days ago, I met it on the hills with a shepherd and gave him 4 Rupees for it. It's like a huge thickly-made Collie but with a head just like a bear and hair like one too. He's fretting for his home poor soul very much, but he will soon be all right when I get away from here.

There is such a beautiful view of the snow-topped mountains from here about 50 miles off, what a pity you can't see it.

In December, Hal received a letter from Colonel Watson with the good news that he had passed 'most successfully. You were easily first of the Dalhousie Class, a gain of 'Special Mention' with an aggregate of 82%. You were: 1st in Fortification, with a star; 3rd in Tactics and Topography, with stars in each;

4

Name of Stages.	Stages M.	Stages F.	Total M.	Total F.	Remarks.
Goojur Khan ... p.o.	9	0	111	6	Supplies procurable, water plentiful, road as above.
Suhawur ... p.o.	11	6	123	4	Supplies and water procurable, road as above.
Deena ... p.o.	14	0	137	4	Supplies and water procurable, road as above.
Jhelum ... b. p.o. r.s. t.s.	12	0	149	4	Small Cantonment and Civil Station, supplies and water plentiful, road as above
Nourungabad * p.o. r.s. t.s.	3	6	153	2	Supplies and water procurable, road as above ; Jhelum crossed by ferry boats.
Kharian ... p.o.	9	2	162	4	Supplies and water procurable, road as above.
Lalla Moss ... p.o.	9	6	172	2	Supplies and water procurable, road as above.
Gujrat ... b. p.o.	9	6	182	0	Small Civil Station, supplies and water procurable, road as above.
Kuthala * ... p.o.	6	0	188	0	Supplies procurable after due notice, water procurable, road as above.
Wazirabad ... b. p.o. r.s t.s.	4	4	192	4	Supplies and water procurable, road as above, Chenab crossed by ferry train.

* Except during the rains there is no occasion to halt at Nourungabad and Kuthala.

5

Name of Stages.	Stages M.	Stages F.	Total M.	Total F.	Remarks.
Ghukur ... p.o.	10	2	202	6	Supplies and water procurable, road metalled & bridged
Gujranwala ... b. p.o. r.s. t.s.	10	6	213	4	Small Civil Station, Supplies & water plentiful, road as above.
Kamokee ... p.o.	11	2	224	6	Supplies and water procurable, road as above.
Mooreeake ... p.o.	12	3	237	1	Supplies and water procurable, roads metalled, nullahs bridged or the banks sloped away.
Shahdera ... r.s. t.s.	13	0	250	1	Supplies and water procurable, road as above.
Mean Meer ... b. p.o. r.s. t.s.	8	5	258	6	Large Cantonment, supplies and water plentiful, road unmetalled the greater part of the way ; Ravee crossed by ferry about 1¾ miles from Shahdera.
Chubeel ...	8	1	266	7	Supplies and water procurable, road metalled & bridged.
Churenda ...	12	2	282	1	Supplies procurable, water good from wells, road as above.
Amritsar ... b. p.ó. r.s. t.s.	11	4	293	5	A small Cantonment and Civil Station, supplies and water plentiful, road as above

A booklet printed for the march from Nowshera to Sipri, via Jhansi and Nowgong in 1893. Each stage of the march is identified, along with the distance to be covered and the facilities available at each camp site.

and 3rd in Law. In the latter subject you only missed a star by a few marks. Let me congratulate you on your brilliant and well-deserved success.' So the young man who failed his Sandhurst entry was rapidly learning his trade.

During the cold weather, the battalion left Nowshera on 2 November, to march to Jhansi, Nowgong, and Sipri, a distance of over 900 miles. It marched down the Great Trunk Road which Kipling had the *Ressaldar*[13] in *Kim* describe:

> For most part it is shaded … with four lines of trees; the middle road – all hard – takes the quick traffic. In the days before the rail-carriages the Sahibs travelled up and down … in hundreds. Now there are only country-carts and such like. Left and right is the rougher road for the heavy carts – grain and cotton and timber, bhoosa, lime and hides. A man goes in safety here – for at every few kos [less than two miles] is a police-station. … It runs straight, bearing without crowding India's traffic for fifteen hundred miles.

In the 1840s, the East India Company spent an average of £400,000 a year on road building, with the largest sums being expended on the Great Trunk Road between Calcutta and Delhi. It had, unusually for India at the time, a tarmac surface which cost £1,000 a mile and required an outlay of £50,000 a year to maintain. Metalled roads had an obvious military value and also helped internal trade run smoothly.[14]

Frank Richards described the procedure for a battalion on the march:

Large marquees were removed and we were issued with mountain tents which could be erected in five minutes and struck and packed up in the same time. Large bags called 'sleetahs' which held the kit and blankets of four men were issued: these were carried by the Battalion transport on the line of march. The heavy baggage was dispatched by rail. Transport in India was supplied by the Indian Supply and Transport Corps, which was either bullocks, camels or mules. Bullock transport was very slow. We always had to wait an hour or two for the wagons after we had completed our days march. Camels were much quicker, but the mules were quicker still and arrived in camp on the heel of the Battalion.

The dairy, bakery, cooks and camp-followers moved off each evening twelve hours in advance of the Battalion, so that… breakfast was ready by the time the Battalion arrived. There was no breakfast before we started out on our march, [at 3.45am] which on some days was stiffer than on others, but any man who chose to do so could give his name to the Colour Sergeant who would put it down on the list of men who would be daily supplied with a good meat sandwich and a pint of tea at the coffee halt, for which two annas a day was deducted from their pay. The Battalion coffee bar supplied the sandwiches and tea which were issued out after half the day's march had been completed. We always knew when we were approaching the coffee halt, where we had half an hour's rest, by the drums striking up with the tune of 'Polly put the kettle on and have a cup of tea'. There did not seem much difference between the line of march and a standing camp; the mucking and other wallahs came around shouting their eatables, the Canteen was opened at the usual time and the shopkeepers from the Regimental Bazaar, who also travelled in advance, had erected a smaller edition of their shops. It was rarely that we pitched camp; the nights were warm enough to sleep out in the open.

A regimental canteen on a line of march.

We started each day's march at dawn and the only parade we did after arriving [at about 9am] at camp was rifle-and-foot inspection. Unless a man was on guard he had the rest of the day to spend how he liked. We were allowed in the small villages near which we camped, but a large-sized town was always out of bounds for us.

Most men spent the rest of the day playing card games and gambling for small stakes. The officers spent their afternoons hunting, playing polo, shooting, pig-sticking, etc and were entertained most hospitably by the regiments quartered near their overnight camp.

Attock Camp, 5 November 1893

Here we are, four marches out of Nowshera. I joined the regiment here with the company from Attock Fort where I've been in command for a day or two.

This morning we had a most tremendous earthquake while at breakfast. It lasted two minutes and it was so severe that although we were in camp the tea slopped out of the cups and the coffee pot nearly fell over, and there was a noise like an express train passing through a station in England.

We have just had news from Peshawar that the huge Government mobilisation storehouses have been burnt by incendiary. It has rather a political bearing as there were enough stores to last a whole Army corps six months, that is, 40,000 men with fodder for horses and transports. They say too that they are trying to do the same at Rawalpindi.

I shall be very glad to get down to Lahore or down country because up here it is so dirty and dusty that one cannot get comfortable.

You must not expect me to write every mail as one has so little time and only very limited time to write as everyone is jostling to get at the only writing table in the Mess, and in the Mess tent there is hardly room to turn in.

Camp Gujarat, 20 November 1893

Many thanks for your last letter dated from Harden.[15] I missed last mail as there was very little time for writing, and only one writing table for us all and of course a regular rush for it.

Here we are in Gujarat, the scene of the great Sikh fight which took place after Chillianwallah.[16] A beastly camping ground, sand up to one's knees. I am going down to the city this afternoon to have a look round. In a camp the other day where we stopped I picked up about 50 old coins which had been dug out of an old fortress there. They were about 3 rupees, among them were two silver ones and three Greek coins which I expect are valuable.

It's awfully hot in camp during the day but very cold at night. We're hoping to get some pig sticking tomorrow when we get to Wazirabad.

Our men are playing a match (cricket) with the Gujarat College team.

I expect you find Yorkshire rather dull and little Freedom[17] too. She said something about your going to spend Christmas with Ynyr and her going down to Molly at Eyre Park. That would be very jolly.

If I am not able to write again next mail you must take this as a Christmas letter, little Mother, and with heaps of love and wishes for a Merry Christmas and Happy New Year. It does not feel much like Christmas here as the sun is so hot you can't go outside without a hat like a mushroom on your head without fearing the sun. We have a terrible lot of men down every day with fever and ague, the results of the outbreak in Peshawar last year which they will never recover from.

Camp Delhi, 1 January 1894
Many thanks for the Christmas letter. I hope mine reached you somewhere near the day. I am sending you a stupid little present, it is a thimble from Delhi and Dolly and Fritz two little brooches from Delhi. They are pretty little things and the stones are real although not good stones

Lt Hal Cadogan wearing the ribbon of the India General Service Medal (awarded for the Black Mountain Expedition) and the gold watch left him by his father.

in colour. I have put in a little brooch three little bears which, if you wouldn't mind sending on to little Gladys, Sid's god daughter.[18] I could not help buying them, I thought they were such sweet little things.

We've been stopped here by the rain and it could not have been at a better place as there is so much of interest to see here. The old Fort, the Palace, Hindhu Rao's house[19] on the Great Ridges just opposite our camp. This is where the old native infantry lines were and there is nothing left but the old balls of arms (musket balls?) and a few tumbledown old bungalows.

We are due at Agra on the 12th but shall not get there now until about the 14th or so, that is if it doesn't rain any more.

It's very hard to write on the march as one is always on the move and march every day, not even excepting Sundays.

There are a good many globetrotters in Delhi, and it's very nice to see pretty English faces again after being in the jungle all the time.

We have been doing a little pig sticking and have just got into the country for it. I dare not do too much myself as I am afraid of laming the ponies. You see being such a heavy size has a disadvantage.

The new station, Jhansi, was spoilt by the battalion having to find a detachment of a wing (four companies) at Nowgong and one company at Sipri. Sadly, this interfered with all forms of regimental and team sports. Jhansi was, and is, a great railway centre. A large half-caste population lived there, running the huge Indian railway network.

Jhansi, 10 February 1894

As you will see by the heading, we have arrived at our destination at last. We got in on the 8 February. I've not had time to write since then as there has been so much to do, the others have gone on again to Sipree and Nowgong, and my company here consists of 209 men, counting attached ones.

It's quite hot here compared with up country places. We played against Jhansi at cricket yesterday afternoon and beat them. I couldn't play myself as I was on duty. I shall be full of work for another fortnight because the General is coming down to inspect again on the 24th and there is much to be put straight.

It is a strange place this, such a change from up country, red soil, no grass and ragged rocks and stones as far as the eye can see. We had the most awful thunderstorm two nights ago just after getting in, the unfortunate half battalion which was going on were in tents and every tent was laid flat and all their kit was under two feet of water. The lightning also struck the guard room roof knocking all the tiles down nearly onto a man in there. The lightning hopped from the roof to the punka pole and thence to the barred door, on again from there to the piled arms with fixed bayonets on which were resting the Colours, which were not damaged in the least.

There is a great colony of half-caste people here. It's the great railway centre of India and they say it is to be the Headquarters of the Bengal Army next year.

Jhansi, 18 February 1894

Many thanks for your last letter. How glad you must be to get back into the house again after being so long away. I heard from Molly last May, she seems very happy and busy at West Park. There are some people here who are great friends of theirs named Foley. He is in the 45th Sikhs and just married before he came out the other day.

It is such a change this place, like no other place I have been quartered in yet. There are very few nice people but there are crowds of railway people here, all sorts of shades of black which I have never seen before in India. Regular ''Arrys and 'Arriets' who all turned out at the Assault at Arms in the sealed pattern English 'costers out for a holiday' kit. One heard the same sort of talk going on as you would hear at some show at home.

I am going away again this year to a musketry class at Pachmaree in August I think, but have not heard for certain. It is an awful nuisance in some ways as there will be no chance of any leave again but it is really a capital thing to get over and done with, as it will be the last exam I shall have to go through before getting my company, which I expect to get in three years' time.

Jhansi, 15 March 1894

Many thanks for your last letter from Woodlands. I was so pleased to see you were back there once more. You must have been pleased to get back after your long exile up in the north.

An overnight camp, possibly on the Grand Trunk Road, in northern India.

I am going away I think for two months' leave in central India. It's not a long or an expensive trip from here and really one gets so awfully bored with the perpetual routine of barrack work and parades. I am going down with a very nice chap from the regiment named Dobell[20] and we are going in from Jubbulpore and Inumdla so you can look them up on the map. It is a great district for bison, buffalo and tiger and we hope to make a bag there.

Jhansi, 12 April 1894

You will be surprised after my letter to find me still at Jhansi, but the fact is that I have got laid up for a few days with a slight strain and could not go on the 6th with my friend. I trust I shall be all right in two or three days and then I shall follow him.

Mr Hall comes out tomorrow and with him a new boy of the name of Kean but he does not interest us very much as he goes to the Staff Corps next cold weather. I hope by the time you get this I may be well into the Lalpura Hills.

P.S. You will have a caller in the shape of my Colour Sergeant. He has got six months' furlough and lives near Stratford and I asked him to call and look you up and tell you all the news about me.

After he recovered, Hal joined Charles Dobell.

Sarangarh, 13 May 1894

I have not written to you for ages but I have been in the jungle and it is very difficult to write, in fact to send letters to the Post Office. We are now some 70 miles from any Post Office.

We came here yesterday after a march of about 12 miles and have had quite a disappointment as we had heard a great deal about this, and now having got here find that all the jungles are burnt and no sambur or bison. We have got a fine bag at present, four bison, four sambur, one bara snipe stag, one kalikur, six antelope, and one bear. No tigers yet, such bad luck we have had. We were in one piece of jungle with six, and the beaters drove two out but they got away unseen. I lost a tremendous bison bull two days ago, they are very wary and my shot went too high. I tracked him for seven miles by marks and blood but never saw him again.

It's quite cool here, of course, the sun is very hot but the nights are bitterly cold. We are going on to a place called Airy, where there are lots of tigers and chietel [deer]. The latter are lovely deer spotted like the deer in English parks but with branching horns instead of the flat ones.

I have to be back in Jhansi by the 5 June so not much time. Our camp is pitched under an enormous 'peeple [peepul] tree' in a village, the houses are entirely built of split bamboo plaited and each surrounded by a fence of bamboos and the whole village also to keep out the wild beasts. There are tigers here and bears as I have seen the marks of three bears this morning and also of a tiger on the road yesterday, but they won't kill the buffalo we tie up. They have so much game to eat. I hope we may get one before we go back.

I hope you will be able to read this but we have only one ink pot between us and that is nearly empty and so have to write in pencil, except for the address.

Jhansi, 11 July 1894

Many thanks for your letter including Freedom's. I am so glad you have taken Woodlands on for another three years especially if Miss Forster makes herself a good landlady.

The rains are still on here and it has rained harder than it has done for years and we have almost had the average rainfall already. It has cooled it down wonderfully though. Unfortunately it rains every night just when one wants to get out for polo or something, and is fine for parades in the morning.

No, we did not get our tiger although we saw six, but I never had a chance of a shot. It was very disappointing as several other fellows shooting within 20 miles of us got four, three and two tigers each and there was no lack of them but were very cautious indeed and would not come back after they had once killed.

We are hoping to get in a game of polo today as it is fine at present, but it usually comes on just before we start.

Jhansi, 9 August 1894

I'm off to the hills tomorrow for a couple of months. I am going to the old place, Kasauli, address Moreton's Hotel. You must excuse a short note today but the mail goes out today and there is still some packing to do. I thought however you would like a line, I shall be quite fit when I get up there. This place is so hard to pick up when you are a bit downhill.

Kasauli, 20 August 1894

Many thanks for your letter, how pleased you must have been to have had old Sid at Woodlands after such a long absence. I hope you will go down to them at Tenby,[21] it will do you so much good.

I am very thankful to get up here, I feel better than I have felt for months. The first week I got down with fever again but got up three days ago and feel now points better and I think it will continue now all right. This place is much the same as four years ago and I notice some of the same faces too; the fat Padre here on leave who was here before, as Chaplain. The hotel is very full, there being 42 people in it, all soldiers and a few wives. I intend to get over to Simla if possible to see the football tournament and also the races. At present everything is hidden in fog and it rains daily in torrents.

Patiala, the Maharaja, is making a polo ground here but it will not be ready until next year. When it is it will be a great success and an excellent thing for the station.

I have been writing to Molly – fancy their not being able to let West Park. I suppose there are so many fine places to let.

Moreton's Hotel, Kasauli, 4 September 1894

My Dear Old Blanche,

Many thanks for your letter, I am so glad you feel fitter. It has rained here perpetually since my last letter, every day and is simply beastly. I am much fitter, however, which is the great thing and I really think that I have got rid of my fever at last.

I am going to try to get over to Simla for a few days to see the inter-regimental football which comes off on the 17th and there are about 12 teams up for it so it will be very interesting, especially as our men are up for it as well which makes it all the better.

It is rather amusing up here in a social way, there are so many of us, about 30 officers staying in the hotel. They are up for both garrison and signalling. I am glad to say I have got through both.

I heard a report the other day that we were going to Poona after leaving Jhansi. It sounds too good to be true.

The same old game – I bought a shawl this morning. I did not intend to, but the man asked a huge price the other day and I told him I would give him less than half. He went away and today he has returned and said, 'Take Sahib', and I did, and now I must send it home to Mother.

Madho Roa Scindia whose coronation Hal attended in December 1894. See Biographies.

Jhansi, 3 December 1894

A Merry Christmas to you and a Happy New Year. I wish I were at home to spend it with you.

I am going to spend a few days at Gwalior. A certain number of us have been asked to his 'Institution Coronation' or whatever it's called.[22] There will be about 200 people in all there and he has contracted with the Buzzard of India, Peliti, to feed everyone at 50 rupees a head a day, so one ought to be well done, and he sends a special train here for us.

I am sending you a little shawl for Christmas to try and keep the cold out.

It's quite bitterly cold here now especially at night and a change to a short time ago.

Since I wrote to you I'm sorry to say we got beat at Jubbulpore by the Munster Fusiliers by three goals to two. I hit a goal, it was very sad being beat, however we can't always win.

I wish we were up in Waziristan now, they are having some good fighting there. That was a great business at Waino. They say some of the levies deserted and of course knew the camp thoroughly. It was more or less of a surprise there is no doubt.

Jhansi, 28 March 1895

I have missed a mail but I was at Kasauli. I went away for a week on duty to take sick troops up to the hills. I stayed one day and came back again, it was quite cold up there, almost too cold to be nice.

I am going away on 10 days' leave on Monday I hope, so that I shall not be able to write next mail. I want to get in a small shoot before the hot weather comes as I do not expect any long leave as we are so short of officers now, only four at dinner each night.

One or two of our fellows have gone up to Chitral and I have applied to go but I doubt if I·shall be able to get up. Everything is done here by interest. There is more gibbery now even than in old Bob's time, and that is saying a great deal. The new man is a Highlander[23] and is all for Highland regiments. It's rather a shame I think and a great pity as he is a very good man otherwise.

Most of the fellows are out pig sticking today. They've killed several fine bulls this year already and have only been out a few times.

Pachmarhi [School of Musketry], 1 May 1895

Many thanks for your last letter. I have reached here as you see and we have a pretty stiff time as on parade one is treated just like an ordinary soldier and have to drill like a recruit with a rifle and side arms. They are quite the nicest lot of men I ever came across and not a single 'stiff' as we say.

It is such a pretty place, it's a plateau on top of a hill about 3,500 feet high and about six miles square and the scenery is like an English park. Beautiful riding and walking, capital golf links – I have taken that up. There is a nice little club and tennis courts and a cricket ground and lots of sport within reasonable distance but we don't get any leave during the course.

No time for any more, we work from 6.30 a.m. to 1.30 p.m.

Jhansi, 26 September 1895

Again I have missed a mail but I am busier than ever and have been for the last fortnight. They put me in command of the Rest Camp, rather a good business as it is the biggest but one in India and there is extra pay of 250 rupees a month. But when I had all the dirty work such as pitching the camp, nearly 300 tents, done, down came a Major from Simla and took it over from me and now the pagoda tree has disappeared into space. However, at present I am doing Station Staff Officer until the permanent one comes back, he is very sick at present and I may possibly get it permanently if he can't come back at the end of another month.

The rains are over at last and it's rather hot again and in the evenings there is quite a feeling of the cold weather and it will soon be round again.

I had a letter yesterday dated from the House of Commons. What a 'devil of a cove' he is now.[24] He seems as keen as mustard.

I fear I will not get home again until the Regiment comes again or until I get my promotion home, but I don't know yet what will happen as to the promotion. I'm trying to get it in the next six months or so.

Jhansi, 12 November 1895

Just a line to tell you how I am and I have never in all my service been as busy as I am now. It takes me to get through the work from 6.30 a.m. to 2 p.m. daily and it's a record year for heat and much more like September than November. I go out about once a fortnight after snipe and have made all the best bags this year that have been got to one gun.

$23^1/_2$ couple before 10.30 a.m.

$16^1/_2$ couple after 1 p.m.

$43^1/_2$ couple all day.

$17^1/_2$ and 8 duck in one hour and a quarter.

So I am very pleased. Unfortunately the last time I was out my coolie broke my gun. I had made a journey of 25 miles by train and a walk of 9 miles out from the railway and then only got one hour's shoot and a broken gun. I had to walk all the way back.

I have met a most interesting man here, Captain Speedy, late Consul in Abyssinia and a great African explorer. He has come out to shoot a tiger and is a most amusing man. He must be nearly 60 but as hard as nails and ready for any amount of roughing it. He wanted me to go down into central India with him shooting but it is in the drill season and I can't do it, I am sorry to say. Among other things I am practising for the Queen's Cup Rifle, shooting for the Regiment, which comes off on the 19th. I am rather pleased as it is the first time I have shot for the Regiment.

I won the Jhansi golf medal the other day, and now I think I have exhausted all about myself and hope you are both well as I am, but not 14st 6lb, like poor me!

Jhansi, 1 December 1895

Here we are again close on Christmas. I am going to spend mine with any luck out in the jungle with two fellows who manage the railway here. We shall be very comfortable as they have their private carriages, and I believe are going to have a private engine and we ought to have a grand time knocking about up and down the line after snipe, sambur, cheetahs, etc. I am rather exercised in my mind as up to date my gun has not come back and the man says he cannot let me have it in time and one never gets on as well with anyone else's gun as one does with one's own.

What sport your hockey matches must be. I should like to see Fritz and all of them whirling around.

I have been over to Sangor for two days to play cricket and am beastly seedy as I have got a bad go of chill and dysentery for the last five days but I am all square again apart from feeling weak and that sort of thing.

There are two generals in the station now waiting to devour us tomorrow and the next day, so we are very busy getting everything square for them. But it makes things very busy and our new CO[25] has never soldiered in India before so most things are strange to him.

Jhansi, 7 April 1896

Many thanks for your letter. I have been away for two days in the jungle as usual and got five fine sambur stags. Such beauties.

I am also busier than I have been for a long time as there is a lot of cholera among the newly-arrived troops from home. Poor chaps, a lot died directly they reached Jhansi.[26] It has not spread, however, except in the case of two men who took a case to hospital and both these have died. Luckily this is not a great place for cholera and [we] usually escape, but there is a tremendous lot all over the Districts this year. There has been no rain, you see, and to obviate famine the Government has started huge relief works where there are as many as 10,000 to 20,000 people employed, and of course that is a rare chance for cholera.

The cantonment cemetery at Jhansi and the grave of the Royal Welsh soldiers who died of cholera in April 1896, shortly after their arrival from Britain.

Jhansi, 18 March 1897

Many thanks for your jolly letter. I am so glad to hear you are fit and none of your rheumatics in spite of the weather which has been so bad. Here we are beginning to fry up again, it gets hotter day by day.

I was away last week, I went down with our GOC, old Sir Bindon Blood,[27] to shoot with the Central India Horse, but we had the most atrocious luck all through and did not get a single tiger although three came out the last afternoon but broke back through the stops and did not get fired at.

You must excuse bad writing but I got a spill at polo, my pony coming down, and I have sprained my thumb and it makes it hard to write.

I am hoping to get away shortly to shoot in central India for a couple of months, and I trust may then get some tigers. We are going into a good district for them.

General Sir Bindon Blood, KCB.

The plague does not seem to get much worse but has broken out near here at a village called Rajpur, and in the last four days 60 people have died out of a total of 500 and it is now in full swing. It was brought in from Bombay by some Brahmins, who avoided the inspection here by getting out at the station before, which these brutes are doing now, and then walking for about 30 miles and getting in again at the station after.[28]

Jhansi, 7 July 1897

I have not written for ages I am sorry to say, chiefly on account of a whitlow on my right thumb, which I have had for almost six weeks. It is almost all right now.

I got back here at the end of the month and had fine sport but no tiger, which was very disappointing and so last month I got nothing at all.

I was not sorry to get back as the cholera and starvation there was horrible. In many places bodies had not been buried and were lying in the water, and in other places they had been buried so shallow that the dogs, pigs and jackals had dug them up again.

I have not any idea as yet when I rejoin my Regiment or when they go home,[29] some say October and some say not till the Spring. I am not really anxious to go, I don't look forward to soldiering in England, and I don't suppose I will stop there long.

I am very busy – a lot of work has accumulated since I have been away.

Probably Hal was thinking of applying to serve in Africa or to join the 2nd Battalion, so that he could serve abroad again – shortage of money being the drawback to serving at home.

Jhansi, 19 August 1897

I join the Battalion for home at Aden and I think start from Bombay about the 7 November but of course nothing is certain just now, as we may be on the point of war with Afghanistan. In fact the Indian Government has sent them an ultimatum I believe, and there are now nine brigades on the Frontier ready and they are talking of mobilising the first Army Corps which has not been touched yet. Should there be war I don't think they would send the Regiment home so soon as it means being relieved by another regiment from England, and I don't think they would care to do this. The natives are very unsettled all over the country.

I had been hoping that General Sir Bindon Blood would take me up on Service,[30] but I am afraid it is no go now. I see in today's paper he has had a good fight near Malakand but no particulars except that poor McLean of the Guides has been killed and also Greaves of the Lancashire Fusiliers. McLean I knew very well, he was hit in the face at the fight at Malakand about a month ago. A bullet went into his mouth when open and came out under his ear. Bad luck being hit a second time.

I am very busy as I had to open the Rest Camp here in 12 hours' notice and send up 300 troops. It was an awful business.

Hal rejoined the battalion in Aden, and then continued to Britain, arriving in Devonport on 9 December. Headquarters and four companies marched to Fort Tregantle. Of the other companies, three went to Millbay, and one to Bull Point.

Fort Tregantle, Devonport, 10 December 1897

At last I write from England and hope I shall see you in a fortnight from hence. I am going down to Gayhurst for three days only on Monday next, and thence I shall come on to you and stay for Christmas if you will have me. I should have come straight down to you but Walter and Blanche are going to Pangbourne so I thought you would not mind my going there first for a couple of days. Besides, old Walt has a shoot on.

We had a very bad time in the Bay. We got into a really big gale and it lasted about 24 hours. There were a good many wrecks I'm afraid. We saw one on the rocks outside Plymouth, and the lifeboat going out.

This is an awfully out of the way place, it's about six miles outside Plymouth, along a most fearful road. I landed my dog all right thanks to old Walt who did the whole thing for me and sent Rogers[31] down and he took the dog away.

Tell dear old Fritz I will write but am awfully sleepy tonight. I have no kit up as yet, not a pyjama, not a toothbrush or anything. The Customs did not allow our things through tonight.

On 10 January, Hal with another officer and thirty two NCOs and men went to Aldershot to attend a mounted infantry course.

Mounted Infantry, North Camp, Aldershot, 25 February 1898

I am afraid it's ages since I wrote but you've no idea how busy we are and how little one feels inclined to write when one gets in. I am going up to town on Saturday to see Reg chiefly. I saw old Syd last Sunday, what a cripple she is at present poor old thing. I do hope it is only temporary and only a matter of time. Reg tells me they are going back to Tenby at once as the change has done her no good. I am sorry – but I think as much merry making as she could put in would do her good; and the more the better. He says it's impossible for her to go abroad, but I can't help thinking that it takes a very ill woman to be too ill to be taken abroad. I shall see Reg, however, and have a talk with him and see what he thinks.

What a small place the world is. The wife of our Colonel is Miss Emeline Sergeant that was, of Turweston near Brackley. She is such a nice woman and so kind.

This course will only last about three weeks more I am sorry to say. It is a very pleasant course and all the riding keeps one so very fit.

Fort Tregantle, Devonport, 14 April 1898

Your letter had something of a rebuke in it and I deserve it for I have not written for a long time, but writing is a difficulty when one has nothing to say and I find in the life here nothing but monotony. It may be otherwise when one gets into a decent place but I cannot stand soldiering at home at present at any price. There is literally nothing to do in the way of work or play, and as far as the work goes one takes as much time over it as if one had to do as much as there was in India. I mean you dress for parade and walk out to it, when you get there you have to peacock about before four sergeants, eight corporals and two men, then you leave the two men to be drilled by the four sergeants and eight corporals and walk back to change again. That is the routine of the week.

The former owner of Cuffles[32] has claimed him and has come over from Ireland and wants him sent out. It's awfully sickening but what can I do? I hope he is not much trouble to you at Woodlands.

What a pity Hal was not encouraged to work for the Staff College entrance exam. With so few men and so little work, his existance must have been stultifying. In any case, Tregantle Fort was a large, damp building some six miles across the Tamar from Plymouth. Those officers with private money could hunt, go racing or go up to London on the train, but many of the less well off must have taken to the bottle!

Things looked up, however, when, on 9 September, the scattered elements of the battalion were reunited at Raglan Barracks, Devonport.

Raglan Barracks, Devonport, 23 December 1898

This is to wish you a Merry Christmas and a Happy New Year and many of them. I wish I was going to be with you for Christmas. Do you remember what a merry one we had last year when I got the thimble I think and no-one got the money.

> I wish I was going with Fritz to her dances too but really can't afford to come rushing down for a couple of days and then away again.

The Battalion Trooped the Colour on the 1 March 1899. Many former officers of the Regiment were present including General Bulwer, and Colonels Holroyd, Creek, Williamson, and Norman.

As part of their Saint David's Day celebrations, the Battalion held its first Red Dragon Cup Meeting since its return. Many of the officers hunted with the Dartmoor Hounds and kept their horses at Ivybridge. The officers took their guests out from Plymouth by special train to Buckfastleigh, and entertained them and others from the surrounding country to lunch and tea on the course. There was a very large attendance and the meeting was a thorough success.

> Raglan Barracks, Devonport, 10 March 1899
>
> Yes, thank goodness our big day is over,[33] all except the bills. I did not see Walt next morning, he had to start by a fairly early train and at a time when we were all busy at office so I could not go and see him off. We had between 60 and 70 to dinner and it was a most amusing dinner. I'm afraid Captain Cowan cut his arm rather badly but I did not see him in the morning either.
>
> We had a great week of route marching, every other day we marched 15 miles. Not bad, and you can imagine it takes a deal of time up because 15 hours means five hours marching in the day and then there is the work to be done. We got back today at 1.30 pm having started at 8.30 am.
>
> We are going to have some Regimental races this year and I am going to enter my old horse.

At the annual inspection of signalling in 1899, the battalion's Figure of Merit was 132.66 out of a possible 135. No doubt Hal, with his signalling experience at Hazara, would have contributed to this remarkable achievement.

Notes

1. Lieutenant-Colonel C. Norman had assumed command on 2 April 1891.

2. HRH Prince Edward died just before his marriage. Princess Mary subsequently married his brother, Prince George, who became HM King George V.

3. Mary, Hal's sister, became engaged to Sir Eyre Coote (1857–1925) of West Park, Salisbury. West Park came down to him from his grandfather, Sir Eyre Coote (1726–83), the victor of Plassey and Wandiwash (1760), and C-in-C India (1771–83).

4. R. B. Mainwaring, see Biographies.

5. H. H. Edwards, see Biographies.

6. This was probably either amoebic or bacillary dysentry.

7. 'Garrison Class' was one of the qualifications for promotion to major.

8. When young ladies 'came out' they were presented to the Queen at a Drawing Room. *Webster's Dictionary* (1913) defines it as 'A ceremonious day reception, attended by both Ladies and Gentlemen'.

9. His Highness Raja Jajatjit Singh (1872–1949), the ruler of the Indian state of Kapurthala since 1890. He eventually bore the incredibly unwieldy title of Major-General His Highness Farzand-i-Dilband Rasikh-al-Iqtidad-i-Daulat-i-Inglishia, Raja-i-Rajagan, Maharaja Sir Jagatjit Singh Bahadur, Maharaja of Kapurthala, GCSI, GCIE, GBE.

10. 'Eyre Court', i.e. West Park, at Damerham near Salisbury, the home of his sister Mary and Sir Eyre Coote. It was a large Georgian pile which was pulled down after the Second World War.

11. A reference to his mother's investments.

12. Route March programme document, p.94.

13. *Ressaldar*, native officer of British Indian Army. *Kim*, Chapter III.

14. *Raj*, Lawrence James, part III, sec. 3, note 29, British Parliamentary Papers 15, 680 and 682.

15. Harden Cottage, Austwick, Nr Settle. Ynyr (Hal's eldest sister) and her husband, Arthur Ingleby, had moved there from Hawkland Hall.

16. The Battle of Chillianwallah, Second Sikh War, 13 January 1849.

17. 'Freedom' also sometimes 'Fritz', Hal's youngest sister Frances.

18. Hal's niece, Gladys, daughter of Frank and Edie Cowper.

19. This house was built by Sir Edward Cole Brook, the British Resident in Delhi. In 1835 the Maratha chief, Shri Hindu Rao Ghatake, bought it and during the Mutiny was gallantly defended by a Gurkha battalion for three months.

20. Lieutenant C. M. Dobell, see Biographies.

21. Reginald and Sidney Hulton lived in Tenby, Pembrokeshire. Sidney died there in 1954, aged ninety-two. She was unable to move from her chair for some fifty years because of arthritis.

22. Madho Roa Scindia, also known as Madhavrao II (see Biographies and photograph p.101) had inherited in October 1876 at the age of ten. The coronation of 1894 marked the end of the regency.

23. General Sir George White, VC, see Biographies.

24. 'Quite a chap', a reference to Walter Carlile, MP.

25. Lieutenant-Colonel C. C. H. Thorold, see Biographies.

26. See photograph of their tombstone in Jhansi Military Cemetery, which bears the names: L/Cpl Thomas Follis, aged 24; Pte Robert H. K. Seagrey, aged 21; Pte Percy Evans, aged 21; Pte Albert York, aged 20.

27. Major-General Sir Bindon Blood, see Biographies.

28. The bubonic plague had broken out in Bombay in the autumn of 1896. In an effort to halt its spread the *Haj* was banned in February 1897 and passengers on the railway forced to take disinfectant baths at stations. Search parties, which could include British troops, disregarded *Purdah* and Hindu women had to strip to the waist so that their armpits could be inspected for the swellings that were the first signs of the disease. These 'outrages' were used by the local newspapers to whip up hatred of the government. *Raj*, L. James, p 357.

29. The battalion, under Lieutenant-Colonel Thorold, had left Jhansi for Aden on 16 October 1896.

30. Sir Bindon Blood was one of the most trusted and experienced commanders on the Indian Frontier. Back in England, fresh from the storming of the Malakand Pass in 1895, he met Winston Churchill and his mother, Lady Randolph. Winston obtained a promise from Blood that he would take her son on his next expedition to the North-West Frontier. Winston virtually forced himself onto the general's

staff. The book Churchill wrote on the campaign, *The Malakand Field Force*, was widely read and established him as a war correspondent. Sadly, Hal did not have such a well-connected mother.

31. Walter Carlile's chauffeur. In 1946, aged over ninety and with only one eye, he was still driving Walter in his 1913 Rolls-Royce.

32. The dog Hal brought back to England.

33. 1 March, St David's Day.

Chapter 5

China

September 1899–November 1902

Very probably because Hal had applied to serve overseas, in September 1899 he was posted to the 2nd Battalion, Royal Welsh Fusiliers in Hong Kong. On 8 October, just after Hal had left them, the 1st Battalion was mobilised and sailed for South Africa. With his desire for active service, his posting to Hong Kong must have been a bitter disappointment, even though his appointment as adjutant was an important step in his career. In the Victorian army, a commanding officer ran his battalion through his adjutant, quartermaster and largely the warrant officers and senior NCOs. An adjutant had even more prestige at the turn of the twentieth century than he has in today's army; his appointment appeared in the *London Gazette* and he received extra pay. But, missing out on active service was frustrating to say the least and even Walter Carlile's visits to the C-in-C failed to get his posting altered.

> Gayhurst, Newport Pagnell, 26 September 1899
> So many thanks for your sweet letter today. I do not think of money matters unless you are in trouble about them yourself. If one was full of the necessary stuff one might not be any more happy and after all that is the great point.
>
> Now little Mother I trust you will not think lack of heart but I am not coming again to Woodlands before I go out, for I don't think I could stand saying goodbye again without losing composure. For as you know what with this Cape business and other things too my cup is almost full and it is the last straw which breaks the camel's back. I don't think I shall be away for more than three years and that will mean returning when the Regiment comes back to India, or perhaps somewhere closer.
>
> I may not write again before starting for I have many letters to write.
>
> Walter is in town but returns today. He went to have another dig at the C-in-C[1] about South Africa, dear kind fellow, and returns today.

> SS *Maba Maru*, 23 October 1899
> So many thanks for your letters. I got both of them, one at Port Said at one end of the Canal and one at Suez at the other.

I told the photographer [to send the photographs to] Port Tewfik or Suez as that is the last place we touch until Colombo. I sent you some of the photos which came out best but they're mostly bad except old Burr and Fritz, who were quite good. The groups were taken on too dark a day and are black but recognisable.

The heat today is tremendous. Curiously enough we have come in for the monsoon which is most unusual at this time of year. We reach Colombo tomorrow and stay there a day and a night starting off again on the 25th at noon I believe.

I wish I were on my way home instead of on my way out, or going back to India would be preferable to this. It's such a mighty long way off as it's over 6,000 miles away now. The journey gets very boresome too. You see there are so few passengers, in fact I don't know what I should do if it were not for Lord H. Thynne who is on board and is full of anecdotes and stories. He lives near Worthing and knew Mrs Thwaites. He told me Mrs T. was his cook and that the story of his marrying her was that he swore one night before some friends that he would marry the first woman who answered his bell. He rang it and the other servants were all together and busy and they asked the cook to answer it which she did, with the result above stated.

We don't know at present if there is a war or not and of course are anxious for news at Colombo. I wonder what it will be!

I turn over and find this page filthy dirty but the ship rolls so and it is so hot. Will write a long letter and tell you about things in general when I reach Hong Kong. Until then I shall have little news to give you.

Love to Fritz and Burr, keep fit dear little mother. I don't think I shall be away very long, possibly not over a year, we shall see.

With his previous battalion on active service in South Africa, Hal chafed at the inactivity in Hong Kong. Moreover, his new commanding officer, Lieutenant-Colonel the Hon. R. H. Bertie, who took over on 15 December, proved to be a pernickety superior.

Hong Kong, 20 November 1899

I am afraid I have been dilatory in writing again and now it is the Christmas mail and I am writing to wish you a very merry Christmas and Happy New Year. I am doing so several days before the mail goes, but then I am full up with work and I have many letters to put in and yours is first and foremost.

I have taken up the adjutancy of the Regiment as the real adjutant, my great friend out here, Dobell, has gone on a year's leave, and I wanted something to fill in the time and I have got it.

We had a bad time coming up from Singapore. We got into a typhoon and had a tremendous sea. Another steamer was with us at the same time and had all her boats, all her bulwarks and her deck houses cleaned right off and is still here patching up and they say she will be here for months.

This is a very pretty place. I am sending you a Christmas card which is little views of the place, which may be more interesting to you than others.

Murray Barracks, Hong Kong.

I feel a little out of my element as I know none of them here and this Boer business naturally hits one rather hard – just being out of it. Major Morris[2] is here of course, he was at home with us and she is a very good little sort so one sees a lot of them. But otherwise it is 'no pigeon' as they say. Pigeon meaning business.

Everyone says there is going to be a big row out here. There is a big Chinese secret society which made trouble a few months ago and they are on the move again. I hope it may be so. Otherwise I hate the place – polo is villainous and there is nothing else to do except there is a very fine Club, into which, if one puts one's foot people invite one in to have a drink with them, so I usually keep away.

The Murray Barracks (Hong Kong), 5 January 1900
I was much surprised at finding in my pigeon hole the other day a note from Reg and a card of Sam Hulton and he came and dined with me last week and was very cheery. He went off next day to enlist in the new Mounted Corps at the Cape. I did envy him, I would like to chuck up everything and go too if I could afford to do so. It is a grand 'neck or nothing' chance which won't come again in a decade I am afraid.

It is a very pretty place this, quite lovely, but I don't like it. I mean I can't get on without heaps of exercise and there is none here – no shooting, no riding to speak of, it is a mountain sticking out of the sea. People very hospitable, and damp and humid – a combination calculated to give one liver, and it does. I loathe the place, and I think most people do who do not care about tea fights and dinners and poodle faking.[3]

There is a chance of 400 of our people going to Borneo to put down an insurrection under that Salat[4] [sic] I think he calls himself.

Young Baker is quite fit again – he has been bad with fever but is all right, tell his mother. I think he is quite one of the most promising sergeants in the Battalion. He is not a colour sergeant yet but will be before long. He is doing Provost Sergeant at present to the Batn. and I shall keep an eye on him as I am adjutant now.

> The Murray Barracks, Hong Kong, 14 Jan 1900

I have not written to you for two or three weeks I am afraid and I feel very neglectful, but I have much 'pidjin' to do now-a-days and my time is occupied most of the day.

Old Li Hung Chang[5] is in the harbour. He is on his way to take over the Governorship of Canton and the people hate him so that the authorities are much afraid that they will try and shoot him [so] that we have to line all the streets tomorrow with troops until his visit to the Governor here is ended. What rot it seems all this for an old Chinaman. But they are funny fellows these Chinamen, they are very clever though as obstinate as mules and sulky tempered.

I am still in a vortex of gaiety. Last night I dined with Sir T. Jackson, tonight American Consul, tomorrow Laytons, Thursday night Government House, Saturday with the Grays, who are friends of Sid's I believe, but I have not met them yet. There are a great number of people here and some very nice people among them.

We have the very poorest wires about the Front and never get any good news until the papers come, and then we have the best of them. Papers of every country come to the Club so there is very good reading.

The weather has been bitter cold. It is like cold Feb. weather at home when the wind blows from the North. There was a frost at the Peak the other night and there has been deep snow in Shanghai lately.

We have many entertainments in aid of the War Fund such as theatricals, concerts, boxing bouts, etc. and the fund has reached very high figures out here, higher I believe than the whole of India.

> The Murray Barracks, Hong Kong, 11 Feb 1900

Just a short letter to say how things are going on and to thank you for all your letters – it is so nice to get them and one seems so beastly far away and out-of-the-world, in this spot.

I went on a big lunch picnic today. Some went on bikes, some rode ponies and some went by steam launch – I with the latter. We had lunch and played games all the afternoon and finally after tea, all returned as we went out. It is a great game here this picnicking and later on the favourite thing is bathing picnics, though in most parties the bathing is done in separate parties and mixed parties are thought to be fast by the steadier-going people.

I went to a Chinese dinner a night or two ago and have hardly recovered yet. We ate sharks fins, eggs a hundred years old, sea slugs, sinews of whale, fungus from the elm tree, toad stools, tripe made of fishes insides, brains of the octopus and many other odd dishes too numerous to mention, which we ate – or at least tried to. Chinese singing girls discoursed sweet music or otherwise, and although I would not have missed it for anything, never again.

The Mail this week does not come in until next Wednesday, three days late. That beastly French Mail always is late and the P and O which is supposed to come in a week later arrives on Saturday only three days after the mail of the week before.

I went down to the China Town on the Chinese New Year night and bought a few odds and ends but nothing much. The shops here are absurdly expensive. They are so spoilt by the Americans and globe trotters that they don't care if you buy or not.

Inspection comes off soon.

Hong Kong, 8 April 1900

Just a line to say how things are going on, but I am afraid it wont be an amusing letter, it is such a dull place, There is no shooting and no riding except the polo which is very poor. The one thing one looks forward to is the Mail from home which brings us our letters and news from S. Africa. Thank goodness I am doing adjutant for otherwise I don't know how I would fill in my time.

We had Mr Smith Ryland[6] here the other day. He was on his way travelling and I dined with him at the Club. He was very pleasant and had taken to drinking water, poor chap. He has had a … kidney complaint or something.

It is very sad about Col Thorold.[7] I am so sorry for her, she was so absolutely devoted to him, and there were so many bachelors who might have gone out without anybody troubling except their pals. It is terribly sad I think.

Goodness only knows what is going to happen. I believe there will be a big blaze up before long, although I can't believe the French want to start fighting with their Exhibition in full swing. But the Italian Reserves have been called up and the Italian War Vessels are being called home and there must be something in the wind. Also I believe the Imperial Govnt. have been enquiring what extra troops the Colonies can find. I do trust it may be France if it is anything. Now is the time to humour them, directly this business is over. It will, of course, be a big business, but the sooner it is over the better – it will have to come before too long.

Young Flower[8] is here and is pretty fit although he has had fever.

Sgt Baker is very fit now and rather fat, a bit too much so. But he is a real good fellow. He is quite one of the most promising NCOs out here.

Although Hal had been in Hong Kong for only fifteen months, he decided in April to return to Britain on leave. This seems extraordinary; perhaps he was hoping to persuade the War Office to send him to South Africa, where his contemporaries were commanding companies or Mounted Infantry columns and winning DSOs. His friend, Charles Dobell, who had shrewdly gone on a year's leave in November, was in South Africa doing just that.

In about 1895, Hal's great aunt, Elizabeth Townsend (daughter of Henry

Lt Hal Cadogan, c.1899

Cadogan, one time Consul at Calais, and the organiser of Emma, Lady Hamilton's funeral) had died, leaving him and his brother, John, each £3,000 (£180,000 approximately in 2009). This must have transformed his life and from this time he does not seem to have been so penny-conscious.

Hong Kong, 13 April, 1900
My dear old Freedom,
I owe you a letter … and have owed one for some time. … I hope [have left] for home before this reaches you. Of course one cannot say for certain, for things in the Army are very much upset but I trust it will be all right.

You will ask 'what the Dickens are you coming home for.' Well I am coming on a five months leave and I am homesick. I wanted to come all the time but doubted if I should be able to. In any case I have taken my passage in the Messageries Maritime SS *Ernest Simon* sailing from HK on the 7 May and reaching Marseilles on 4 June. So I trust I shall see you before very long. It will give me nearly three months at home.

This is rather a rotten place – all right for a week, but to live in – no. There is so little to do and so little sport. The acme of sport is to keep half a dozen China ponies a whole year until the Races and then win a lot of dollars with a miserable looking pack pony. Polo we play a bit but there is not much of it and bad what there is.

We are all wondering when we shall be out of this, and where we shall go to when we go.

Poor old Fritz, I sent you an Indian fan the other day but all things here are so absurdly expensive. I mean a Mandarin coat which you can get at Liberty's for about £2 they ask here $50 or £5. For the truth is it is filled with Americans on their way to Manila and they give any price asked for anything. Later on when one gets away one will be able to pick up pretty things and cheap no doubt. But here you ask the price of indifferent silk handkerchiefs and they say $18 a dozen. You can get the same thing in any shop at home for about 1/5d [8.5p] and a dollar is 2/- [10p].

In China in the summer of 1900, an obscure but formidable peasant sect – nicknamed 'Boxers' because of the martial arts they practised – instigated a rebellion with the intention of expelling all foreigners from China. In May, sensing the gravity of the situation, many British subjects from the outlying communities surrounding Peking took the advice of the British Legation and gathered for protection within the Legation Compound. On 20 June, with the encouragement of the elderly Empress Dowager Cixi, the Boxers besieged the foreign community in Peking's diplomatic quarter. The siege lasted for fifty-five days.

The 2nd Battalion was warned on 9 June to prepare to sail for North China, and a detachment of 336 officers and men left on 16th on HMS *Terrible*.[9] On 21 June, they landed at Taku, and embarked on HMS *Fame*,[10] whose captain was Commander Keyes, later the renowned Admiral of the Fleet.

On 11th July, Battalion HQ, with the commanding officer, Colonel Bertie, and H Company sailed from Hong Kong for Taku. Joining the first detachment to arrive in China, the contingent, now numbering ten officers and 451 NCOs and men marched to Tientsin as part of an international army.

As Hal got home to Britain on about 10 June, he must have been in a fever to return to Hong Kong as soon as he arrived and by early July he was on his way back to the Far East.

Marseilles, 5 July, 1900

Just a line to say that I am on board the *Australia* and we sail in an hour. A magnificent boat and I think some nice men on board. I have a cabin to myself thank goodness, so I can have a little peace.

At present there are crowds of small French children on the jetty playing

A group of RWF officers aboard HMS Terrible *en route to Tientsin. [RWF Archives]*

God Save The Queen and other tunes on the strings of a violin. It is a little trying.

We had a dirty but otherwise comfortable journey for I came down on the *train de luxe*.

Dear old Walt came with me as far as Dover which was awfully good of him, and I have just sent dear B a line.

SS Chusan, Singapore, 29 July, 1900

You see we are getting on but the journey seems very long, almost as long as it seemed coming home and yet for what a different reason.

We are running along the coast of the Malay Peninsula, such a low lying swampy looking shore. We reached Penang yesterday and get to Singapore today and I hope shall get some news, for we have heard very little as yet, and that seems all the news that is going. They told us at Penang that the telegraph wires north of Hong Kong had been cut and that old Nien Li had arrived at Hong Kong on his way north. I trust now they have him there they will keep him as a hostage. I believe he is responsible for a great deal that has been going on.

We have about fifteen or twenty officers of the Indian Staff Corps on board, among them are General Creagh[11] and his staff of the 3rd Brigade. They think they will go to Wei Hai Wei, but don't know anything yet.

I suppose I will go up at once to Taku where I see the Headquarters of the Regiment have gone, but I don't know anything until I reach HK this day week I trust. They have had a great many casualties at Tientsin among the British, but of course we have not got particulars yet so don't know if it is among our men or not.

We had a very rough time from Aden to Penang as of course the monsoon is on and they must be having a very fair one in India by the look of it out at sea. We did not have a really fine day all the way.

There is rather an interesting crowd on board taking them all round, for there are two men, a doctor and an engineer, going out to join an expedition for the exploration of Borneo arranged by the Colonial Office. They expect to be out about 18 months and they are both explorers. Then there is another engineer going to build a railway in Borneo, and he has been building that railway from Beira to Salisbury in Africa and knows all that country. Then there is a Circassian lady who was in the hareem of one of the late Rajahs of Johore and, since his death, is the wife of the Turkish Consul at Liverpool. She unofficially was bought for 1,000 dollars and now wears jewels to the value of £50,000 on her. She wears an emerald brooch about the size of half a piece of soap.

The Allied force marching and fighting their way from Tientsin reached Peking on 14 August. Hal caught up with the battalion in Peking a week later, when the fiercest fighting was over.

Peking, 28 September 1900

The Chief of the Staff, General Bower, told me today that more troops were

*Tientsin railway
station badly
damaged in 1901.
[RWF Archives]*

*Badly damaged
native quarter in
Tientsin, 1901.
[RWF Archives]*

*Coolie transport
used by the Royal
Welsh Fusiliers in
Tientsin, 1901.
[RWF Archives]*

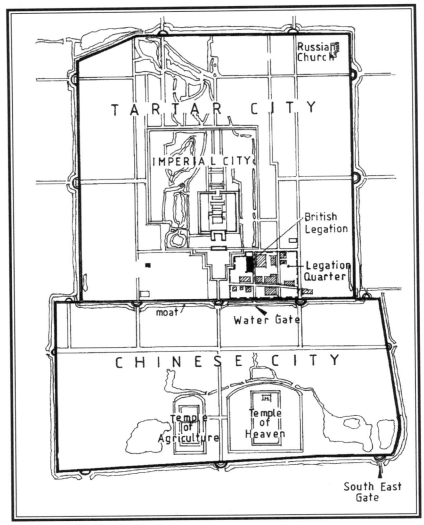

Sketch map of Peking, 1900.

coming up into Chihli[12] – one can't understand why because the Chinese up here are quite demoralized and it is enough for 1,000 men to go out 20 miles to put to flight 6,000 Chinese without our losing a single man. All their guns and breech loaders – and all their … rifles almost have been captured. Also all their arsenals and cartridge stores are in our hands, so that the rifles they have with them will soon be useless as they have no chance to get ammunition . The only reason I can see is that we wish to keep a garrison here as strong as that of Russia or Japan.

I am still in the Quarter of the Russians, French and Germans, Austrians, Japs and Italians with my 110 men and it is very interesting as I have officers of one or the other dropping in. I had an awfully nice French naval officer this afternoon to sit with me for half an hour. He spoke English wonderfully well.

I have been sick for about a week but nothing much, and hope to be off the

Royal Welsh Fusiliers inside the British Legation, Peking, August 1900.

list again the day after tomorrow. I have had a little go of dysentery which takes it out of one a good deal.

We have most of us collected a good deal of loot. When I say loot I mean one has bought many valuable things from soldiers of other nations for about $1/10^{th}$ of the real price. For our people are supposed to send all loot into a big store where it is all sold by auction and the proceeds are to go to Prize Fund to be divided among officers and men of the Expedition. It is a stupid way for so systematic is it that each house is visited in turn and the things just picked out and sent in, giving the servants left in the houses time to bury watches, pearls and all small precious things. The result is that in our force there is little of real value except big bronzes and clocks and old china and things that one can't easily remove.

Three or four days before I arrived silver was being sold by the soldiers in the streets. Blocks worth £8 at 10/- [50p]. I have managed to collect a certain amount. I have about £40 worth I have paid about £15 for, and I wish I could

Chien Men Gate, Peking, burned down during the 1901 fighting.

get a little capital. I bought about 100 real pearls for £2, two as big as small peas but they are pierced. I got about 30 pieces of carved jade for about £2. It may be worth £500 or more, or only £50 to £100 but only Chinamen really understand what expensive jade should be. The only difficulty about these things now is that they may be stolen on the way down. A great many officers have had their boxes broken open and everything of value taken. I fancy it is done by these infernal European China merchants up in Tientsin who I fancy are fit for anything in that line and if they don't do it themselves, they are not above paying the Chinese to do the dirty work for them.

Just before I got seedy I was asked, as OC British Troops up here, to attend the *Te Deum* service in the French Cathedral, the Peitang, where they made such a marvellous defence. It was held in the Cathedral itself with no glass in the windows, half the walls down and the organ pipes looking like nutmeg grinders caused by the bullets. The place was full of Chinese native Christians and there were a great many losses during the siege. Four large mines were exploded under parts of the outlying defences. One caused a crater about 30 yards across and probably 30ft deep, and it is lucky the Relief came when it did for they found no fewer than 4 mines under the Cathedral itself ready to explode when the powder had been put in.

After the Service I had an invitation to attend a big *dejeuner* given by the Bishop, but as there was no one present who spoke English and my French is very poor I made excuses and came away.

At the present there is little going on. A small Expedition goes out 20 miles now and again on hearing that some Imperial Troops or Boxers are in some temple or other, and they kill perhaps 10, 20, or 100 and burn the temple and then return. The troops (Chinese) are merely armed bandits and the ordinary Chinese peasant is only too pleased to see them ousted. The Germans are the most active of any but then they were too late for the heavy fighting, not having got up until I did, so that they are anxious still to carry out the orders of their Emperor, I suppose, but then a terrible lot of inoffensive Chinese have been

Damaged barricades on the south wall of the Tartar City, Peking. [RWF Archives]

The view along the canal towards the British Legation. The Prince Su's Palace was separated from the Legation by the canal which was usually empty during the summer. [RWF Archives]

shot down by them and in fact by most of these foreigners. They don't seem to understand. I marched two days with a German Battalion, and at one place they shot two quiet peaceful natives before their wives at their own door because they found a few Chinese crackers (used to celebrate festivals like fireworks). The German Major came to warn me and another officer, as we were sleeping in the next house, that we should come in further as we were in great danger and he told us the story and showed us the crackers which he was carrying.

The French troops are too despicable for anything. They are infinitely worse than the Chinese – most of them are perhaps a few inches longer than their own rifles, all along the line of communication they spend their time looting and shooting at everything: Chinamen – dogs – cats- pigs or anything else to the detriment of travellers. When marching they look like nothing so much as those pedlars one used to see years ago at home who mended tin pots, for they are slung all over with pots and pans and old boots and as all their helmets are made the same size as the biggest man, they cannot hold their heads up for the kit behind comes up nearly to the top of their helmet. Their clothes are made of butchers blouses, and the cover of their helmet is rolled up behind and shows white.

The Germans have adopted our khaki, but think it never should be washed and they have bought their men globe trotters' pith hats in Ceylon as they could get none in Germany, with the result the rain has melted them and they are now like bits of wet biscuit.

The Russian men are very soldier like. Most of the officers … always look clean.

Above: Royal Welsh Fusiliers aboard converted junks approaching the Yangtsun railway bridge during the first week of August 1900.
[RWF Archives]

Left: A paddle steamer used to transport the British force up the Peiho river.
[RWF Archives]

Graves of some of the Royal Welsh Fusiliers killed during the relief campaign.
[RWF Archives]

Cheng Wang Fu's Palace, 6 October 1900

My dear old Reg,

Many thanks for your letter, you have been awfully good about writing and I have been a hog over it.

I wish you were up here, you would revel in the sales and curios that are being sold at the corners of the streets and that are shown you by soldiers and different people.

I arrived up here very late, nearly a week after they had got into Pekin, so missed most of the looting and all the good fighting. We have lost very heavily as a Regiment. The casualties have been about 63 out of 350 who came up, curiously enough no officers. 8 of our men were killed and wounded by one shell in the Railway Station at Tientsin and five more were killed by an explosion of gunpowder at Tung Chow about three weeks ago and Ivor Hill of the Wei-Hai-Wei Regiment. I have a sort of idea you knew him. He belonged to the East Surrey Regiment, the 31st, and was a brother of Clegg-Hill.[13]

Things are quiet here now except that small expeditions go out for two or three days and attack the Boxers and Imperial Troops but they never stand now and have come to an end of all their European arms and ammunition almost and have lost most of their fuses.

I was in command of two Companies at Coal Hill (the North Gate of the Palace) and it was amusing as one was in the middle of the foreign troops – Russians, French, Italians, Germans, Austrians and Japs, and managed to get a good deal of jade and little curios. I sent out three boxes of stuff about a month ago and the swine of an orderly (an American) looted one en route, and the worst of it is I don't know which. Two were filled with embroideries and fur lined coats – sables, sea otter, grey fox, white fox, white squirrel and seal. Also some cloisonne vases, one of the Ming Dynasty worth they say 800 taals and some old red lacquer. The other contained bronzes and buddhas and a set of centre piece and two candle sticks. The centre piece an elephant with howdah on and the candle sticks were men holding the stand and all their trappings were set with Turquoises. They were very old bronze. This box I am afraid is lost. However I think that it would be better so than either of the others. Since then I have sent another full of jade and things and I have not heard if it has arrived safe or not. I have now enough to fill two more boxes with snuff bottles and china and bronzes etc. I hope I shall get them home without another mishap but one never can tell. There are some lovely things for sale but there are a lot of Shanghai and American dealers here and prices for well known things are big – good sable lined coats are going for $300. $2,000 was offered and not taken for a vase.

It is getting bitter cold up here and the Russians and most of the Americans have gone down and the troops here are settling into winter quarters. We hope to go down about the end of the month, as at present we have no winter clothing. They can hardly keep us up here much longer.

This place we are in is the Palace of a Prince and some parts of it are very fine. We divide it with the Gunners. They have much the best half, but we are very comfortable and they talk of sending the Head Quarters of the Regiment

Officers of 2nd Battalion aboard SS Salamis *returning from Tientsin to Hong Kong, October 1900. Back row (L–R): Capt H.O.S. Cadogan; Lt H. Grant Smith, East Yorks; Capt H.M. Richards; Lt W.G. Vyvyan; Capt & QM J.F. Clieve; J.M. Browne, RE; Capt Prynne, RAMC. Middle row (L–R): Capt J.H. Gwynne; Lt-Col Hon R.H. Bertie; Maj Reilly, RAMC; Maj C.M. Dobell; Capt A. Hay. Front row (L–R): Lt C.S. Owen; Capt O.S. Flower; Lt F. J. Walwyn; Lt R.B. Johnson. [RWF Archives]*

Officers relaxing aboard SS Salamis *en route for Hong Kong. [RWF Archives]*

out from the Legation, and later I believe the Australians will take the place over from us. I don't know how they will like coming up for the winter. They are getting rather bored with the show – you see they were too late for the fighting.

I think you knew young Higgon, he got married on the sly to an Australian girl – a Miss Moses. I believe she is not a bad sort – but well known I am told. He leaves the Regiment directly things are settled a bit. Bancroft has married the sister and he also goes. Neither will be a great loss I think.

Last Sunday our people occupied Shanghai Keran. It will be rather a blow for the Russians as they consider it in their sphere of influence and it is the only ice free port on the Gulf of Pechihli. They are a rum lot, they still say they are not at war with China but on the contrary are the only power who are really friendly and that they are helping the Empress against her rebellious subjects. And when they left Pekin they declined to hand over the various Palaces they occupied to any Power. They said they intended to hand them back to the Chinese. So that the Powers that took over the various Palaces had to force the sentries left behind. I went to the Summer Palace which the Russians had occupied and they have looted the whole place and ripped the silk off the chairs, and torn the hands off the clocks because they thought they were gold and torn all the works out to get the jewels out. You never saw such a wreck.

[To Reg Hulton], 8 October 1900

The cold is infernal and we are still in khaki and no warm clothes on their way up. It has been raining all night and one is very miserable this morning.

We have started polo in the Temple of Heaven but I have not played as I have not been fit since it has started. I had a go of dysentery which pulled me down a good stone and a half.

The Battalion left Peking on 18 October, embarked at Tientsin on the SS *Salamis* and arrived at Hong Kong on 3 November. After landing in launches at Murray Pier, headed by the band and drums, and behind the commanding officer, Colonel Bertie, the officers (including Hal) and men marched to a position close to the Queen's statue. Major-General Gascoigne and his staff inspected the parade, and the General made a welcoming speech, '… gave us a lot of wind' as Lieutenant Charlie Owen irreverently put it in his letter home. The General ended by saying: 'Now, men, we have been standing in the shadow of the statue of the Empress-Queen, whose servants we are proud to think we are. Raise your helmets and join with me in giving three cheers for Her Most Gracious Majesty Queen Victoria.' They gave three cheers and, on the call of the General, the Band played the National Anthem. The General then marched at the head of the column back to Murray Barracks, where they received a great reception from members of the rear party who had remained in Hong Kong.

A celebration dinner in the Sergeants' Mess was followed by a 'smoker' which the officers attended. According to next day's local paper:

> Colonel Bertie, who was suffering from a cold, was received with cheers, and ... after thanking the NCOs for their hospitality made suitable remarks about their return to Hong Kong. Colonel Bertie referred in brief to Major Dobell shortly vacating the post of adjutant, and said that all ranks would miss him.
>
> Major Dobell feelingly replied, and said that he could only congratulate his successor, Captain Cadogan.

Hong Kong Club, 5 November 1900

Just a line to say we are back from the North again and I suppose we shall all sit still until the Spring and goodness only knows what will happen then. I believe there will be a rumpus between all the Powers; there is no doubt that old Li and the Chinese are trying to make it so. They are cute as foxes.

I take over the Adjutancy[14] permanently from Major Dobell this week as his time is in then. We are full of officers just now, having about 26 here, so that it is rather amusing, and some of them are old friends I have not seen for some years as they have been in the Egyptian Army or seconded on some staff billet or other.

It is curious out here, foreign troopers come in nearly every day and the place is full of Germans, French and Russians.

It is quite hot here and muggy, such a change after the North where one was starved with the cold with no warm clothing. The poor ones left there will have a terribly cold time I'm afraid, as it freezes hard so much so there is skating all winter and bad blizzards.

I have not heard the result of the Election yet but I feel sure it is all right.

Look in the *Sphere* of about this date and you will see me in a photograph standing against a pillar in a veranda, it was taken by Lynch when I was out at Coal Hill on detachment. I don't know how it turned out, but just behind me was a table with a lot of loot on it, and he said he would call the picture 'Loot', but I fancy he was only pulling my leg.

Hong Kong Club, 23 November 1900

I have come across young Lionel Cowper[15] and he is such a nice boy and he seems very popular on his ship. I intended to call on his Captain but he was never at home in the afternoon and I was always busy in the morning, in fact since I have taken on the Adjutancy I have hardly been out of the office before 3 p.m. He is very shy and I could not get him to come along to the Mess but we had several evenings together, and I like him very much. He has plenty of grit.

I must write to Edie and tell her all about him, I am sure she will be pleased to hear. He is very fond of her and sent me her photograph, the only one he had, before he started for Vancouver.

I have been playing polo this afternoon and breaking in a new pony which I brought down from Peking. He will take a lot of making but is a real fine pony for a Chinaman.

I am so glad to hear dear old Walter got in again, he deserves to do so

Officers and men of the 2nd Battalion parade at Murray Pier, Hong Kong for inspection by Major-General Gascoigne on their return from Peking, 3 November 1900. [RWF Archives]

thoroughly; but I expected he would do so by a far larger majority. I suppose, however, that a good many of his partisans are in the Volunteers in South Africa.

Hong Kong Club, 22 December 1900

Just a line to say things are going on fairly well and one is full of work and business. I don't think I like the place at all, there is too much tea party and such like and too little sport for me and one gets out of sorts by not having sufficient exercise. I have played a little polo but I have only one pony and I am not going to get any more

I was much surprised to find in my rack last night a note from Reg and a card from Sam Hulton who is globetrotting. I have not seen him yet but have asked him and he is coming to dinner tonight so I shall hear a bit of news I expect. Then Hobson of *Merrimac*[16] fame is also dining with me, he is a very nice fellow and not a bit spoilt by all the kisses he got on his return to America after his incarceration in the forts in Cuba. I must say one meets most interesting people out here and amusing, but I am sorry to say it is not all I want. I want to be doing something, or I worry. I have the Adjutancy and that keeps one fairly on the warpath and one usually gets to bed sleepy.

Prince George of Prussia has gone home. He used to play polo mounted on other people's ponies, he never kept one himself.

I had an amusing dinner at the German Consul's and another at the American Consul's, in fact if one chose one could be away every night almost somewhere dining. I was asked to go up the West River into China for eight days at Christmas but I shall be too busy. Colonel Bertie has just come out, you see, so it makes it difficult to get away.

Hong Kong Club, 21 March 1901

I fear I have been a bad correspondent lately, there is little to say about the place and less news and I am thoroughly sick of being here. As you know, half the Battalion of ours has gone North again to Peking and this time unfortunately Headquarters has had to remain behind, so here I am. Things look rum, with Russia, but I don't believe there is likely to be anything in the way of trouble with them, as the Japs would take advantage of it at once and at present I believe the Japs could see them out of western Asia altogether.

We have been having inspections lately and I'm glad that the General has been pleased to say he's been exceedingly pleased with the Battalion.

Today the Royal Artillery have had some sports to which I went for a short time but they are the most boresome things to watch. The Governor has also given 'The Gun Club' here a silver cup to be fired for, but they have made it a handicap so that I am handicapped out of it being two yards further off than anyone else.

I am dining with Sir Boucher Wrey on the *Brisk*[17] tonight, and tomorrow we have a party dining at Mess and afterwards we go to the theatre where the Dallas company are playing 'The French Maid'. The last time I saw it I was with B and Walter.

RWF officers, Hong Kong, 1900. Back row (L–R): Lt J.A. Higgon; Lt G. J.P. Geiger; Lt H. Hill; Lt H. M. Richards; Lt R.B. Johnson; Lt C.S. Owen;
Bt Maj C.M. Dobell; 2Lt G.H. Gwyther; Capt C.H.M. Doughty (later Doughty-Wylie); Lt & QM J. Clieve; Bt Maj Sir Horace McMahon, Bt.
Seated (L–R): 2Lt C.I. Stockwell; Lt O.S. Flower; Maj S.G. Everitt; Lt-Col Hon R.H. Bertie; Capt & Adj H O.S. Cadogan; Lt A. Hay; Capt J.H. Gwynne;
Capt C. Bancroft. Front row (L–R): 2Lt M.E. Lloyd; Lt F.J. Walwyn; 2Lt J.R. Minshull-Ford. [RWF Archives]

HMS Terrible, a first-class cruiser (launched 1895), at Hong Kong, 1902. Some of her crew had served as a shore-based naval brigade in South Africa in 1899–1900 and in China in 1900. The message has been formed by members of the crew suspended over the side of the ship.
[RWF Archives]

What a winter you seem to be having lately and how strange it seems to talk about the King and the dear old Queen no more. He seems to be going on very tactfully at present and no doubt he will do, until the next time he falls in love.

Young Flower goes home to the Depot next month and young Lloyd[18] is due out here next month, also Major Beresford who was in the other Battalion with me.

Hal was a remarkable shot. In spite of his low handicap, he won, *inter alia*, in July the following year a handsome silver cigarette-box inscribed:

HONGKONG GUN CLUB
July 1902
SOO. KUM. POO. CUP
100 CONSECUTIVE RISES
Won by
Capt. HOS CADOGAN RWF
SCORE 86. Handcp. $16^{1}/_{4}$ Total $102^{1}/_{4}$

Murray Barracks, Hong Kong, 22 April 1901
We have very little news as yet from the fellows gone North but they seem furious with the conduct of the French, who apparently spend their time spitting and throwing brickbats at British officers from behind walls. Nothing seems to happen and I believe that all our native troops will be withdrawn and the half Battalion left up there. The Germans I believe will stick there and perhaps it is our policy to allow them to do so, so as to make a cushion between us and the Russians.

I believe the Emperor and Empress will not come back to Peking; anybody that knows anything about the matter says no, but nobody knows anything about it or in fact China in general, even old Sir R. Hart[19] is an ignoramus as far as China is concerned.

I am going to go up to Canton for a couple of days on the *Isla de Luzon*, an American man o' war. I think it would be rather a good way of seeing it for the hotel is full and staying there most uncomfortable.

Murray Barracks, Hong Kong, 18 May 1901

We are having a warmish time of it and so beastly damp and wet which makes it ten times worse. There is little news from North China except that they are thoroughly sick of it and also the troops of the various powers are being gradually withdrawn.

I am riding over to the other side of the Island today and shall lunch there and come back by launch. It is rather a pleasant trip and so pretty.

We can get no news as to where we are to go after this, I suppose the War Office have not the slightest idea yet where to send us. I hope, however, it won't be Singapore. It would be baddish luck after being here all this time and then probably we should be split up again as they say they are going to send a couple of companies to Penang again.

Most of the men have gone to the Peak and only one company remains here. I am afraid we shall have to go in a day or two as Headquarters have been ordered to go as well – it is nice and cool at night but continually buried in fog and cloud.

I have not packed up my Peking stuff yet, it is such a business for one does not know what is worth selling and what keeping. I should have liked to have come home with it and then one could have settled.

Murray Barracks, Hong Kong, 19 July 1901

Many thanks for your letter … Yes I have got a good many things I got in Peking still, in fact I have sold nothing. The things I got there are a collection and it seems a shame to sell them. I have not sent them home as I really have not had money to afford to – I sent one bronze to B and have asked her to get rid of it if possible and it cost me £22. I'm not going to question her about them yet, however, as it is very good of her to take the thing on at all and if she had not I don't know who would, but I must sell some things as to buy them I had to spend almost £210 and I am in debt. I shall know more when I hear she has got them all right. A great many of the things too are not intact, they require re-setting on stands and this all costs money. It is a mistake to call it loot, it was originally loot, doubtless, but it has all been bought one way and another and the getting abroad of the idea that it is loot

The Military Order of the Dragon, an unofficial medal awarded by an American society for the relief of Pekin, 1900.

pure and simple does infinite harm to the name of the Regiment, and the British troops in general.

It has not been very hot this year, at least compared with what they say it is most years, but there has been lots of rain and that makes the atmosphere damp and humid. The half Battalion is still at Peking. … We believe we are going to Singapore next cold weather.

Hong Kong, 21 November 1901

It feels little like Christmas here, it is very hot still in the sun. The inter-fort cricket week has just come to an end. It has been a most successful one. Hong Kong beat Singapore, then Shanghai beat Singapore and finally Shanghai beat Hong Kong, but they were all most exciting games and fought out to a finish.

It is a great nuisance being split up still – the half Battalion is still at Peking and Tientsin. The latter lot were burnt out the other day, it was thought it was an incendiary but it appears not to have been one.

They are just packing off another regiment to Tientsin and we are all very sorry they are going as they were a very nice lot and we shall miss them sadly.

Hong Kong, 4 January 1902

Just a short line as I am very busy with two companies going into camp and the end of the year and so on. No news about moving except that they wrote from Singapore asking us how many helmets we required in the coming year as they said they had been informed we were going there. I can hardly believe it myself for the men are very sick with fever and ought to go to some cold bracing place like a hill station in India for a bit – it would set them up again.

The Admiral, Sir Cyprian Bridge, and his staff, dined with us last night and I sat next to him. He seems a jolly old chap and as cute as you'll find them I fancy. H.E. the Governor, Sir H. Blake, goes off today by the mail, home for three months and his duties will be carried on by the GOC. We have to provide a Guard of Honour to see him off.

Things don't seem to be quietening down much in South Africa. That ass Firman[20] who got his brigade cut up the other day, used to be in this Battalion of my Regiment. He was never a soldier and I don't think was ever keen. He retired as a captain and here we learn the weird procedure of War Office

routine. He had a good deal of interest so they go and stuff him in as commanding the Middlesex Yeomanry, is there any wonder that the man was found out?

The Government at home do not appear to be too popular now, there is a growing feeling against the Cecil family monopolising the Cabinet.

Hal's remarks about Firman may have been tinged with jealousy and ignorance because, whatever Hal may have

Another unofficial medal, the Hong Kong Coronation Medal awarded by the Governor for the coronation of King Edward VII, 1902

thought of him, Firman was awarded the DSO in September 1901 and had commanded 11th Battalion, Imperial Yeomanry (Middlesex) from August 1900. On Christmas Day 1901, his companies were decimated by de Wet at Tweefontein. Firman had positioned them on 'Christmas Hill' as it came to be known, on General Dartnell's orders, but he, Firman, had been ordered to proceed on leave and so was unable to avert the impending disaster.

The *Times History* records that:

Until his departure on leave in the second week of December, Colonel Firman, an officer who had done good work in organising Rundle's (8th Division) Yeomanry, had commanded the column ... In April (1901) 3,000 unorganised and untrained Yeomanry of the second draft had been sent to him, but twenty percent, including the majority of the officers, had to be sent back as inefficient. The rest, principally by the exertions of Colonel Firman, had been formed into three Battalions (1st, 4th and 11th), officered afresh and trained under great difficulties. Some of the best squadrons were taken from Rundle and sent to other districts.

Firman's command and organisation of the Yeomanry should not be underestimated as, by this stage of the war, apathy was shrouding England and the standard of Yeomanry Volunteer had reduced substantially since the war-crazed days of January 1900.

The IY was often referred to as 'Ignorant Yahoos' or 'Innocent Yokels'.[21] This was because, against the C-in-C, Wolseley's, advice and in a surge of patriotic fervor, huntsmen and other country men joined to be sent directly to the front.

Hong Kong, 9 March 1902

Back again from our five days trip in the New Territories.[22] You know we have all been out manoeuvring and we managed to force out way into Hong Kong, much to the annoyance of the Engineers who have led the fortifying of it, so I suppose there will be a lot of new works made in defence.

It is a marvellously unhealthy place this Hong Kong, we have now at the same time plague, smallpox and cholera.

The General inspects us next Friday and I trust it may go off all right but it is difficult to know at present what is out of date and what is up to date.

It still keeps fairly cool here but we've had no rain, except a little Scotch mist when bivouacking out the other day, since last August and the whole Colony is dried up and parched and we only get water for about an hour a day.

There is no news about the Battalion returning from the North.

In November 1902, the Battalion moved to India, arriving at Calcutta on 24th, and then making a five-day rail journey to Meerut.

NOTES

1. Field Marshal Viscount Wolseley.

2. Major F. Morris, see Biographies.

3. ie. continual socialising.

4. This is a reference to the rebellion in North Borneo led by Mat Salleh, a leading local disident. His relative, Mat Sator, had provoked the troubles in late 1899 when a force of natives under his control (mostly Tagas) had murdered three native runners. Shortly before Christmas, a small force of 100 Sikhs and 600 native carriers (mostly Dyaks), under the command of Captain Harrington, was sent into the interior to try and crush the rebellion and capture the ringleaders. Following fighting on 8 and 9 January 1900, Harrington's force captured two enemy forts, two villages and blew up their main ammunition magazine. At the end of January, Harrington trapped Mat Salleh in a fort which was bombarded for several days. On 31 January, Mat Salleh was killed by Maxim-gun fire and the bulk of his followers surrendered. Mat Sator, the instigator of the troubles, continued to operate with a small force until early April when he was killed.

5. A reference to Li Hung Chang (1823–1901), a former soldier who had been virtual head of the Chinese government since 1870 with responsibility for foreign policy.

6. Probably Mr Charles Smith Ryland of Sherbourne Park, Warwickshire.

7. Lieutenant-Colonel Thorold, CO 1 RWF, was KiA at Colenso in South Africa, on 24 February 1900. See Biographies.

8. Lieutenant O. S. Flower, see Biographies.

9. HMS *Terrible,* a First Class cruiser, launched in 1895. See photograph p.132.

10. HMS *Fame*, a D Class destroyer, launched in 1898.

11. General O'Moore Creagh, VC. See Biographies.

12. The province in North China, adjoining the province of Shantung, in which the Boxer movement first began.

13. See Biographies.

14. Published in the *London Gazette* 6 Nov 1900.

15. Hal's nephew, second son of Frank and Edith Cowper. He died in 1906 aged 26.

16. During the Spanish-American War of 1898, Assistant Naval Constructor Lieutenant Richmond Pearson Hobson, USN (1870–1937), executed a plan to scuttle the US Navy Collier *Merrimac* in the entrance to Santiago harbour in Cuba in an endeavour to trap the Spanish fleet in its port. The ship was sunk but failed to block the harbour entrance and Hobson and his small crew of volunteers were taken prisoner. Hobson was awarded a very belated Medal of Honour in 1933 for this action.

17. HMS *Brisk,* a torpedo cruiser of 1,770 tons, launched 1886.

18. 2nd Lieutenant M. E. Lloyd, see Biographies.

19. Sir Robert Hart, Bart, GCMG (1835–1911), the former Inspector-General of the Imperial Maritime Customs, was the British Minister to China at the time of the Boxer Rebellion.

20. Captain R. B. Firman, see Biographies.

21. *London Gazette*, 10 September 1901.

22. Under the convention for the Extension of Hong Kong Territory, the territories north of Boundary Street and South of the Sham Chun River, and the surrounding islands, later known as the 'New Territories' were leased to the United Kingdom for ninety-nine years, and became part of the crown colony of Hong Kong. The lease expired on 30 June 1997.

Chapter 6

Calm Before the Storm
November 1902–July 1914

The Battalion arrived in Calcutta on 24 November and then went by train, taking five days to reach Meerut. Almost immediately, on 2 December, Hal accompanied three other officers and 100 NCOs and men left for Delhi for duty at the Durbar. Lord Curzon, the Viceroy, had arranged the Durbar of December 1902 to celebrate the coronation of King Edward VII and the achievements of the Raj. HRH The Duke of Connaught represented the King. One of the officers accompanying Hal was Lieutenant W. M. Kington who, extraordinarily, conducted the massed bands at the Durbar. Gertrude Bell wrote in her diary:[1]

> It was the most gorgeous show that can possibly be imagined …. First soldiers; then the Viceroy's bodyguard, native cavalry; then Pertab Singh at the head of the Cadet Corps, all sons of Rajas; then the Viceroy and Lady Curzon, followed by the Connaughts, all on elephants; and then a troop of some hundred Rajas on elephants, a glittering mass of gold and jewels. The Rajas were roped in pearls and emeralds from the neck to the waist, with cords of pearls strung over their shoulders, and tassels of pearls hanging from their turbans; their dresses were shot gold cloth, or gold embroidered velvet. The elephants had tassels of jewels hanging from their ears. There was also an exhibition of carpets, jewellery paintings, gold and silverware to show the genius and progress of India.

Private Frank Richards was in the company, having recently arrived on a draft from England. His account of the Durbar is much earthier and more amusing than Hal's bald reference.

> A well-known Delhi prostitute, after working for 36 years, announced her retirement. To celebrate this happy day and also out of loyalty to the Crown, she decided to make a final appearance that night and give all soldiers who wished to take advantage of her offer free access … between 6pm and 11pm. Preference was given to old customers. She posted notice to this effect on the door to her room, and if I related here how many men applied and were admitted and went away satisfied in those short hours, I should not be believed.[2]

2nd Battalion corporals, Chakrata, India, summer 1903. The officers seated, to the left of the Colour Sergeant (wearing a sash) are (L–R): Maj W.R.H. Beresford-Ash; Lt-Col Hon. R.H. Bertie, CB; Capt H.O.S. Cadogan; Maj S.G. Everitt.   [RWF Archives]

Meerut, India, 25 January 1903

Such a bitter cold day, it has been raining the last two days, the first we have had since we arrived. We are beginning to settle down after our gaiety at Delhi. It really was a very fine show, and we have got two beautiful tents for mess tents, half price and only pitched one for the Durbar.

I shall not be sorry when we get up to the hills, it seems such an endless business being always under canvas, and it is so uncomfy living in a little tent with all one's kit packed up so that one does not know if it is spoiling or not.

I saw Willie Fletcher at the Durbar, just his old self, such a good sort. He was travelling with an old lady cousin of his, Lady Boumphrey, such an amusing old thing and full of go. She was never satisfied unless she did everything, drove elephants, drove miles sightseeing and danced in the evening.

The 15th Hussars and the Rifle Brigade are the other two regiments here and they both seem an awfully nice lot.

McMahon,[3] of my regiment, has got some foxhounds and took them out for the first time yesterday. He had about 40 people out, among them eight ladies, and they had quite a good run with several casualties.

On 12 March the battalion marched to Chakrata, about 8,000 feet above sea level, arriving on the 24th. Richards describes this march and life in this hill station most vividly.[4] In August Hal wrote:

Chakrata, 10 August 1903

Here … it rains and rains and when there are no rains the clouds are so thick that one gets fully as wet. We are so high up here that we are bound to catch them. Between the clouds one can look down over the plains and see what looks like a network of rivers. Really they are the water courses, all full, and they are 50 miles from here at least – it has a very quaint effect.

The flowers are very fine now, forget-me-nots, asters and dahlias in any numbers besides many others like wild jasmine and passion flowers.

The ponies keep very fit up here, my charger was so full of bounce I could hardly do anything with her on parade this morning. I wish I could send one of them over to you to drive about.

On 21 August, Lieutenant-Colonel the Hon R. H. Bertie, CB, handed over command to Lieutenant-Colonel H. T. Lyle, DSO. Bertie's departure was celebrated throughout the battalion and Richards says that he was most unpopular, being a fussy martinet. Colonel Tommy Lyle was well liked and proved to be no less efficient.

Chakrata, 23 August 1903

We have been isolated up here recently, there has been so much rain that the causeway on the far side of the Kalsi Bridge has been washed away and they have to bring the mails across on elephants – no dongahs can go.

General Gaselee[5] comes up here on 1 October to inspect. Not a word yet about that Delhi billet and I have not written again as I don't think it is diplomatic to worry too much.

We have a Mansourie[6] and Chakrata week coming off on 20 August. I should have gone to play for Chakrata but the General coming the week after makes this difficult, besides, my exam comes off the first week in October.

We go down to Meerut on 25 October and have manoeuvres all the way down. One battalion of Gurkhas coming up to join us and another trying to stop us marching down.

It would seem that at the end of a tour as adjutant, an officer was considered for a (probably interesting) staff job. Hal did not get the job he was hoping for. Perhaps he did not have enough 'interest'.

The qualifications for promotion to major he refers to below involved the successful completion of various courses, including garrison, musketry, signals, and mounted infantry, and probably the appointment of adjutant.

> Chakrata, 5 September 1903
>
> I have not succeeded in getting that billet I had hoped to have got and I should not have minded if the fellow who got it had prior claims, but he is junior to me by five years as a captain and has only two qualifications while I have six. It really knocks me a little flat.
>
> The rains are still in full swing and they have got cloudy and damp now, perpetual clouds instead of rain which is far worse.
>
> The chikaw season (partridges) commenced on the 1st and I am going to try and get a shoot tomorrow – Sunday. It will sound funny to you at home, but it is really the only day in the week one gets to oneself, and I have not had one day, Sundays included, to myself since the Delhi Durbar. Thank goodness the little Colonel has left so we are breathing a little more freely, especially the men.
>
> We are going to have a great week in Mansouri after the 15th and I shall go there and stay there for my exam[7] which takes place on 1 October. It is a nuisance for the exam to be directly after the week and it is a nuisance to have one's other work at the same time as one is preparing, but it cannot be helped and I hope I shall pass. I think I shall.
>
> We are to be divided up in the cold weather, worse luck, just as we are getting into trim; four companies Meerut, and Headquarters and two companies at Delhi and two at Chakrata in the snow.

On 29 October the Battalion marched to Meerut arriving on 12 November. En route, they took part in hill manoeuvres between Chakrata and Dehra Dun.

Facing page: The 2nd Battalion on the march at Chakrata, 10th August 1904. This superb photograph gives a good impression of the quality of the military roads constructed in India during the nineteenth century. [RWF Archives]

Two scenes of a British force on the march in northern India in the early 1900s. The officers in the above photograph, from 2nd Battalion, are watching a dongah cart being assisted across a stream. In the lower photograph an Indian Army lancer is being photographed in front of the horse lines. [RWF Archives]

Meerut, 22 November 1903

Colonel Lyle has now come back and has taken up command and reigns again after Colonel Bertie's time. Thank God he has gone.

Chamberlain is excellent, he is so full of originality and does not care a fig for all the whims and cobwebs that stick to those other politicians. He strikes out his own line which is so refreshing, after witnessing old Devonshire toddling back into his shell like an old hermit crab when it has reached too far out.

I am going up to the hills for a couple of days' shooting with Major Ash and Capel and Hayhurst of my regiment tomorrow morning, a thing I never asked for when Colonel Bertie had command. He always made such a palaver of it one never asked him.

The following letter to Mrs Dickson,[8] mother of Captain George Dickson, is an example of the kind of office work that kept a conscientious adjutant so busy.

Meerut, 8 December 1903

I am sending you a letter I received enclosing a note from the doctor who is looking after your son, Captain Dickson, thinking that you will be glad to hear any news that is available and especially good news. Major Shakespear is a friend of mine, and I have asked him to let me have news at intervals. It is always more satisfactory to have news from an outside source, than from the patient, as they often think that they are better, or worse, than they really are.

He is in Colonel Wright's house, and Colonel Wright is the doctor to the Goorkhas, so that he is in capital hands, and as you will see by the letters enclosed he is likely to be with us again in the course of the month. I trust by Christmas.

To avoid the hottest weather, on 12 March the battalion again marched to Chakrata, arriving on 24th.

Chakrata, 11 April 1904

We are going to Agra this cold weather, not a bad place at all although very hot during the hot weather. There is plenty of sport such as shooting, pig sticking and polo and on the whole I think it will be preferable to Meerut, and anyway one will be settled down for a couple of years which is a great thing.

I fear I shall not get home this next winter, there is a chance of my getting a billet when my adjutancy is up and if one were to be out of the way they would probably not think about one again. However, I trust it will not be long before I get back to see you all again. If one gets a billet one will be able to get home on eight months' or six months' leave and that is quite long enough to be away from one's job here.

I went up for a walk to the top of Deoband yesterday, it is 3,000 feet higher than this and about 10,000 feet and found snow four feet deep up there on the shady side. It was rather funny as here the sun is very hot.

Chakrata showing the parade ground and the camp's position high in the mountains. Frank Richards describes the 'Upper' and 'Lower' camps which are both clearly visible. [RWF Archives]

The Tibet Force gave the poor Tibetans a bit of a doing, did they not?[9] I wish they had been those selfish Buddhist monks and not the poor country people, for the Llama priests are the ones to blame.

The Japs seem to be getting along very well with the Russians who seem to be content with talking and saying what they intend to do.

On 21 October the battalion marched to Agra, where it arrived on 26 November, having halted at Meerut from 3–12 November for 'examinations in tactical fitness for command' (for promotions from captain to major and major to lieutenant-colonel).

Camp Katauli, 1 November 1904

Here we are within 20 miles of Meerut and only two short marches to do. The weather has been lovely and the march would be very pleasant as far as I'm concerned if I did not get these periodic goes of fever about every three days, which make me a veritable worm, and one therefore misses much of the sport.

I expect Lord Kitchener will pay us a visit at Meerut when we reach there, as he will be there.

What a scandalous thing that was of the Russian fleet firing on our fishing fleet.[10] I must say I wonder the weak-kneed Balfour is allowed to bring such a case before the Tribunal if it is given against us, foreign ideas of the right of the individual are very different to our own, our hands will be tied and we can do no more. I must say I think they might have stopped the Russians with more ado with the Mediterranean Squadron and caught them behind with the

Channel fleet and scuppered the lot. It is a pity we have no Lord Palmerston or even old Salisbury.

Agra, 9 December 1904

I have not had fever for the last five or six days I am glad to say, and I feel quite fit and fat again. It does take it out of me in the most extraordinary way, two or three hours' fever takes about half a stone off me and when it comes every night one feels as if there is nothing left.

It is such a pretty place now, so much improved to the last time I saw it in '93.[11] They have made gardens all the way to the Taj so one no longer drives through dirty villages and dried up brown grass and nullahs. It is green all the way from the town.

The people seem very nice and friendly here and I think it will be quite a nice place taking it all in all.

I am sending you my little Christmas presents, a cheque for £5, please give £2 to old Fritz and £1 to old Burrly. I wish it was more.

I have been very busy lately, especially till Pat Mantell comes back. I have had all the Institutes to look after, which means a lot of extra work as all the canteen, coffee shop, etc., are involved. It is quite a cost not having the adjutancy any longer, but of course the pay is different.

I was offered the billet of Attaché at Simla to the Adjutant General in India for nine months, but I have settled to come home and get rid of the fever. I should like to have taken it up immensely as you get to know all the buzzes and hear of anything that's going.

Although his health may have been a factor, he had a hidden agenda. He

2nd Battalion resting on a march, Chakrata, c.1904. [RWF Archives]

Major Hal Cadogan, a studio portrait taken whilst at the Mounted Infantry School, Fatehgarh, 1907. He is wearing 'jodphur' riding trousers and his pith helmet sports the fusilier hackle. The medal ribbons are for Hazara and China.

had met Evelyn Violet Ross,[12] in India, and she had returned to England. He sailed for home on 25 February 1905. They became engaged on 21 October, and were married in Holy Trinity, Sloane Street, on 2 January 1906. Early in 1906, after a short honeymoon in Paris, Hal and his bride sailed for India, where he had been appointed assistant commandant of the Mounted Infantry School. They took with them a small car – surely one of the first in the sub-continent.

Fatehgarh, 15 November 1906

Eve is very keen about her garden and now can be outside most of the day. Blanche sent her some seeds and they are all coming up splendidly.

We have been getting very little shooting here as there is much water at this time of year and the birds are thoroughly scattered. I took Eve out last Sunday for the day. She sat and worked and read under a grove of trees near the jhail while I shot it. I got eight snipe and three teal and a duck only, but we had a jolly little picnic and the car went very well. It is a great boon to us.

Major Parr and some of the class go off to Lucknow for the Army Cup on Sunday and will be away for a week so I shall be alone again for a week. Eve very fit and well.

Fatehgarh, 3 December 1906

A very merry Christmas and happy New Year to you all. How well I remember last year and the plum pudding. I have no little Christmas offering to send to you, I know you will understand however. I wonder who will be with you for Christmas, I suppose only old Fritz.

Major Parr and Eve and I are having our Christmas party in camp… consisting of the fellows of the class and one or two others, and the only thing needed to complete a good time is the birds of which this year there are not a great number.

We went out for the day yesterday, eight guns, and did not do too badly. We got 257 duck and some snipe, had a long day and a long ride back and got back nice and tired. Today I have one part of my Hindustani exam but I doubt if I shall pass this time, it is good practice, however, going up.

Major Delmé-Radcliffe and Major Garnett of the Regiment have asked us to go down to Agra and live in their bungalow for the Durbar there. They are living in Camp. It is mighty kind of them and we will avail ourselves of his invitation. Most people's houses are filled up and our ladies are putting up the 15th Hussars' ladies who will be in.

Eve is very fit and has her garden so pretty now. She is so keen about it and does most of it herself, in fact she has got rid of her male (gardener) now and does all the superintending work herself.

Car still working in excellent order, in fact I think better than ever.

At about this time, Eve gave birth to a daughter, who tragically died shortly after she was born, and Hal and Eve went for a break to the hills to recover.

Hal and Eve's married quarters at Fatehgarh.

Grand Hotel, Naini Tal, 1 August 1907

Here we are after a very hot time stewing below, in a delicious climate and such a lovely place. We are just on one side of the lake which is a blessing I think. People like being high up but still in the rains. When you can't go far it is nice to be among the shops and to sit on our veranda and see the yacht races on the lake.

Eve has of course not been calling but the Gaselees[13] are very kind and I have found one or two married people I knew in Agra and so she gets on quite well. She is wonderfully fit and well and cheery and I am glad to say likes the hospital and nurses which is half the battle. Many ladies have been in this season and one went in from this hotel only yesterday.

It has rained a great deal since we have been here but I am sorry to say they have not had as much rain as they might have had on the Plains.

Fatehgarh, 5 November 1907

We have a very nice new class here now, nine of them, and are as usual at this time, full of work.

I am trying to get my little motor into order as I think I shall sell it now if I can, as goodness knows what may happen next hot weather. I may have to return to the Regiment or anything. If I do, I should like Eve to go home but she is so much against it I fear it might affect her health more than the climate. She has been having a big choir practice and I have been trying to work at Hindustani. It is a capital thing for her and for the men too as it keeps them out of mischief, and they are very grateful for a little kindness.

Everything is awfully dried up this year on account of the shortage of rain and I fear there will be much hardship amongst the poor.

Kasauli, 2 September 1908

We have little news here, rain still goes on daily. We have had only one fully fine day since 6 July but I'm glad to say that they show signs of giving over. The papers say that the rain is now doing damage to the crops.

Eve is very fit still and full of energy. Her doctor thinks that she is out in her calculations and that the event may come off at any time now. She has a great dislike of the native *ayhas* , and I think she is right, and luckily she has got the wife of a sergeant to look after her, a very nice woman who is very fond of her, and as far as I can make out is as keen on coming events as she is.

Major Chichester, my CO, has gone to Simla for 10 days' leave so I am alone here for the work at present. He is a kind man, second-in-command of the Connaught Rangers and a cousin of my late Colonel, Colonel Lyle, who poor soul, he tells me, has not yet got a billet at home. It is such a pity, he is just the man for a Boys' Brigade or anything like that, so popular. His wife drives him to places like Southsea when his one hope is to be in Ireland shooting and fishing.

Kasauli, 16 September 1908

I trust you got the wire all right. The child[14] came at 10 a.m. on the 11th, the waters having broken at 3.45 a.m. and we were rather frightened that the same thing as last time might happen. The doctor came at 5 a.m. and had Eve taken to hospital at once and we moved her, her bed and all. It is a merciful thing that we had such a clever man as Stones the doctor, for it was a shoulder presentation and the cord was twice round the child's neck. He shouted like a man at once and was 8.5 pounds and 22 inches or more long and Stones who has had a lot of cases up here this year, says Eve is the most satisfactory case he has had and the child the finest child. They all tell me it is a very pretty child. I am not much of a judge.

Eve has been seeing people as if nothing had happened for the last two days and says she wants to sit up. She will not, however, get up until the 24th or the 25th. The boy has a fine shaped head and a chin like Grandfather Cadogan.

Kasauli, 30 September 1908

I am sorry to say that little Eve is not at all herself and so I don't want her to write any letters this mail.

Hal with his infant son, Edward,
at Fatehgarh, 1908.

Officers at the Mounted Infantry School, Fatehgarh. Hal is standing second from the right.

The barracks and parade ground at Kasauli c.1900.

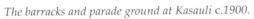

She taxed her strength I fear by seeing too many people at the start and writing too many letters, and then that attack of malarial fever came and it has taken her back and this of course has made her very weak and low. In fact so much so that I have got the doctor to allow her to come back home this afternoon where she will be much happier and will be able to sit out in the garden among the flowers which are lovely, and see the glorious snows which are so clear and beautiful now. She never slept a wink yesterday and she sent for me about 10.30 p.m. When I went down I found her very wide awake, and she told me she had been worrying over whether the child might get affected with malaria in the feeding. I told her not to worry, that the doctor would be sure to let her know if it might be, and that the malaria could not be very strong in her system. She went off to sleep and writes this morning that she is better but her fever is still 100 degrees. I have not been able to see her yet as I am shut up in an exam room for the day superintending a first class school exam.

The boy goes on very well. He has put on 1.5 pounds in 19 days which is quite a record here.

Hal was posted back to the 1st Battalion and rejoined them in Cork in April 1909. He and his family moved into 4 Bellevue Road, Cork which he describes as a semi-detached villa, but with an excellent view.

The Army Hal joined in Ireland was very different to his home posting of ten years before, when he had been so bored in Tregantle Fort. Shaken by the reverses of the Anglo-Boer War, the Government had been galvanised into modernising the army which previously had been nothing more than an imperial garrison. Two reforming Secretaries of State for War reshaped the army and its organisation. Mr Arnold-Foster had launched the Esher Committee in 1903 to investigate the War Office itself, with a view to organising a General Staff. In 1905, his successor, Lord Haldane, saw clearly the pressing need for the creation of an expeditionary force and for a territorial force, organised and administered by the County Associations, to reinforce the regulars when required. At the same time, brigade and divisional level training had been radically improved. At company level, new tactics including 'fire and manoeuvre' rather than 'extended line' were introduced. *Field Service Regulations* of 1909 placed much greater emphasis on the need for a commander to attack and seize the initiative, arguing that decisive success in battle can only be gained by a vigorous offensive.[15]

On 5 August the Battalion marched to Kilworth Camp for annual training, returning on 12 September

Fethard, Co. Tipperary, 10 September 1909

We marched 17.5 miles yesterday and 17 today and it's very pretty country but wild. As we marched yesterday on our left were the Knock-Muldoon Mountains, and on the left Galtee Heights and then we came out into undulating country, much more fertile. Our Brigade is now separated from the rest of the Division who are in the South of the County at North Waterford. I fancy most of these people have never seen troops before for they looked much surprised at our column of over a mile along.

Camp near Carlow, 17 September 1909

We have just marched in from near the late McKavanagh's place (the man who had neither arms nor legs but many sons). We had a great battle yesterday here, up at 5 a.m., fought all day and then marched 15 miles to Camp in the evening, but it is all over now and we get into the Curragh tomorrow.

I am glad to say that before leaving yesterday we were congratulated by both generals on the excellent manner the Regiment had worked which was very pleasing.

Very pretty country on our journey through, much more civilized than most of the parts we've seen.

Hal went immediately to the Curragh for the examination for majors' promotion to lieutenant-colonel, which he passed.

On 3 October 1910, the Battalion entrained at Curragh Siding, Kildare, for Dublin on change of station, and was quartered in Royal Barracks.

In January 1911 Brigadier-General Thompson Capper was posted to Ireland to command 13 Infantry Brigade to which the Battalion belonged. He was one of the most enthusiastic supporters of the new military ideas and for the remaining three years Hal's life, he and the Battalion were very much bound up with this renowned military thinker and dynamic trainer of troops.

When Capper passed into the Staff College in 1896, among his contemporaries were many officers who, like himself, were to hold high command during the Great War, including Haig, Allenby, Robertson, Murray, Haking and Edmonds – a vintage year indeed. Capper developed a passion for staff work and training, but the real lesson he learned was to relate the principals of strategy to practical operations, and in particular to value the morale factors necessary to win a battle. He was considered one of the ablest students; original, imaginative and a master of his profession. At the end of the course he and Haig were selected for special service with Kitchener in the Nile campaign of 1898. His success there, and then in South Africa, where he was awarded the DSO, were followed by the huge impact he made as an instructor at the Camberley Staff College. He then went as the first commandant of the newly established Staff College in Quetta. He concentrated his instruction on the arrangements required for the success of operations in war, rather than in peacetime at Aldershot. Remarkably, this was innovative at the time.

His arrival at Quetta followed the conclusion of the Russo-Japanese War, for which the Germans had trained the Japanese. Capper examined how German doctrine had succeeded or failed under modern conditions, and he lectured extensively on this war. The nub of Capper's beliefs, when discussing the principals of strategy, was that determined courage in leaders and men is the absolutely necessary foundation of all successful warlike action. Such courage nurses and sustains the offensive, and therefore preserves the initiative.[16]

In 13th Brigade he gained a great reputation as an excellent trainer of troops, and proved to be a lucid and practical commander. In 1912 he was one of the first to reorganise battalions from eight companies to four, thereby improving tactical organisation and fire-power. His success in commanding his brigade led to his appointment as Inspector General of Infantry (with the rank of major-general) in February 1914.

3 Harcourt Terrace, Adelaide Road, Dublin, 14 January 1911
At present I am officiating as AAG in Ireland for Colonel Boyle Smith who has gone abroad on leave. He is the man you will remember who was nearly shot by de Wet in South Africa. De Wet hit him across the face when he was a prisoner and he knocked De Wet down.

Eve and the boy are very bright and well and she's delighted with the table cloth you sent.

It has been bitterly cold lately and the ponds at St Stephens have been frozen hard, but it is gone today.

I am glad to say that some nice people have begun to call on Eve. We began to wonder if anyone was coming but there's been quite a rush the last few days.

Albuhera Parade, Phoenix Park, Dublin, 16 May 1911. RWF officers are (L–R): Major Hal Cadogan (standing, centre left); Lieutenant-Colonel Iggulden (mounted). Reviewing dignitaries (L–R): HE The Lord Lieutenant of Ireland, Earl of Aberdeen, KT; Major-General W. Pitcairn Campbell, CB, GOC 5 Division; General the Hon Sir Neville Lyttelton, GCB, C-in-C Ireland.
[RWF Archives]

To the Victorian army, Dublin had been regarded as a first-rate station. The peacetime officers had little work and less responsibility. The drill and discipline, the feeding and well-being of the men, were all left to the commanding officer, his adjutant and various NCOs. What with cricket, hunting, balls and dinners, every officer had more than enough to do.[17] No doubt General Capper shook the Province to the core.

Dublin, 25 January 1911

I have been very busy finishing an essay I have to write on the Russian-Japanese war.

Eve has some friends staying and lots of nice people have called. We had a charming dinner at the Lytteltons[18] and Lady L was very nice to Eve. Then we lunched with General Monro[19] last Sunday so I think that Eve will enjoy herself here after all.

On the back page of Hal's essay are the comments of Colonel Iggulden, his Commanding Officer. Opposite this are favourable comments in green ink, and annotated 'TC'. Perhaps his essay became a decisive factor in Hal's promotion to lieutenant-colonel and command of the 1st Battalion the following year. At the same time, one wonders how many brigadier-generals at that time took the trouble to train their officers in this way.

On 22 June, a representative detachment from the Battalion under Hal with fifty NCOs and men, and the goat, attended the coronation of King George V. They camped in Regents Park East, and were posted at the southern end of Whitehall. 'The Goat excited much curiosity among the foreign Royalties in the procession.'[20]

On 11 July the battalion took part in a royal review in Phoenix Park, Dublin for the King and Queen who were accompanied by Prince Edward and Princess Mary. An hour after returning to barracks, the battalion embarked for Wales, reaching Caernarfon at 11 p.m. where they camped at Coed Helen, alongside the Regiment's 3rd (Special Reserve) Battalion.

On 13 July the battalion lined Castle Square in Caernarfon and also found the Guard of Honour at the Water Gate for the investiture of Prince Edward as Prince of Wales. The next day, they left by train for Bangor where they mounted another Guard of Honour at the opening by the King of the new university buildings. Both officers and men were given tea through the generosity of Colonel Platt, Hal's old Commanding Officer from 1887. They returned to Dublin that night.

A month later, on 18 August, the battalion was suddenly warned just after midnight to embark at 6 a.m. on account of a threatened railway strike. In fact they embarked at 4.27 a.m., crossed to Holyhead, reached Chester at 1p.m. and camped on the Roodee (Chester Racecourse). After various excursions to

Men of the 1st Battalion line the processional route through Castle Square, Caernarfon, during the Investiture of the Prince of Wales, 13th July 1911. [RWF Archives]

1st Battalion provide the Guard of Honour, commanded by Capt A. Hay (extreme left), with 2Lt M.D.G. Parry carrying the King's Colour, at Bangor railway station for the King's visit to open the new university buildings, July 1911. [RWF Archives]

Warrington and Manchester to protect signal boxes from rioting strikers, they returned to Dublin on 24 August.

On 20 September, Major-General Luke O'Connor, VC, CB, attended a parade to mark the anniversary of the Battle of the Alma.[21]

Hal's Company (B Company) won most of the military competitions that year including the brigade shooting competition, and the Monro Challenge Cup (for gymnastics, cross-country, and rifle shooting), by a considerable margin.

A group of the Battalion about to depart Dublin for Manchester during the 1911 railway strike. The men are in their khaki uniforms but are wearing their busbies (see also photograph on p.159) as this was the easiest way to transport them without getting them damaged. [RWF Archives]

Royal Barracks, Dublin, 7 April 1912

We sent you a wire for we knew how pleased you would be. It is not out yet but I have a letter from Delmé-Radcliffe, the Colonel of the other Battalion, who said he had had a letter from the War Office saying that Lloyd, who is senior to me, had been passed over and that I had got the command of this Battalion in succession to Iggulden. He goes on 8 May so that it is less than a month now. I must say I shall be a very proud man indeed for I shall be one of the youngest Colonels in the service, being only two days over 44. So that all going well I shall be entitled to my pension two days after reaching my 48th year, which is a blessed thing – £420 a year is a very different pension from £200 which is all I should have got if I had been passed over.

I do hope we shall be able to see something of you at Portland,[22] though I believe we spend most of the summer away in camp, which is rather sad for that must be the best time of year at Portland for it must be a rough, windy spot in the winter. It will be a blessing to get away from this country anyway where we are so far away and yet so near.

The 2nd Battalion was based in Quetta at that time; it is extraordinary that they heard news of Hal's appointment so much earlier than he, with barely one month's notice before the handover. No doubt, as usual, the 'char-wallahs' were the first to hear!

Soon after the death of Burr in October 1911, her maid and companion of more than thirty years, Hal's mother received more sad news; her son, John, who had left to find his fortune in Canada after some unfortunate business at home and a failed marriage, died of pneumonia in Edmonton, aged only forty-six.

Royal Barracks, Dublin, 19 April 1912

I can't tell you how I grieve for you, you poor lonely Little Mother. How I wish you could come over here to us.

Poor old Jack, do not regret his going over to Canada however, for there is one point we must be thankful for and that is that he died a man in every healthy shape of the word; I fear had he stayed at home he would, poor chap, have only sunk lower than he was.

I have heard nothing since I heard from him when he wrote that burst of letters at New Year. I wish I could get over to you, dear Little Mother, but I am very busy taking over, for Colonel Igg goes on 3 May and all is in the transition stage.

I am looking forward to the time we shall get to Portland and you come and stay with us.

What a dreadful thing is this *Titanic* catastrophe.

Much love and sympathy from us both, and do not blame the parents of poor old Jack. He started square enough, poor old chap.

Hal obviously managed to get over to see his mother, for he wrote four days later on his return.

Royal Barracks, Dublin, 23 April 1912

I reached home this morning at 8 a.m. and found the little party very fit.

I had a dreadful journey. They told me at Pershore station that I should get a train at once at Worcester but it did not run, and I had to wait till 12.40 before I got a train. … I had four hours to wait at Crewe as well which was a cheery spot to stay at. A very nice crossing over and a lovely morning.

The others have all gone to Punchestown Races and have a beautiful day for it.

His mother was ailing, and died on 24 March the following year. She was buried at Wicken with Edward, her husband, and near Edward and Dorothy, two of her children who had predeceased her. The family paid for a window and a bell in the church in memory of their parents.

In early May Hal's great friend, Charles Dobell, who was a fellow company commander in the battalion, was appointed to command the 2nd Battalion, The Bedfordshire Regiment.

On 12 May Hal took the battalion to the musketry camp at Kilbride in Co Wicklow. In his last letter to his mother to survive, he wrote: 'We have had an influx of generals today – Sir A. Paget, General Campbell, General Capper, General McKracken, and others.'[23] None of Hal's letters written after her death have survived.

On 18 May the battalion moved to Doolystown Camp, near Trim, for battalion training until 3 July. No sooner had they returned, than the brigade commander carried out his annual inspection on 10 July, beginning with a formal parade on the Esplanade. Afterwards, General Capper[23] commented on the smart and soldierly appearance of the Battalion, and expressed his regret that they would shortly be leaving the Irish Command.

Hal's tour in command was marked by a remarkable run of successes in shooting and sports. While at Dublin in 1912 the battalion won 13 Brigade shooting and bayonet-fighting competitions, and *inter alia*, the Irish army football and boxing cups and the Monro Challenge Cup again. It also won the Dublin Garrison and Irish Junior League Football Cups, the Brigade Commander, General Capper, presenting the cups.

On 21 November the battalion moved to Portland, Dorset, with two companies in Dorchester. Major-General Capper, in his farewell speech, praised the battalion on its '…smartness on parade, and zealousness in performing [its] duties …' He accompanied the battalion from the Royal Barracks to the North Wall where it earned further praise for embarking in only seventeen minutes.[24]

While at Portland, the battalion continued its successful sporting run. The regimental football team won the Dorset Senior Cup in March (without a goal being scored against them) and they were runners up in the Army Regimental Boxing Championships. In July, a team was sent to the Army Athletics Meeting at Aldershot, where, among other successes, 2nd Lieutenant John

1st Battalion parade in Dublin prior to their move to Portland, November 1912. The two officers seen here are (L–R): Capt W. B. Garnett; Capt T. J. de P. O'Kelly. [RWF Archives]

Courage won the Officers' High Jump.

Perhaps this is a moment to pause and consider the regiment of which Hal had been appointed to command the 1st Battalion. In 1912, it was well officered, well manned and particularly well trained, after its time under General Capper. The regiment had a tremendous fighting reputation, having taken part in most of the great campaigns since its formation in 1689. Its sporting achievements were renowned. In the class-ridden world of the late nineteenth century the Royal Welsh came after the Brigade of Guards, the Rifle Brigade and the 60th KRRC and some, but not all, cavalry regiments. It roughly ranked alongside the other old fusilier regiments – the Royal Fusiliers and the 5th Northumberland Fusiliers – and several Highland regiments. Of a total of some thirty officers who went to Belgium with the 1st Battalion in October 1914, nearly all had been privately educated, with at least twenty attending a major public school including some five each from Eton, Winchester and Wellington. While a good public school education is by no means an indication of ability or efficiency, the records of those officers show the majority to have been able men and talented sportsmen, while many were remarkable linguists – for example Richard Barker, who was a scholar of both Winchester and New College, Oxford, handed over as adjutant of the 1st Battalion in 1909 to Eric Skaife, another Wykhamist. He in July 1914 handed over to Claud Dooner, a scholar of Tonbridge. An able bunch indeed. Some had other talents. For example, W. M. Kington, who took over B Company from Hal and who had won a DSO in South Africa, besides being a talented cricketer, actually conducted the massed bands at the Delhi Durbar of 1903 while still a subaltern. Very few of the officers lived in Wales, and only a few

Alma Day, Windsor, 20 September 1913.
Above: Maj-Gen Sir Luke O'Connor, VC, KCB (in frock coat), escorted by Lt-Col Hal Cadogan, inspects the Battalion. The Flash can clearly be seen attached to the back of each collar. O'Connor is not in uniform probably because he was standing in for Maj-Gen Hon Sir Savage Mostyn, KCB, Colonel of the Regiment, who was prevented from attending because of a rail strike. [RWF Archives]

Below: 1st Battalion presenting arms, Windsor, 20 September 1912. [RWF Archives]

had a Welsh connection of some sort. It was truly a 'family' regiment; many officers were the sons and grandsons of former officers of the regiment, and others were recommended by members of the regiment or by others who knew of the regiment's good name. Several married their brother officers' sisters or widows.

Warrant officers and senior NCOs were as much the backbone of the battalion as they are today. Many had served in India, South Africa, China or Crete. Although the majority of the men came from Wales and the borders, about fifteen percent came from Birmingham, and the remainder from Manchester, London, Ireland or elsewhere.[25] The men were much better educated than their fathers, although many still joined for two square meals a day and a roof over their heads.

Hal had had a small car in India after he was married. But in January 1913 he bought a Ford Model T, a two-seater, which he used regularly to drive from Portland to Wool, visiting the detached companies, and to Parkstone on 15th March to watch the final of the Dorset Senior Cup. It did not take him much longer to get to Gayhurst in Buckinghamshire than it might today on a bank holiday, although his top speed is recorded as being thirty-five miles an hour.

After training at Bovington, and later at Bulford for some six weeks, the battalion took over public duties at Windsor in September 1913. While there, a special Review Order Parade was held on 20 September to celebrate Alma Day. Major-General Sir Luke O'Connor, VC, KCB, who had been knighted in the Honours List that year, and had won his Victoria Cross at the Battle of the Alma fifty-nine years before, inspected the battalion and gave an address. In addition to Eve, Walter and Bee Carlile, and Eyre and Mary Coote attended the memorable occasion.[26]

On 10 January 1914, Hal, accompanied by Eve and Edward (aged five), sailed with his battalion from Southampton bound for for Malta, on HM Troopship *Rewa*. They arrived a week later and occupied Sliema Barracks. The Battalion became part of a static brigade of five battalions, commanded by a brigadier -general. Due to the heat of the summer and the shortage of space for field training, the winter was the main training period, although there was

Hal dressed for motoring.

Officers, families and friends, 1st Bn RWF, Windsor, Alma Day, September 1913.
BACK ROW: *Capt C.E. Wood; Lt J.G. Bruxner-Randall; 2Lt J.M.J. Evans; Lt E.C.L. Hoskyns; Lt M.I.H. Anwyl; Capt E.J. de P. O'Kelly. Third row: Lt A.E.C.T. Dooner; –?–; Capt W.M. Kington; –?–; Capt & Adj E.O. Skaife (behind HOSC's left shoulder); 2LT D.M. Barchard; –?–. 2ND ROW: Lt & QM E.P. Parker; –?–; 2Lt H. R. Hardie; Lt G.O. de B. Chance; Capt J.H. Brennan; Mr Walter Carlile; –?–; –?–; –?–; H.O.S. Cadogan (behind O'Connor); Capt W. Harris-St John; Sir Eyre Coote; 2Lt J.H. Courage; Capt J.R.M. Minshull-Ford; Lt M.D. Gambier-Parry; Lt R.E. Hindson. FRONT ROW: –?–; –?–; –?–; –?–; –?–; Blanche Carlile; Eve Cadogan; Maj-Gen Sir Luke O'Connor; –?–; Maj G. Norton (Military Knight of Windsor); Mary Coote (with dog); –?–; –?–; –?–.*
[RWF Archives]

scope for limited exercises up to company level. However, good ranges meant that their shooting was first class.

The Battalion quickly made its mark in the sporting world of the island, Captain Eric Skaife, Hal's adjutant, won the half mile, among other events in the Malta Athletics Meeting of February 1914. In March, the battalion won the football competion.

St David's Day, was especially memorable in 1914. Returning home from India, the 2nd Battalion, under command of Major Archibald Hay, arrived in Grand Harbour, Malta at 8 a.m. and disembarked six sergeants and 327 junior NCOs and men who were to reinforce the 1st Battalion. The Governor[27] detained their ship until midnight, so that the officers of the two battalions were able to dine together. The sergeants held a smoking concert. This was the first time since 1880 that the battalions had met.

Hal, now aged forty-six, kept himself very fit, and was playing cricket for the Battalion twenty-six years after he first did so in Lucknow. Few of the Royal Welsh team would be alive five months later.

Hal's car was a boon and was much used to visit ranges or training, not to mention taking Eve and Edward to seaside picnics, which were among Edward's earliest memories.

In July, Hal appointed as his adjutant Claud Dooner who, in 1910, had passed third into Sandhurst where he won the drill prize, and was

The 1st Battalion soccer team that won the Governor's Cup, Malta, 17 March 1914.
Back row: L/Cpl Cathrine; Dvr Price; Cpl Brackley; L/Cpl R. Davies; L/Cpl Osborne;
L/Cpl Howel. Middle row: Capt & QM Parker; Lt–Col Cadogan; QMS Cottrill.
Front row: Pte Kelly; Sgt J. Austin; Pte G. Austin; Pte Hill; Pte A. Davies (possibly
the orderly buried next to Hal in Hooge Cemetery). [RWF Archives]

MT Rewa, the ship that transported the 1st Battalion to Malta in 1914.

commissioned in 1911. He was a first-class interpreter in German, and on his appointment was thought to be the youngest adjutant in the British army. During the four months they worked so closely together, culminating in a final three weeks of horror, being twenty-four years younger Claud Dooner must have become like a son to Hal.

This happy peacetime soldiering in Malta was not to last, however, for the storm clouds were gathering.

CRICKET.

A match was played at St. Andrew's on 16th May between the Royal Welch Fusiliers and the Scottish Rifles, resulting in a win for the Royal Welch Fusiliers by 53 runs.

Royal Welch Fusiliers

E. C. L. Hoskyns ct and bd de Blaquiere	19
J. H. Courage ct Evetts bd Clarke	33
Capt. R. V. Barker l b.w. bd Maunsell	37
Pte. Kelly ct Shields bd de Blaquiere	88
J. M. J. Evans bd Maunsell	0
Col. Cadogan bd Evetts	12
Capt. Harris St. John bd de Blaquiere	4
C. G. H. Peppé ct White bd de Blaquiere	1
Sergt. Dr. Chapman l.b.w. bd de Blaquiere	9
A. E. C. T. Dooner not out	6
Pte. Newton bd de Blaquiere	3
Extras	8
Total	**220**

BOWLING.

	Wickets		Runs
Evetts	1	for	48
de Blaquiere	6	for	77
Clarke	1	for	62
Maunsell	2	for	25

Scottish Rifles

Capt. Maunsell ct Hoskyns bd Barker	33
Pte. White bd Barker	1
W. J. Kerrct Courage bd Barker	39
A. C. L. Stanley Clarke ct Peppè bd Barker	56
Hon. J. de Blaquiere ct Chapman bd Barker	14
J. F. Evetts bd Barker	3
Capt. Kennedy bd Barker	0
Bds. Shields ct Kelly bd Barker	7
Bds. Thompson not out	6
Bds. Gardner bd Dooner	1
Corpl. Rose l.b.w. bd Barker	4
Extras	3
Total	**167**

BOWLING.

	Wickets		Runs
Barker	9	for	69
Newton	0	for	48
Dooner	1	for	49

The score-card for the match played in Malta against the Scottish Rifles, 16 May 1914.

NOTES

1. *Daughter of the Desert*, Georgina Howell, p.65.

2. *Old Soldier Sahib*, pp.107–8.

3. Major Sir Horace McMahon, Bart. His wife, Ellie, with Elsie, Charles Dobell's wife, remained great friends with Hal's wife, Eve, (whom he married in 1906) for the rest of their lives. All three attended the Regimental Cocktail Party at the Hyde Park Hotel in 1962.

4. *Old Soldier Sahib*, pp.125–38.

5. General Sir Alfred Gaselee (1844–1918); commander of the British expeditionary force during the Boxer Rebellion.

6. A fashionable Hill-station.

7. Captain to major.

8. Dickson letters, RWF Regimental Archives.

9. An expedition under Colonel Younghusband was sent to Lhasa in 1904 was sent by the Viceroy, Lord Curzon, to forestall Russian interference in Tibet.

10. In poor visibility, the Russian Baltic Fleet en route for the Far East at the start of the Russo-Japanese War, took fright in the North Sea and fired on British trawlers, mistaking them for the enemy. The Russian fleet was defeated off Japan, at the battle of Tsu Tshima, the following year.

11. The Taj Mahal had been restored and its surroundings hugely improved by the Viceroy, Lord Curzon.

12. Evelyn Violet Ross, was the daughter of Harry Thornton Ross of the Indian Civil Service, and his wife, Lena Caroline Outram (née Battye). Most of her mother's family had served in the army in India.

13. Probably Lt-Gen Sir Alfred Gaslee who commanding British forces in Peking.

14. Edward Henry Cadogan, born 11 September1908.

15. FSR, Sect 99.

16. Capper Papers, II/4/16.

17. *All Sir Garnet*, by J. H. Lehman.

18. General Sir Neville Lyttelton, C-in-C Ireland.

19. He became General Sir Charles Monro, an army commander in France, and was the man who planned and executed the faultless withdrawal from Gallipoli. See Biographies. In 1937, Eve married Maurice, 3rd Lord O`Hagan, whose sister, Mary, had been married to Monro (he had died in 1929).

20. *Regimental Records of the Royal Welch Fusiliers*, Vol. II

21. See photograph p.160.

22. 1 RWF was due to move to Portland in November 1912.

23. Letter dated 16 May 1912

24. See Biographies.

25. Precis from *Regimental Records of the Royal Welch Fusiliers*, Vol. II. In *Old Soldiers Never Die* (p.21), Frank Richards says 80% were from Birmingham, this is an exaggeration. For example, in 1914–15, eighty of the 535 dead of the original 2 RWF were from Birmingham. 1 RWF was probably similarly constituted.

26. See photograph p162.

27. His Excellency General Sir Leslie Rundle, Governor and C-in-C.

Chapter 7

Active Service
4 August–14 October 1914

On 4 August Britain declared war on Germany. Although it was not immediately obvious to him in the heat of a Maltese summer, Hal's supreme test as a soldier, and the one for which he had trained all his life, was near. No doubt the young bloods itched to get to the front before the 'show' was over, especially when, on 11 August, they heard that the 2nd Battalion was ordered to France as part of the BEF. But the 1st Battalion did not have long to wait.

The Hultons, at home in Tenby, received a telegram at 6.55am on 18 August: 'Hal and Goat returning England, Parker.' Captain Parker was the battalion's excellent Quartermaster, and the coded message is clear.

The Battalion sailed on the SS *Ultonia*, a Cunard immigrant ship taken off the Trieste–New York service, and arrived at Southampton on 16 September. Hal left his car in a garage in Malta, never to be seen again.

Eve arranged for several large items of furniture which she had bought in Malta to be brought back on one of HM ships – 'It was so kind of nice Admiral de Robeck', she would say. It was his ships which failed to break through to Istanbul nine months later, at the start of the disastrous Gallipoli campaign.

Private Jack Ellis of Moel-y-Don, Deganwy recalled:[1]

We were at Malta when war broke out. While there we saw a German transport ship, laden with arms and ammunition bound for Austria, brought into port by two British torpedo boats. We left Malta and had a royal send-off. Thousands of inhabitants lined the bastions, and the Governor of Malta came out in a motor launch, boarded our ship and gave us a farewell speech. We arrived at Gibraltar, and on our way a French warship steamed up to us and the crew lined the deck and cheered us. We returned the compliment. We were at Gibraltar for three days and while there saw *Highflyer*, the cruiser which sank the *Kaiser Wilhelm der Grosse*[2] off the coast of West Africa. We left Gibraltar escorted by a cruiser, but did not know our destination. However, we landed at Southampton from where we went to Lyndhurst, where we underwent stiff training in preparation for the front.

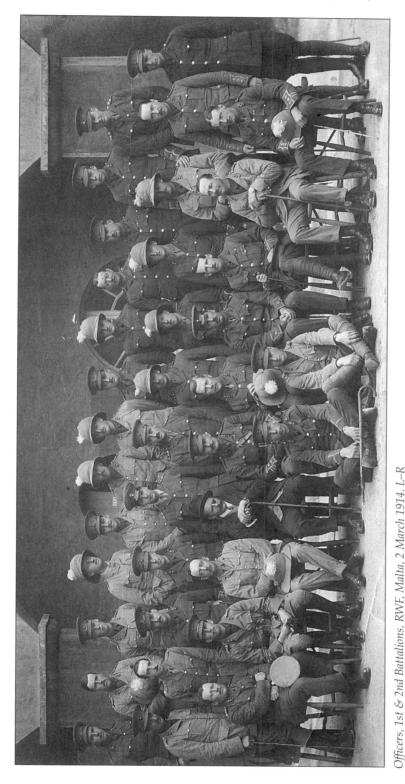

Officers, 1st & 2nd Battalions, RWF, Malta, 2 March 1914. L–R
Back row: 2Lt Courage; 2Lt Antwyl; Lt Wodehouse; 2Lt Holmes; Lt Peppé; Lt G. Parry; Lt Barchard; 2Lt Hardie; Lt Mostyn; QM Yates; QM Parker; 2Lt Evans;
Lt Ormrod. Second row: Lt Alston; Lt Soames; Lt Chance; Lt Snead-Cox; Lt Fitzroy; Lt Thomas; Lt Childe Freeman; Lt Wynne-Edwards; Lt Maltby;
Capt S. Jones; Capt Phillips; Lt Hindson. Seated: Capt Jones Vaughan; Capt & Adj Skaife; Capt Knox-Gore; Maj Gabbett; Lt-Col Cadogan; Maj Hay;
Maj Williams; Capt Kington; Capt Vyvyan; Capt & Adj C. Owen. Front row: 2LT Poole; 2Lt Ackland Allen. [RWF Archives]

Men of the 1st Battalion approaching Lyndhurst after disembarking at Southampton,
16th September 1914. The road signposted to the right is the road to Beaulieu

On 19 September, Captains M. E. Lloyd, J. H. Brennan and 2nd Lieutenants
R. le B. Egerton, Hon C. R. B. Bingham, A. Walmsley, T. Taylor and a draft of
342 other ranks joined from the Depot at Wrexham. Many of these men were
reservists, and would have been well known to the battalion. They brought the
battalion up to its War Establishment – it sailed 1,150 strong.[3] In 1914 a man
served for three years with a commitment of nine on the Reserve. Therefore
those who had left after serving in South Africa with 1st Battalion, or at Peking
with the 2nd, were able to be recalled quickly to the Colours, and were as
quickly assimilated, bringing their great experience with them. Despite the
huge physical and mental demands shortly to be made on them, they would

not be found wanting either on the march or
in battle.

The battalion spent two weeks training
and drawing its mobilisation stores, while
other regular battalions returned to England
to join the newly-formed 7 Division commanded by that old friend of the battalion,
Major-General Tom Capper. They joined 22
Brigade under Brigadier-General Sydney
Lawford (late Royal Fusiliers).[4] The other
infantry battalions in the brigade were the

Maj-Gen 'Tommy' Capper, GOC 7 Division.

2nd Battalion The Queen's Royal West Surrey Regiment, the 2nd Battalion The Royal Warwickshire Regiment and the 1st Battalion The South Staffordshire Regiment.

7 Division was composed of men averaging five year's service, from healthy stations, with comparatively few reservists. Four of its infantry battalions were in the UK when war broke out. Two others came from Gibraltar, two from Malta, including 1st Battalion The Royal Welsh Fusiliers, three battalions from the Cape and one from Egypt. Some of the smaller divisional units and the two field companies of the Royal Engineers came from South Africa. Signals, Ordnance, Stores and Transport joined in October, at the last minute. The greater part of the division was in the New Forest for about three weeks before embarkation – time for some brigade and two divisional exercises. By 4 October the division was complete, except for the gunners who had only forty-eight field guns, six short of establishment.

The Signals Officer of 22 Brigade was none other than Lieutenant Richard O'Connor, the desert victor of 1940. He, too, had been serving in Malta with his regiment, the Scottish Rifles. He was an admirer of General Capper and described General Lawford as 'a wonderful man.'[5]

Divisional HQ was set up in the Crown Hotel, and many officers had their wives staying in other hotels or with friends nearby in the New Forest. Hal, with Eve and their son, Edward, then aged six, stayed in The Grand (now renamed and very much larger).

General Capper had little time to train his hastily assembled division. An officer in the 2nd Bn, Scots Guards, in 20 Brigade, later wrote:

> General Capper took infinite trouble over divisional training at Lyndhurst on really sound lines, the value of which was proved in Belgium when they had

A group of fusiliers relaxing in front of their tent lines at Lyndhurst, September 1914.

Hal at Lyndhurst, September 1914, probably mounted on Hadji, his favourite horse. Note Hadji's cropped tail, ready for active service.

to fight against great odds. He was a man with a wonderful personality, and could be relied on to get the best out of any man he had dealings with. He was always very straight and fair, and if he once made up his mind that a thing was possible, and that the cost was worth it, he would say so and carry it out to the end. From what one saw of him from my view as a Regmental Officer, there was nothing that one could find fault with.

Hal, too, exercised the battalion hard, and included weapon training and route marches. One footsore soldier recorded that he marched 300 miles round the New Forest. There is no evidence that the division practised digging trenches or they would surely have rectified the shortage of entrenching tools before embarking. While exercising Hadji, one of Hal's two horses, Eve nearly lost him in Matley Bog near Beaulieu Road Station.

As the division departs for the front, it is a good moment to point out that the *Official History*[6] claims that the BEF that left England in 1914 was:

… the best trained, best organized and best equipped British army that ever went to war … except in the matter of numbers; so that though not 'contemptible' it was almost negligible in comparison with continental armies, even of the smaller states. In heavy guns and howitzers, high-explosive shells, trench mortars, hand grenades and much of the subsidiary material required

Camp of the 7th Division, Lyndhurst, September 1914. The road in the foreground is the Lyndhurst–Cadnam road.

for siege and trench warfare, it was almost wholly deficient. Further, no steps had been taken to instruct the army in a knowledge of the probable theatre of war or of the German Army.

The destruction of the British professional army, which began at Mons and was completed at the First Battle of Ypres, can largely be attributed to the lack of preparation by the British government in the years before the war. In round numbers, the BEF totalled some 160,000 men including recalled reservists. Compare this figure with the French Army's 1,071,000 men in five armies, or the Germans, who had 850,000 with the Colours and who could mobilize a total of 4,300,000 trained men in a matter of days.

The complicated factors leading up to the declaration of war in 1914 is beyond the scope of this narrative. But what is worth remarking here is why the officers and men of the BEF willingly and happily embarked, certain that their cause was just and with no trace of the cynicism that appeared the following year. Their sense of obligation and unquestioning sacrifice is to us, in the twenty-first century, almost impossible to understand. However, the regular army, bolstered by excellent reservists, was very professional and took huge pride in its skills. It was every officer and man's job to fight, and it was the chance for which they had been waiting. Unquestioning courage was expected of every soldier, especially of officers who led from the front. No one could see in September 1914 that this war was going to be totally different from the small wars which the army had fought in defence of the Empire, or even from the Anglo-Boer War which had shaken the complacent Victorians.

A group of officers, photographed by Lt Dick Hindson at Lyndhurst, the day before they left for France. L–R: Maj R.E. Gabbett; Capt R.V. Barker; Capt E.O. Skaife; Mrs Dooner; Lt A.E.C.T. Dooner; Capt W.M. Kington. Matilda Dooner, the mother of Claud Dooner, was visiting from her home in Kent. This would have been the last time she saw her son.

Officers 1st Bn RWF, photographed by Lt R. E. Hindson (therefore missing, as was 2Lt G. Snead-Cox, on sick leave), at Lyndhurst on 3 October 1914.
Above (L–R): Back row: Capt J.H. Brennan; 2Lt Hon G. Bingham; 2Lt E. Wodehouse;
2Lt H. T. Ackland-Allan; Capt J.G. Smyth-Osbourne; 2Lt R.E. Naylor; Capt R.V. Barker;
Lt B.C.H. Poole; Lt E.C.L. Hoskyns; Lt J.M.J. Evans.
Seated: 2Lt R. de B. Egerton; 2Lt A. Walmsley; Lt G.O. de P. Chance; Capt S. Jones;
Capt W.M. Kington, DSO; Maj Gabbett; Lt–Col H.O.S. Cadogan.

Below (L–R): Back row: ; Lt E.C.L. Hoskyns; Lt J.M.J. Evans; Lt L.A.A. Alston;
Capt Robertson (Med Officer); Lt D.M. Barchard; Capt M.E. Lloyd; Capt E. Skaife;
2Lt H.R. Hardie; Lt C.G.H. Peppé.
Seated: Lt–Col H.O.S. Cadogan; Lt A.E.C.T. Dooner (adj); Capt Harris-St John;
Capt W.G. Vyvyan; Capt E.A. Parker, DCM; Lt J.H. Courage.

In the last letter Hal received from his father before he died in 1890, his father had written '… I earnestly wish you could get active service …' For regular officers it was the quickest way to get ahead, and to escape the long wait for promotion into dead men's shoes. Moreover, the field of battle was still the field of honour.

There was another reason, too, which was felt deeply at the time. Long after the war, in *Goodbye To All That*, Robert Graves wrote of his feelings in 1914: 'I was outraged to read of the Germans' cynical violation of Belgian neutrality. Though I discounted perhaps 20% of the atrocity details as wartime exaggeration, that was not, of course, sufficient.' That even with his family background, (his mother's family was of German descent, and he had close links with his German relations before 1914) he mentions the German atrocities as a major reason for his having enlisted fourteen years earlier, reflects his horror at the acts of cruelty perpetrated by the enemy. To civilized Edwardians the war was the defence of civilization against barbarism. By 1915, and even more in 1916 with the Battle of the Somme, cracks appeared in this national consensus; a huge semi-trained citizen army was by then fighting the war after the destruction of the regular army, and these valiant civilians had experienced the full horror of modern war.

But back to Hal and his battalion training at Lyndhurst. When orders to embark were received, at 2.40 p.m. on Sunday, 4 October, they were unexpected and caught many officers on weekend leave visiting friends in the neighbourhood – servants were dispatched in all directions in cars. Nevertheless the battalion was ready to leave camp at 3.40 p.m. However, due

1st Battalion on a route march at Penerley on the Beaulieu road, September 1914.

Lieut-Col Hal Cadogan, followed by Capt W.G. Vyvyan, OC A Company, at the head of the 1st Battalion, marching through Lyndhurst, September 1914.

to delays in the division's embarkation, they did not leave Lyndhurst until 9.30 p.m., behind the drums and fifes, and with the pipes of the Scottish regiments to encourage them. On entering Southampton, O'Connor records: '… the crowds were in the streets, and broke into the ranks, embracing all and sundry.' In fact the town was up all night, for the vanguard of the marching division had embarked before the tail had left Lyndhurst. A number of men were in Southampton on day passes, but only a few failed to reach the ship. 2nd Lieutenant Rowland Egerton of Oulton Park in Cheshire, known to his friends as 'Rowley', had just joined from Sandhurst. He was left at Lyndhurst to bring them on, and they arrived at Zeebrugge on 7 October, the same day as the battalion.

Bert Judd, a coal merchant of Lyndhurst, years later remembered:

> They were the last of the Old Contemptibles, were those soldiers. The finest body of men I ever saw. Drunk as lords every night, but each one as fresh as a band box next morning. They marched out of here on October 4, 1914. I saw them go. All those proud men. They marched out of here to Southampton Docks and got caught in the First Battle of Ypres.

The Battalion embarked on the Leyland Line cattle boat, *Winifredian*, and once aboard learned that their destination was Dunkirk.[7] They sailed at 8 a.m. next morning, thousands of sailors on destroyers moored in Southampton Water cheering the ships as they steamed past. Early on 6 October, the convoy, including the *Winifridian*, was ordered to return to Dover, entering the harbour at 6 a.m., and remaining there until 9 p.m. Despite their impatience to be on

HOSC and members of the Sergeants' Mess at Lyndhurst, 1 October 1914. Seated (L–R from directly below the gap between the huts) are: Sergeant Major Williams; Lt & Adjt Dooner; Lt–Col Cadogan; Maj Gabbett; Capt & QM Parker, DCM; QMS Cottrill, DCM.   [RWF Archives]

their way and the tedium of the inexplicable delay, the day passed pleasantly enough while 7 Division rode at anchor. There was plenty to see – there were so many ships that it looked, in the words of one soldier, like a ruddy review of the Fleet – so many cutters plying to and from the shore, carrying so many senior officers that they seemed likely to sink under the weight of gold braid. No doubt the soldiers shouted irreverently to the tars on the warships, and rumours were swapped. While in the harbour, Hal practised his battalion in boat drill; a cargo ship had been blown up on a mine outside Dover the day before and no doubt this acted as a spur. It is unlikely, however, that any of the rumours about the delay were near the mark. In fact 7 Division's original task was being changed.

Finally, the convoy of some fifteen ships sailed, docking at Zeebrugge at 9 a.m. on the 7th. The distant thunder of heavy artillery could be heard from the direction of Antwerp.

7–14 October: Zeebrugge to Ypres

There were now in effect two Expeditionary Forces operating on the Continent; one under Field Marshal Sir John French already in France, and the second, from 9 October, including 7 Division under Lieutenant-General Sir Henry Rawlinson, directed by the Secretary of State, Lord Kitchener, from the War Office. This was designated IV Corps. 7 Division was initially bound for Antwerp with orders to reinforce the Royal Naval Division that was already defending that city. Before General Capper embarked on 4 October, Kitchener had summoned him to the War Office where both he and the CIGS impressed on him the importance of not becoming trapped in Antwerp; 7 Division being positively the country's last reserve of regular troops. As the division had been about to embark on 6 October, Capper, who had gone ahead by fast destroyer, learned that the fall of Antwerp was imminent. So, while a revised role for 7 Division was determined, the division had been held safely at Dover.

On disembarking, the Division entrained for Bruges to link up with the French and to cover the retreat of the Belgian Army and our Naval Division from Antwerp.

The Battle of Ypres 1914, known as 'First Ypres', was considered to comprise three phases:[8] Langemark [21–4 October], Gheluvelt [29–31 October] and Nonne Bosschen [11 November]. It is the first two phases which particularly concern this story. These were the times when the fighting was at its peak, but it did not stop between those dates. 7 Division fought in the Battle of Langemark as part of IV Corps, under General Rawlinson, and thereafter in I Corps under Lieutenant-General Sir Douglas Haig. For each belligerent these operations were the outcome of a definite plan of attack against the northern flank of his opponent; for the French and British against the German extreme right flank, and for the Germans against the Allied extreme left flank.

Facing page: 7 Division unloading on the quayside at Zeebrugge, 7 October 1914. [IWMQ57134]

This was known as 'the Race to the Sea'. Unfortunately, the Allies were always twenty-four hours and an army corps behind the enemy, sometimes more.[9] Thus, instead of being able to outflank and envelop the foe, the French, Belgian and British Armies in the north were themselves for many days in October and November 1914 in imminent danger of being broken and rolled up. The period was one of the most momentous and critical of the war, and only by the most desperate fighting did the Allies succeed in maintaining their front. Had they given way, all Belgium would have been lost and the Germans would have reached Dunkirk and Calais – which were their objectives. If these ports had fallen to the enemy, the effect on our sea communications and on operations generally might well have changed the course of history.

For a week after landing the Battalion marched or was moved by train round the marshy Belgian plain. On 9 October, 20 and 22 Brigades, the other two brigades in the division, were ordered to cover the retreat of the Belgian Army from Antwerp. 22 Brigade entrained for Ghent, arriving at 6.30 p.m., passing other trains carrying the Royal Naval Division back from its aborted defence of Antwerp. The Brigade bivouacked a mile south-west of the town. The enemy was reported to be ten miles south of them and no fires were allowed, and there was a steady downpour of rain. At 2 a.m. on 10 October the battalion marched some six miles to a ridge which was about a mile south-east of the village of Melle where they entrenched with the Royal Warwickshires on their left, in support of Belgian and French troops, who were in contact

7th Division transport on the move, Belgium, October 1914. [IWM Q05714]

with the enemy. The French and Belgians were going to attack a small German force, and the British were to cooperate by striking the German rear and left flank. The Germans, however, attacked first, and were surprised by the French and Belgians as they were coming over a railway embankment. The Germans left about 200 dead behind. This was the nearest encounter the Battalion had had so far. No British artillery had accompanied them to Ghent.

On the 11th the Battalion was ordered forward to cover the retirement of the Belgian and French troops and itself began to retire at about 4 p.m., marching west, via Ghent and Tronchiennes to Hansbeke. Civilians, transport and other troops were streaming along the roads. 'A battalion of [French] Marine Fusiliers marched parallel to us through the broad boulevards [of Ghent]. We were impressed with their rapid and easy marching.'[10]

The column was badly guided, and the Brigade marched some distance out of its way, only arriving at Hansbeke at 7 a.m. on the 12th. The place was crowded with troops and billets were hard to find, but they had little time for rest before the brigade continued its retirement at 2 p.m. The Battalion's task was for three companies to hold some important crossings over canals on the Germans' lines of advance, between Hanime and Neyele, until the morning of 13 October while Belgian engineers blew up the bridges. But at 5 p.m. further orders arrived to hand over to the Northumberland Hussars and to retire at once on Thielt. However, the Hussars were delayed on a patrol, so the battalion did not finally leave until 10.15 p.m., and after again marching all night reached Thielt at 5.30 a.m. on 13 October. Corporal Hugh Roberts, of Four Crosses near Welshpool,[11] a veteran of the South African War, was a section commander in a platoon forty strong who dug in to cover this withdrawal. The Germans attempted to surround them, but the position had to be held '… to give the Warwicks at least an hour's start. As luck had it, orders had been given [for the Royal Welsh to withdraw] when the Germans advanced in thousands and we had to run about two miles before we rejoined the Regiment.'[11]

The 13th at Thielt was an even wetter day than usual. There Private Ellis had the thrill of shooting down a German *Taube* plane '… with a maxim gun, fired from an attic window of our billet. The airmen were killed and the machine was smashed and burnt.' Corporal Roberts also saw this, noting that '… the driver of the aeroplane was shot, and as the machine was falling, one of the three men in it jumped into the pilot's seat, but in vain.'

At 11.15 a.m. orders were received to move to Roulers, again as divisional rearguard. The roads were so congested with refugees that the Battalion only arrived there at 8 p.m. after a tiring march, although the distance is no more than ten miles. By that evening, the cavalry holding the canal crossings defended by the battalion the day before had been driven in.

At 3 a.m. on the 14th, orders were received to march to Ypres at 8 a.m. One

7 Division at Thielt, 13 October 1914. [IWM Q57184]

hundred and fifty men per company went by train, leaving the transport and details to march by road. Private Ellis remembered: 'When we reached Ypres, at 2 p.m., we were ordered to march in ceremonial order into Ypres. This was to signify that we had retaken the place from the Germans, 800 of whom had evacuated the town [shortly] before our arrival. The party that came by train had no sooner landed [sic] than they shot down another *Taube*. One of the airmen was killed and the other taken prisoner after trying to escape.'

The battalion had now marched some 126 miles in six days in filthy weather and with little hot food. Moreover, the pavé roads were particularly hard on the feet of marching men.

At Ypres they were billeted in the Kaserne for the night.

A unit of the 7 Division resting near Gheluvelt, October 1914. [IWM Q57207]

NOTES

1. Private Ellis, reported in in the *Liverpool Echo* and the *Caernarvon & Denbigh Herald* of 11 November 1914.

2. In August a number of German merchant ships were each equipped with ten 4-inch guns. Most were bottled up in German ports but the *Kaiser Wilhelm der Grosse*, a liner of 14,000 tons managed to escape.She had snatched the prestigious Blue Riband trophy from Britain's Cunard line in 1897. Her task was to sink British shipping between the UK and the Cape of Good Hope. She had great success, sinking three large liners within ten days but was eventually caught coaling off Las Palmas, Gran Canaria, by HMS *Highflyer*, a light cruiser of only 5,600 tons, but armed with 6- and 12-inch guns and was sunk.

3. *A Short History of the Royal Welsh Fusiliers*, Eric Skaife.

4. See Biographies.

5. *The Forgotten Victor*, John Baynes, Brasseys, 1989.

6. *OHW, Military Operations*, v. I, pp.10–11.

7. Many major units were divided, half going on a separate boat, so that should one be sunk then the other half could form a nucleus of the reconstructed battalion. The 2nd Bn, Royal Welsh Fusiliers had sailed in two ships, on 11 and 13 August, for Rouen. There is no evidence, however, that the 1st Battalion was divided.

8. By the 1921 Battles Nomenclature Committee.

9. *Memoirs of General Galieni*, p.197.

10. *Regimental Records of the Royal Welsh Fusiliers*, Vol. III.

11. *Oswestry Advertizer*, 18 November 1914.

Chapter 8

Armageddon
15–30 October 1914

Ypres lies in a saucer, overlooked from all round. Undulating slopes lead away to the north-west, and south-west towards the River Lys. The main ridge runs east on which lies the Menin road running through the villages of Hooge and Gheluvelt. The country was far more wooded than it is today, with interconnecting hedges, and dotted with large farm buildings.[1] In the low ground many small streams restricted movement. All this was good ground for defence, but it was very difficult spotting for the artillery, still firing over open sights as at Waterloo nearly one hundred years before. The biggest problem, however, was that of communication. Even orders down from division were normally sent by runner or motor cycle; telephones were few and unreliable and radio was in its infancy. This meant that artillery fire could not be brought down quickly and units reacted ponderously to orders. Nor could vital information be passed back quickly, therefore brigade commanders and the commanders of higher formations, found it extremely difficult to know what was going on during a battle.

On the morning of 15 October it was learnt that a German army corps was moving on Menin. 22 Brigade, in reserve, spent the day in the orchards round Zillebeke, returning that evening to billets on the south-east side of Ypres. At 9 p.m. they were ordered to be ready to march at 3.30 a.m. next day.

Early on the 16th, the Division marched east out of Ypres through the screen found by the Royal Scots Fusiliers. The Royal Welsh was the brigade's advance guard. Private Jack Ellis later recorded: 'My company was in front. In the distance we could hear the sound of firing. Nearer and nearer it sounded, and suddenly we came across a party of half a dozen Uhlans[2] who managed to escape.' This was at Zonnebeke at about 6.30 a.m. Captain Eric Skaife, probably the second captain of A Company, Ellis's company, also had under him Private Tom Jones,[3] who followed Skaife's lead into a farm just vacated by the Uhlans where they found the bayoneted bodies of the farmer and his family.[4] Tom Jones had previously been a boy in the battalion, but had been just old enough to accompany it to Belgium.

Elements of 7 Division approaching Ypres from Roulers, 14 October 1914. Note the rough pavé road. [IWM Q57189]

The enemy was reported to be in strength at Roulers, Wervicq and Menin. and the battalion was ordered to take up an entrenched outpost position from a point midway between the 6th and 7th kilometre stones on the Wervicq–Passchendaele road, north to where the railway crossed the main road. It was close country, with houses and gardens to the left and a wood to the front. Hal deployed three companies in the front line, each with two platoons in the trenches and two in close billets immediately behind them. He sited the reserve company with Battalion Headquarters in a sand pit, about 400 yards to the rear on a reverse slope. The soft sand made digging difficult and they did not have time to dig communication trenches. It did not help that the infantry entrenching tool at that time was inadequate and that there was no revetting materiel. Battalion QMs had scoured the hardware and agricultural stores in Ypres, but this yielded only twenty spades and no wire. What little wire they had, had been retrieved from farmers' fences, but only enough for occasional strands to be twisted round improvised posts forward of the trenches. These were hung with empty tins to warn of a night attack. Relieved to see the departure of the Germans, the local Belgians welcomed the arrival of the British and gave them food and drink as they watched them dig. Farmers worked their fields nearby.

20 Brigade, meanwhile, was deployed between the Menin road and the village of Zandvoorde, with the 2nd Battalion, Scots Guards digging in to the east of that village. The trenches were '… in short lengths, not continuous, on

the forward slope facing Wervicq and Comines.'[5] This position was the one occupied by Hal's battalion ten days later, and in which they were to be annihilated.

By the 16th, the German front lay south along the River Lys, with a line of posts, America–Koelberg–Kezelberg, north of the river covering Menin. By making a general advance, General Foch, the French C-in-C, saw the chance of separating the German III Reserve Corps advancing from Antwerp, from the main German armies further south. The bulk of the Allied troops would force the passage of the Lys, and strike north of Menin. Sir John French manoeuvred the BEF in accordance with this plan, but neither he nor Foch knew of the approach of the German Fourth Army between Menin and Antwerp. General Rawlinson's corps, therefore, was about to attack Menin across the front of an unexpected enemy army.

On 17 October, Sir John French ordered IV Corps to attack Menin, while the French III Corps which had occupied Armentières (some ten miles south of Ypres) was to move east down the River Lys towards that town. Reconnaissance by armoured cars on 18 October revealed that Menin had not been substantially reinforced the previous day.[6] General Rawlinson therefore ordered 7 Division to act quickly. To avoid enfilade fire from Wervicq on his right flank, General Capper decided to attack first from the north. His plan, issued at 8.30 p.m was for a three-phase attack:

Phase 1 – 22 Brigade to attack the enemy trenches known to be at Kleythoek (i.e. from the north) against the outpost trenches of the German's XIII Corps.

Phase 2 – a combined attack by 20 and 21 Brigades against Gheluwe (i.e. from the west)..

Phase 3 – a combined attack from Gheluwe and Kleythoek on Menin.

Map overleaf: The movements of the 1st Battalion 14–30 October 1914. Direction of German advance shown by black arrows.

14 October 1914 – March and train from Roulers to Ypres.

1. 15 October to Zillebeke and return to Ypres.

2. 16–7 October Broodseinde.

3. 18 October Becelaere.

ERRATUM

The daily movements of the 1st Battalion shown on page 185 should be altered as follows: delete

4. 19 October to Kleyhoek via Stroolboom, Dadizeele, Kezelberg and return via Dadizeele, Terhand, Becelaere to Broodseinde late p.m.

insert:

4. 19 October to Kezelberg via Stroolboom, Dadizeele, Kleyhoek and return via Dadizeele, Terhand, Becelaere to Broodseinde late p.m.

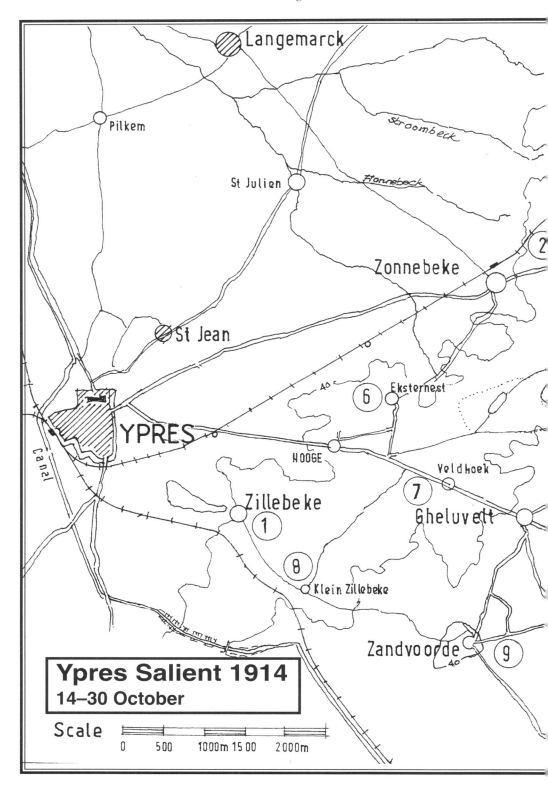

Ypres Salient 1914
14–30 October

Scale

0   500   1000m 15 00   2000m

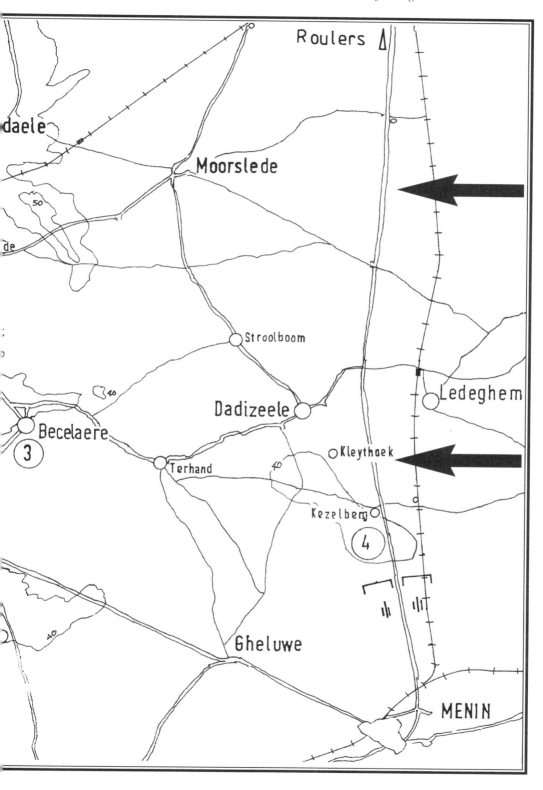

The Operation Order is at Annex B. It was the only one issued by 7 Division in October; from then on in the First Battle of Ypres, under-strength battalions and companies were deployed, often piecemeal and at short notice, to 'putty up the front', in the jargon of the time.

To prepare to attack, 22 Brigade went into reserve and marched to the area round Hooge, with the battalion at Veldhoek where the men received their first pay since landing in France. There were few sounds of battle, but much speculation about where and how they would be used in the battle that all knew was imminent.

Late that evening, the battalion marched to Becelaere and billeted there for the night. Battle orders arrived about 2 a.m. on the 19th.

19 October: Attack on Menin and withdrawal to Broodseinde

There could have been little sleep that night for the officers in particular; orders had to be written and issued, and everyone was up and on the move at 5 a.m. As the brigade advance guard, the battalion was clear of Becelaere by 5.30 a.m. heading for Dadizeele and Stroolboom, which were reached without contact with the enemy. The order was given to attack Kleythoek, and the battalion deployed to the north of the road.[7] The Royal Warwickshires were on the right, and the South Staffordshires in support. The Queen's were the left rear battalion, covering Ledeghem, on which the 3rd Cavalry Division, who were covering the left flank, had orders to move.

The Royal Welsh cleared Kleythoek, crossed the main road, wheeled south and pressed on towards Kezelberg with the enemy retiring before them. The advance was now against rifle fire, and made in short rushes. Casualties began to mount up, and the South Staffordshires were called up to reinforce the front line. At this point, A Company, who were the left forward company, were deployed to cover the eastern flank, while the Royals and 10th Hussars, part of the cavalry screen to the north east, put in a spirited charge to clear the village of Ledeghem of some 200 enemy. This diversion delayed the advance from the cross-roads west of Kezelberg until 10 a.m. A and D Companies were forward, with B and C Companies in support. At 10.30 a.m. Hal received word by runner that the 2nd Queen's were to come up on the battalion's left, with the Menin–Ledeghem

QMS J. Cottrill, DCM

railway as the inter-battalion boundary. They were now approaching the second milestone north of Menin, on a forward slope overlooking the town and the German trenches defending it.

The men in the leading company with Private Ellis '... were eager for the experience of battle, and they advanced in artillery formation[8] until they were within rifle range.' His company first dealt with a party of snipers in a farmhouse. Then, as they advanced further, '... shells wrought great havoc, and Lieutenant Chance was killed leading the men into action. Captain Skaife called on a section of A Company to follow him, to capture two of the guns which were doing most of the enemy's mischief.' They got to within five yards of the guns when Skaife was hit. As the section was well ahead of the battalion the Germans swept them with fire. Ellis's friend, Private Chris Pepper from Caernarfon, was wounded. Private James Cowan,[9] another of the six men with Skaife, thought he was the only one left alive. They could get no further.

At 10.30 a.m., as the battalion had Menin in its sights, alarming news reached General Rawlinson; air reconnaissance reported that the head of an enemy column, estimated to be a division, had reached Gulleghem four miles north-east of Menin and that other columns were approaching Roulers and moving up from further east. 7 Cavalry Brigade and the French cavalry on their left were already falling back. In sum, considerable forces had suddenly materialised on the front of IV Corps.

At noon, General Capper received orders to halt the attack on Menin. He therefore ordered 22 Brigade to break off the engagement and to fall back with its right on 21 Brigade at Terhand, but facing east, and in touch with the right of 3 Cavalry Division at Moorslede. There was naturally some confusion at this sudden change of plan, but General Lawford managed to extricate his brigade. Messages left brigade headquarters with orders for a withdrawal, but the runner bound for the Royal Welsh was killed en route. Somehow the order still managed to reach the battalion although it does not seem to have come directly to Hal or to any of his staff. The surprise it caused may be imagined; the battalion had made such excellent progress and Menin lay in full view just ahead, now it was ordered to cover the retirement of the brigade, and so all began to dig in the area of Dadizeele windmill, awaiting the enemy's advance. The Germans, however, made no attempt at pursuit, but their accurate shelling caused many casualties during this difficult phase, and a number of men were picked off by snipers. Our artillery was unable to locate the enemy guns and so there was much grumbling in the ranks about the absence of the promised artillery support.

Corporal Hugh Roberts, under this withering shrapnel fire, got his men to crawl on their stomachs through a turnip field to the windmill where they found some shelter although many fell dead and wounded around him.

Lance Corporal Marchant,[10] a Special Reservist from Cardiff, was wounded in the forearm here when:

> … two men of our Regiment were shot by a young German (prisoner) not more than sixteen years of age, who we foolishly allowed to pass on account of his youth. We allowed him no more mercy after this, and soon put him out of his misery. The Germans do not show any respect to the wounded. On one occasion I saw them cutting off the head of a poor soldier who had been unable to get away.
>
> I shall never forget the courage shown by one of our officers, Major Gabbett, when he was wounded. Two of our men ran out to bring him in and he appealed to them all the time to sharpen his sword in order to have another 'go' at the enemy.

Private D. Callaghan[11] was wounded when about 700 yards from the enemy at Menin:

> Shrapnel shells began flying all around, and about 140 of our men got knocked out. We were then ordered to retire a bit, and to wait for the arrival of the artillery to support us. I have seen active service in South Africa, Egypt, Crete and China, but those campaigns were a picnic compared with the present. This war is nothing but an artillery duel.

Private George Davies of B Company,[12] later wrote to his mother in Oswestry from Gottingen where he was a prisoner of war: '… it was terrible to see the men die. I shall never forget the sight as long as I live for I never expected to come out of the fight alive.' It was at this time, too, that Lieutenant Roland Naylor, whose family lived in Liverpool and at Welshpool, was wounded, and '… two of his company carried him back to safety.' Very probably one of these was Sergeant Smith, maybe his platoon sergeant, who was awarded the DCM for his bravery. As Naylor was carried past, 2nd Lieutenant Geoffrey Snead-Cox, whose platoon was holding the Dadizeele position, shouted to him 'Are you the last?'

When the rest of the brigade was clear, the battalion withdrew through Terhand and Becelaere – where the villagers still remained, though now thoroughly alarmed as the enemy had begun to shell their village – to the shallow trenches they had left at Broodseinde the day before. They arrived there at 5 p.m. The scene on this last stage was one of great confusion, for the road was blocked with refugees fleeing the advancing Germans, and the battalion transport had to turn off the road and make its way across the fields. All through that night, when the battalion was deployed in its rifle slits, a great stream of civilians flowed past them down the road from Roulers.

Company commanders spent part of the night sorting out their men. In addition to Skaife, Brennan and Chance, it was thought fifteen other ranks had been killed. Major Gabbett, Captains St John, S. Jones and 2nd Lieutenant Naylor, and eighty-four other ranks had been wounded; and eleven other ranks were reported missing. Nevertheless, 7 Division Diary for 19 October records: 'In connection with the fighting on this day, the dash and steadiness of 1 RWF was conspicuous.'

The enemy was now exerting pressure across the division's front. Even so, the true situation was still not fully appreciated by GHQ on the evening of the 19th. Intelligence placed three and a half enemy corps advancing, when there were actually five and a half. Sir John French, mistrusting this intelligence, informed General Haig, commanding I Corps: the enemy's strength on the front Menin–Ostend is estimated at about a corps, and no more. On the battalion's left flank, 3 Cavalry Division moved out early on the 20th to Passchendaele to link up with the French cavalry corps.

20–24 October: The Battle of Langemarck

Soon after 11 a.m. on the 20 October, in the distance, enemy columns were seen approaching, and their artillery opened up on the Royal Welsh. Unknown to the battalion, 3 Cavalry Division and the French cavalry corps on their left had been driven back, and the reconnaissance companies from 20 and 21 Brigades had been called in from their positions on the high ground to the east, where they had been in touch with the enemy. It had been drizzling since the early morning and the battalion waited, crouching in their shallow trenches under the bombardment. At last the shelling ceased, and the enemy infantry advanced. Every man knew that the weight of artillery was against him, but his musketry skill gave him confidence in his rifle; a trained British soldier could fire fifteen or more accurate rounds a minute. The German infantry advance was massive – they always favoured superior weight in men and metal – and the excitement was intense in the Royal Welsh rifle slits, from which arose a roar of fire indistinguishable from machine-gun fire. The waves of the enemy drew nearer, then, under the devastating rifle fire, seemed to hesitate as figures darted about unsteadily, and then drew back.

At about midday Hal ordered Captain Peppé[13] to reinforce the frontline trenches with his reserve company. After a pause, there followed more artillery fire, and then at 4 p.m., another attack. The depleted ranks of the battalion maintained their devastating fire and this attack, too, withered. Several more attacks, perhaps weaker in numbers but equally determined, were made before darkness, but these were also repulsed.

During this hectic day B Company alone lost two officers and thirty-two men. One of the men from his company recorded that:[14]

… Lieutenant Hoskyns was killed by a sniper, and about three hours later Captain Kington, DSO was killed.[15] [Kington] was a very popular officer, it made us all mad to avenge his death. We had the devils almost beaten, and they were quite close to us when we received the order to fix bayonets and charge. This bucked us all up. With bugles sounding and a cheer from thousands of throats we ran as fast as we could into them. What a sight it was! The devils turned and fled like birds, but we were close to them and let them have it.

Captain Hindson[16] recorded:

Owing to dead ground, the enemy were able to get up to within a hundred yards of our trench, but we kept them from leaving the shelter of the wood to our front. Our chief danger lay in enfilade fire, as our trench turned abruptly across the Broodseinde–Passchendaele road and our left was exposed. There were numerous cottages which the Huns occupied and were thus able to fire down into the trench from the roofs and upper windows; to our front and within 120 yards was a thick wood in which the Germans were able to concentrate, especially as part of it was dead ground. This wood was occasionally 'searched' by machine-gun fire which covered some of the dead ground invisible from the trench, but with what result it is hard to say. One machine gun was in the main trench on the extreme left, and had an all-round traverse, so as to be able to fire to our front or to our left flank and half–right; the other was in a well concealed pit some thirty yards to our left front, in a cottage garden, and, in addition to lessening the amount of dead ground to our front, was able to bring enfilade fire on any party of the enemy attempting to rush the trench from the wood; it covered some 400–500 yards of the trench front.

... my best machine-gun target [was] a group of thirty to forty of the enemy who were ... behind some cottages about 150 yards away; only a few escaped. About 120 yards to our left front were three haystacks, which the enemy used as cover and so worked round to our flank. We had no wire in front of our trench. About 7 p.m. the Colonel and Adjutant came up to the trenches from their headquarters in the small quarry.

After visiting Hindson's company, Hal spoke to Captain Barchard and Lieutenant Bingham of C Company in their trenches before moving on to Captain Smyth-Osbourne's position at about 10.30 p.m. Private Tom Jones met his commanding officer coming towards him up his trench. 'Do you mind if I crawl over you, my boy?' asked Hal.

While Hal and Claud Dooner were in the forward trenches Hindson recorded that:

... there was a sudden outburst of shrapnel, machine-gun and rifle fire, which lasted for some time, and then gradually died away. Most of the cottages round the trench and cross-roads were burning by now. We carried on digging a communication trench back to the road but this was never finished.

A listening-post of an officer and a private, sent out on our left flank, reported digging some 150–200 yards away; on investigation they were found to be Germans. Captain Smyth-Osbourne, the senior officer in that part of the line, reported this to Headquarters and asked if he should charge, but the Brigadier [Lawford] considered such a step too hazardous with the small number of men at his disposal.

During the night there were several violent outbursts of fire, lasting some time, but nothing followed. The enemy were blowing bugles and whistles most of the night, but with what object I am unable to say.

Hal at his headquarters in the sandpit received a lot of attention from the enemy artillery – a hole definitely marked on the map! He was knocked over once by the burst of a shell, but was unhurt.

It became clear later that 7 Division and 3 Cavalry Division, with little artillery support, had withstood the attack of two German army corps. Dawn revealed thousands of Germans dead in front of the battalion.

The artillery of the German XXVI and XXVII Reserve Corps had moved forward during the night, and early on the morning of the 21st again opened up on 22 Brigade – especially from Passchendaele, whence they enfiladed the whole line. It was a day of furious bombardment and many casualties, with frequent assaults, always repulsed by the Battalion. Hindson noted:

About 10 a.m. the enemy began to bombard us with 'coal-boxes',[17] having previously sent an aeroplane over. They soon found the exact range and began to flatten our trenches very systematically. The brunt of the fire fell on the trenches on either side of the Broodseinde–Moorslede road, held by A Company, who lost heavily, the occupants being killed or buried in their trenches. This bombardment went on until about 2.30 p.m., and machine guns occasionally traversed our parapet. The enemy also fired shrapnel.

My machine guns had both been put out of action, but the Royal Warwicks brought two guns to replace mine. We lost a good many men from snipers, some being in the cottages and roots to our immediate rear, men being shot from behind.

It was a section commander in the 2nd Battalion, Royal Warwickshire Regiment who, using his initiative, came to the rescue of the Royal Welsh. Corporal Loveridge saw them in trouble.

I ran to our Regiment's two machine guns and told the gunners to send a cross fire right along our line. It was a success for it simply mowed the enemy down. Then the captain of the [Royal] Welsh asked who gave the order. Our officer told him that I did. The captain sent for me and made me a sergeant at once.[18]

Private James Cowen of Cardiff, later convalescing at home, reported:

After the first day the firing was so hot that we could not get anything to eat in the trenches except turnips. Then I was ordered to signal to our artillery, as the Germans were advancing on us in the form of a horse-shoe. They had reached a building on our flank, but our artillery succeeded in dropping a shell right into the building, putting about a hundred Germans out of action. It was whilst signalling that I got shot through my hand. … I will be glad to get back although I now know what I have to go through.

He had three brothers fighting, while a fourth was already home, wounded. His cousin had been killed on the Aisne.

By the afternoon of the 20th, Snead-Cox had only sixteen men alive in his trench. During a lull he went along the trench sharing his rations and chocolate and dividing the contents of his brandy flask with his men. When the battle began again, Snead-Cox stood up and looked through his field glasses in order to direct his men's fire. A sergeant, who was next to him, begged him to take cover. Snead-Cox exclaimed, 'All right, I see them now.' At that moment a bullet struck him in the middle of the forehead.

Lieutenant Wodehouse tried to clear the left flank, but his casualties were so heavy he had to give up the attempt. Several efforts were made to occupy the edge of the wood to the Battalion front, and some fifty men succeeded in passing through a raking flank fire to gain the cover of the wood, but were held there. Only half a dozen won their way back. As the day went on we received several messages 'to hold on at all costs', but it became more and more difficult to get messages to and from Battalion Headquarters, and for two hours before we were taken we had lost touch; our only means of communication being by runner ….

After the bombardment we found it impossible to use many of the rifles and we had to hammer our bolts open with entrenching tools: our maximum rate of fire fell (from their usual 15 rounds) to about three rounds per minute.[19]

Private Ellis remembered:

… they seemed to find the range of our trenches to a nicety and continued shelling us unceasingly. Their infantry also made repeated attacks. The shell fire became so hot that we were obliged to evacuate the trenches, and we (were) ordered to form up about 500 yards in the rear. This we did, quite orderly. Up came the Germans. Coolly and anxiously we waited until they were right up by our trenches, and then was given the order to charge them with the bayonet. We chased them. The spirit of battle had gripped us. Into their

2nd Lieutenant Geoffrey Snead-Cox. Killed in action aged nineteen.

midst we hurled ourselves and hundreds of them were slaughtered. In this charge I was put out of action – worse luck. I was shot right through my arm at close range.

Private E. T. Smith probably has the reason for this unusual tactic – a charge in the middle of a tense defensive battle.

Word was passed down the line from man to man from D Company that nearly all the rifles were jammed. The section to which I belonged had only two rifles working out of sixteen when the enemy commenced to attack. We were informed that the order would be given to retire 15 yards behind the trenches, and then, when the enemy was getting well up, we were to dash back and carry out a bayonet charge. The two who were firing kept up [firing rapid] as well as they could, and ultimately we managed to get six rifles into firing order.[20]

Ellis had heard the German officers urging their men on with the command *'Vorwaerts'*, and the men replying *'Nein'*. He then saw the officers, revolvers in hand behind the men, threatening to shoot those who refused to advance. 'Our officers,' said Ellis, 'are in front and not behind.'

Finally, Hindson and the remnants of his company were overwhelmed.

In the afternoon we were being shelled from our left rear with shrapnel – at the time we thought our own guns were bursting short, but apparently they were German guns.

Parts of our line had been reinforced by the Royal Warwicks. About 4.30 pm I was captured with two other officers and 42 men; we had been holding about a hundred yards of trench.

The Battalion's Regimental Goat on the Menin Road, Ypres, October 1914. In the background are members of the 7th Division Cyclist Company.

The battalion's position was critical, and General Lawford therefore withdrew them through the 2nd Queens by Zonnebeke Station, into reserve at Eksternest. After 2nd Lieutenant Snead-Cox and Captain Lloyd were killed there were no officers left in Corporal Hugh Roberts' company. He and a dozen men were manning their trench when one of his men, looking round, exclaimed: 'Good gracious, [no doubt an euphemism!] they have retired', meaning the main body of the battalion. Roberts could not persuade his men to retire with him – they seemed too bewildered to leave the trench. So he shouted:

> I am not going to be captured, let us make a dash for it … so I made a run for 50 yards on the level, a German machine gun playing on me all the time, and then I found a little bit of a gutter, into which I crept, and crawled along for about thirty yards on my stomach, the bullets whistling overhead. The machine gun had stopped, so that the enemy might see were I was, so I jumped across the road into a deeper gutter, and just as I got over the road the Germans put the machine gun on again and the fire from other guns as well were concentrated on me. I had retired about a mile before I could see anyone on the British side. I went through farm buildings, all of which had been shattered by the guns. Scores of British dead and wounded were lying (in the fields).

Roberts tore up his diary before his dash for safety in case he was captured.

The Battalion that mustered at Eksternest was sadly depleted; of the 1150, there remained only Hal, his Adjutant (Claud Dooner), Lieutenant Peter Poole, 2nd Lieutenants Edmond Wodehouse and Rowland Egerton, and Captain Parker, the Quartermaster, with 206 other ranks.

Captains Kington and M. E. Lloyd, Lieutenant Hoskyns, 2nd Lieutenants Ackland-Allen and Snead-Cox, with, as far as was known, thirty-seven other ranks, had been killed; Lieutenants Alston, J. M. J. Evans, Courage, and 2nd Lieutenant Walmsley, with some eighty other ranks, had been wounded; while among the missing were Captains Smyth-Osbourne and Vyvyan, Lieutenants Hindson, Barchard and Peppé, 2nd Lieutenant Bingham and 213 other ranks. Some were able to rejoin and some became prisoners-of-war. In the chaos of that night it was inevitable that small parties got lost.[21]

Early the following morning, 22 October, Hal led parties from the three battalions of the brigade in an attempt to collect the wounded, but was heavily opposed and their efforts had to be abandoned. The battalion was now deployed to the west of Polygon Wood, and apart from shelling and sniping the next two days passed without incident. Parties of Germans tried to establish snipers and machine guns near the British line, but lost heavily. All this time the enemy's aim was to pin down the forces opposite them. At 5.30 a.m. on the 24th the artillery bombardment began again. Trenches had by now lost all regular shape and gave little cover. More serious was the effect of the

Sergeant Major Shem Williams

sand thrown up by the shelling which got into the mechanism of the rifles causing bursts and jams and preventing the fixing of bayonets.

The Regimental Goat, which had faithfully followed the battalion so far, now had to be left with the Second Line transport, otherwise the battalion would have been accompanied by no less than four regimental pets, as the Battalion War Diary describes them. Three other goats, deserted like most farm animals at this time, decided their best chance of survival lay in following the Regimental Goat, and they refused to be dissuaded. The Germans had advanced so quickly that the farmers had flown with their families, leaving meals half-eaten on the kitchen table and abandoning their livestock; tethered dogs remained howling for food, and cows were left un-milked except by soldiers at quiet moments.

Polygon Wood was lost and then recaptured with help from 2 Division; reinforcements arrived at the moment General Capper was preparing his HQ to make a stand with a few cyclists and officers' servants.[22] It is interesting that again and again during the battle for Ypres, the Germans attacked in overwhelming numbers and succeeded in penetrating the line, but did not know what to do after reaching their objective and so became vulnerable to British counter-attacks. The reasons for this hesitancy may have been the poor standard of training of the German Reserve Army, but more probably the Germans' conviction that the British had a large concealed reserve near Ypres. A captured German officer, on being taken to the rear, asked the British officer escorting him 'Where are your reserves?' In reply, the British officer pointed to the line of guns. Obviously disbelieving him, the German then asked 'What is there behind?' On getting the reply Divisional HQ, he exclaimed from the depths of his heart in German 'God Almighty!'[23]

The battalion, now part of the Divisional Reserve found by 22 Brigade, was half-a-mile east of Veldhoek and every reinforcement was eagerly seized; men employed in the services behind the front were ordered forward, stragglers and lost men trickled in, so the strength of the battalion rose to a little over 400. Although later that day 22 Brigade was moved south to support 21 Brigade they were not used. Even so, the battalion's casualties totalled sixteen on the 23 and 24 October, largely due to enemy shelling.

The 24 October marks the end of the first phase of First Battle of Ypres. The

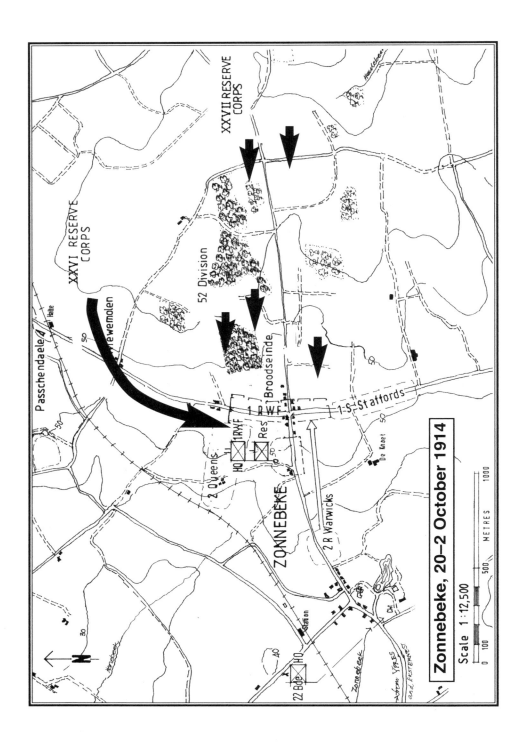

Zonnebeke, 20–2 October 1914

Scale 1:12,500

defences of the city were now in the form of an eastern semicircle, with the British holding the southern half and the French the northern.

24–29 October: A comparative lull in the battle

During the pause in the major attacks between 24 and 29 October, the enemy was preparing yet another devastating assault.

The 25th was a comparatively quiet day – even the Germans seemed to need to catch their breath. The situation was really stalemate. Sir John French signalled London optimistically about ultimate success, in spite of the severe shortage of artillery ammunition. The only sinister signs were air reconnaissance reports of considerable enemy train movements, and news that fresh enemy troops were coming up to their Fourth Army.

After a fairly quiet night, General Haig hoped to regain Becelaere, given up by 7 Division on 19 October. However, German shelling by heavy 8-inch howitzers increased steadily, and at midday on the 26th German infantry swept through Kruiseke, cutting off three companies of 20 Brigade, most of whom were captured. 22 Brigade was ordered to advance through Gheluvelt, south of, and parallel to, the Menin road, to relieve the pressure on 20 Brigade. The Royal Welsh, leading the brigade advance, came under heavy shellfire on reaching the Gueluvelt–Zandvoorde road. After advancing a further mile, it was learned that 20 Brigade was withdrawing, so 22 Brigade pulled back to the area of Point 1660 and one mile east of Gueluvelt, to cover 20 Brigade's retirement. Therefore, at nightfall, 20 Brigade, near Zandvoorde, faced NE, and 22 Brigade on its left faced south. Again, however, the enemy did not follow up their initial success. Late that evening, 22 Brigade was told to cover the re-entrant towards Zandvoorde. This adjustment took all night and further fatigued the troops.

A draft of ninety NCOs and men had arrived from Britain under 2nd Lieutenant E. Procter that morning. Procter was wounded the same day, within twelve hours of joining, as was Regimental Sergeant-Major S. Williams and some nine soldiers. It was at about this time, too, that Corporal Roberts was wounded in the left arm by a machine gun. He bandaged his arm himself, before going to the Regimental Aid Post to get his wound dressed. The Germans shelled the building so all had to run for their lives and Roberts was taken to Ypres where he spent the night in a convent, before being evacuated home.

7 Division was showing signs of exhaustion. The length of the line did not allow commanders to keep a reserve, and therefore there was no possibility of relief from the strain of constant exposure and readiness for action in the trenches. The nights were spent carrying forward supplies, improving or reorganizing positions – endless activities which prevented sleep, while the days were taken up with fighting. By the evening of 26 October, after nine

Scots Guards in a shallow trench in a landscape typical of where the Royal Welsh fought during the First Battle of Ypres. [IWM Q57228]

days of continuous fighting, the Division had lost 44% of its officers and 37% of its men. General Capper favoured siting trenches on forward slopes, protected by overhead cover. This was the method used by the Japanese in the Russo-Japanese War, on which Capper was an expert. In his Operational Report, General Rawlinson points out that 7 Division's heavy losses '… may possibly in some small measure have been due to want of experience in the construction and location of trenches on the part of troops from garrison stations abroad.[24] However, it can be argued that the casualties were mainly a result of the overwhelming superiority of the enemy's heavy artillery, and of the sterling efforts of 7 Division's riflemen to check the huge German assault. The riflemen's efforts became ever more important for, as the artillery became increasingly short of ammunition, the gunners were forced to use what they had against enemy artillery rather than against their infantry.

During the 27 and 28 October, divisional and brigade commanders desperately plugged gaps in the line, so units became very mixed. Bad visibility restricted air reconnaissance, and there was intermittent shelling all the time. On the 27th, 7 Division came under the command of General Haig in I Corps, who readjusted the line, giving the division the stretch from Zandvoorde to the Menin road. 20 Brigade relieved 22 Brigade, a manoeuvre that was not completed until midnight resulting in yet another disturbed night for the battalion. It was during the night of 27/28 October, in pouring rain, that the battalion was relieved by the Bedfords. But one hour later, as Corporal Sutton, Hal's servant, remembered '… the Brigade Major appeared, to order the Battalion back into the line … drenched as they were. The Colonel was furious, saying he had only 205 men left. The trenches were all smashed and broken in by shell fire [so we] had to hurriedly dig what [we] could. [We] only [had] shelter when kneeling.' For the next thirty-six hours the battalion rotated between the front line and Klein Zillebeke where they snatched some rest. Every few hours the rain poured down, trenches were now deep in mud, some 50% of the cartridges proved too large for the rifles and there was no rifle oil.

29–31 October: The Battle of Gheluvelt

The 29 October was the first of the five days when the Kaiser was present in person with his troops opposite Ypres. His intention was to stimulate his army to one supreme and irresistible effort which would carry all before it and open the road to Calais. He proclaimed: 'This breakthrough will be of decisive importance for the War – on this account it must and will succeed.'

The Germans had brought forward a new army group under cover of the cavalry holding their line east of Gheluvelt, with the intention of breaking through south of Ypres. General von Fabeck from the German's XIII Corps had been given command of 'Army Group Fabeck' on 27 October. This comprised: the II Bavarian Corps from their 2nd Army; a corps from the Aisne; VI Bavarian Reserve Division from 4th Army; XXV Division from the 6th Army and 1 Cavalry Corps. These were not the semi-trained reserve formations the enemy had thrown against the Allies in Flanders so far. They were experienced troops, and their arrival meant that the Allies' $11^{1}/_{2}$ divisions now faced $23^{1}/_{2}$ divisions. Fabeck was also given the unprecedented number of over 260 heavy howitzers and mortars, in addition to 484 smaller calibre guns. This was at a time when the acute shortage of shells forced some British artillery to be removed from the front altogether because they had nothing to fire.[25]

As an example of 'puttying up', on 29 October six officers were sent up on attachment, reporting to Hal in the trenches to make up for the battalion's acute shortage of officers. They had under twenty-four hours to get to know their companies or platoons before the great attack came the next morning. All this would have put further strain on Hal and his adjutant, now without the vital support of his experienced RSM, Shem Williams, who had been wounded.

At 10 a.m. on 29 October, 22 Brigade was called forward again to attack towards Kruiseik, to support 21 Brigade which was under severe pressure. The battalion held a position south of Kruiseik until dark when it moved to occupy the trenches east of Zandvoorde on the extreme right of 7 Division. On the battalion's right were the 1st and 2nd Life Guards of 7 Cavalry Division, who had already held the village of Zandvoorde for seven days in

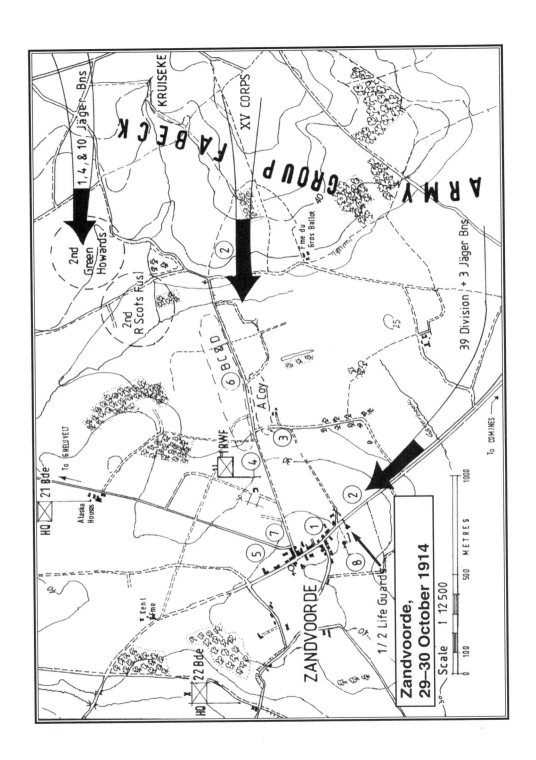

**Zandvoorde,
29–30 October 1914**

Scale   1 12 500

0   100   500   1000

METRES

a dismounted role. Moreover, the Life Guards had been shelled repeatedly from every direction except north! The 2nd Battalion, Royal Scots Fusiliers were on the battalion's left. The Royal Welsh's position was weakened in the middle by a big gap where the road from Zandvoorde to Becelaere passed through it.

The night passed quietly. As during the night before Waterloo, the sodden soldiers huddled under their soaking blankets, waiting for the rations to come up on the QM's wagons, grinding forward along rutted tracks from Kleine Zillebeke. Although the men in the trenches heard the distant rumbling of metal-rimmed wheels on rough pavé roads, few sights or sounds of General Fabeck's new army, supported by his huge concentration of heavy guns, reached the ears of British Intelligence. But the guns were in position and had registered on 29th October. All was prepared for their great effort to break through.

Hal did a round of his depleted battalion late that night. He spoke to Lieutenant Edmond Wodehouse: '… in the trenches in which [he] was captured next day. He [Hal] was in good health and spirits, and at 10 p.m. that night spoke to Captain Peter Poole who was commanding D Company.'

It was a misty autumn morning on the 30th. At 6 a.m. a tremendous battle took place on the Menin road at the crossroads south of Gheluvelt – trenches were taken and retaken. Finally the Germans retained the crossroads. At dawn, Hal made another round of his battalion, to the sound of the barrage five miles to the north. He visited Lieutenant John Evans at about 6.30 a.m.:[25]

Facing page: 30 October 1914: Sequence of Events

1. 0645–0800 hrs. 260 heavy enemy guns bombard Zandvoorde.

2. 088 hrs. Large number of German infantry advance downhill towards 1 RWF from east and south east. They are kept at bay all morning, never closing to the Battalion's front. Massive German infantry assault on Zandvoorde (XXXIX Division and two Jäger Battalions). The four squadrons of 1 and 2 Life Guards are ordered to withdraw, but the two forward squadrons and the Royal Horse Guards machine guns are annihilated (Site of the Household Cavalry Memorial).

3. 0900 hrs. Having occupied Zandvoorde, the enemy occupy farm, fire on A Company from 30 yards range, and close up to within 200 yards to south west (ie behind 1RWF).

4. Approx 0930 hrs. Hal and Claud Dooner, his adjutant, are killed.

5. 1000 hrs. Two German field guns fire from Zandvoorde ridge directly into 1 RWF's shallow trenches.

6. By 1200 hrs, the Battalion's resistance ends.

7. Post-war Commonwealth War Graves Cemetery.

8. Household Cavalry Memorial.

> He came up the trench that I was in and spoke to me for about five minutes. He
> was wearing a soldier's greatcoat and was carrying a rifle on his shoulder as
> though it was a shot gun. After talking to me he passed on to some trenches on
> my right which were separated from me by a hedge.

There he spoke to Captain Barrow, one of the officers attached from the 3rd
Battalion, Duke of Cornwall's Light Infantry, who was commanding A
Company '… which was holding the right of the line …. I was myself with the
half company on the extreme right. After conversing with me for a few
moments he left me to go to his shelter behind our lines.'[26]

The German's early morning attack on Zonnebeke was repulsed. Forty-
five minutes later, Fabeck's heavy guns opened up on the Life Guards and on
Hal's battalion. After this shattering bombardment, at 8 a.m., the massed
infantry attacked. They consisted of two regiments of XXXIX Division and
three *Jäger* battalions.

By 9 a.m. the storm of shrapnel and high explosive had blown to pieces
the trenches of the Life Guards who were ordered to retire. Unable to retreat
from their positions, or perhaps because they never received the order, two
squadrons died where they fought. They included the crew of a machine gun
manned by the Royal Horse Guards, which inflicted huge casualties on the
enemy until the last. Viewed from Gheluvelt some two miles away '… the sky
over Zandvoorde became as black as a London fog.'[27]

The battalion had already been under heavy artillery fire in trenches in full
view of the enemy for some three hours. One of Hal's very last orders was
'Stay in your trenches.' In any case, to retire over an exposed forward slope –
a position forced on the battalion by the need to keep its place in the general
line – would have spelt disaster. Shortly after capturing Zandvoorde, the
German infantry seized a farm to the right rear of the Royal Welsh. Working
forward from there, the Germans could fire from a hedge only thirty yards
away, though to the front they were still kept at a distance. At the same time,
the Germans brought forward a battery onto the high ground on the edge of
the village, and this opened up with shrapnel, raking the battalion's trenches
from end to end. Our men began to run out of ammunition as, once again,
rifles began to jam.

The story is taken up in *The First Seven Divisions*:[28]

> The Zandvoorde trenches passed into the hands of the enemy soon after 9am,
> and the Germans at once swarmed into them and began making their way
> along them to the north, till they reached a position from which they could get
> the Welsh Fusiliers in the flank. Then began the annihilation of this very gallant
> regiment. From the moment that the Zandvoorde trenches went, its position
> was hopeless, its right flank being completely unprotected, and its own
> trenches disconnected and ill adapted for mutual protection. The Regiment

fought as it had fought on the 19th and again on the 20th and 21st. It fought till every officer had been killed or wounded; only 90 men rejoined the brigade. Among those that fell on that day were Colonel Cadogan and his Adjutant, Lieutenant Dooner. The latter was killed in a very gallant attempt to cross the interval which divided the trenches and investigate the state of affairs on the right; and the Colonel fell in an equally gallant attempt to rescue his subordinate after he had fallen.

This of course was written after the war. But at that moment, in addition to Hal and Claud Dooner, eight other officers and 320 NCOs and men had disappeared. Parker, the quartermaster, was the sole remaining officer, who with eighty-six men answered the roll call that evening. Of the missing, only four officers and fifty men were subsequently found to be prisoners, every one of whom had been wounded by splinter or bullet. The balance, 275 of them, were dead.

Such is the story in a few words. But naturally the battalion was not wiped out in so many minutes – officers continued to give orders and sections fought it out, but by midday its resistance was over. The fire of a British battery made the enemy gun crews in Zandvoorde flee for an hour, before a counter-bombardment destroyed our guns. General Haig, 1 Corps Commander, had heard of the Life Guards' withdrawal at 9 a.m., but the news took time to pass down through the HQ of 7 Division and it never reached General Lawford in 22 Brigade. By the time Haig had pulled together what few reserves were available, it was too late to save Hal's battalion.

NOTES

1. Most of the farms were rebuilt in different positions to those of 1914.
2. *Uhlans* were German light cavalry, armed with a lance.
3. Later, Corporal (Acting Lance Sergeant) T. I. Jones. See Appendix 4 Awards.
4. Tom Jones told me this among other memories. Some of his tales of German atrocities perhaps were exaggerated and are not included here, but the invading Germans had been ordered to terrorise the Belgians.
5. *Scots Guards in the Great War*, Loraine F. Petre, Wilfred Ewart & Maj-Gen Sir Cecil Lowther, 1925.
6. This was the first use of armoured cars in warfare.
7. In Vol. III of the *Regimental Records of the Royal Welsh Fusiliers*, Kleythoek and Kezelberg have been transposed. The German trenches were about two miles north of Menin.
8. Infantry adopted artillery formation to avoid casualties from enemy artillery. It meant shaking out, so that each section was in file at fifty-yard intervals.
9. Private James Cowan of Cardiff, reported in the *Western Mail*, 2 December 1914.
10. Lance-Corporal Marchant, reported in the *Western Mail*, 24 October 1914.

11. Private D. Callaghan of Glanamman, Carmarthenshire, reported in the *Western Mail*, 24 October 1914.

12. Private George Davies, reported in the *Liverpool Echo*, 11 November 1914.

13. Captain Peppé, see Biographies.

14. An unidentified private in B Company, reported in the *Liverpool Echo*, 11 November 1914.

15. Hal's successor as commander of B Company.

16. Captain Hindson, see Biographies.

17. Also known as 'Jack Johnsons', after the black American heavyweight boxer. They burst in a cloud of black smoke. German heavy artillery, probably 8-inch howitzers.

18. Sergeant T. Loveridge of Shingrig Road, Nelson, Glamorgan, reported in the *Western Mail*, 1 December 1914.

19. Pte James Cowan of Cardiff, letter published in the *Western Mail*, 2 December 1914.

20. The cartridges now issued were not a problem when a rifle was cold, but as a rifle heated during rapid fire the cases began to jam. A dearth of rifle oil in the BEF added to the problem.

21. In the previous forty-eight hours the battalion had lost ten officers and 250 other ranks (OHW, France and Belgium 1914, p.156).

22. 7 Division, unusually, had a divisional cyclist company deployed with it.

23. *OHW*.

24. *OHW*, p.248. National Archives WO 95/706, IV Corps Report, dated 14 November 1914.

25. The armies of 1914 simply lost control of ammunition expenditure. In the first six months of the War the British Army fired one million shells, nearly four times as many in the whole of the Boer War. It began the war with 1,500 rounds in stock for each of its 18-pounder field guns, but by October these were sometimes restricted to four rounds per gun per day, or less, because of shortages. Many riflemen expended all the 300 rounds they carried in a single action. [*Soldiers: A History of Men in Battle*, John Keegan and Richard Holmes.]

26. From the results of the enquiry carried out in 1918 by Captain Eric Skaife into the fate of Hal and Claude Dooner.

27. *Scots Guards in the Great War*, Loraine F. Petre, Wilfred Ewart & Maj-Gen Sir Cecil Lowther, 1925.

28. *The First Seven Divisions*, Lord Ernest Hamilton, Hurst & Blackett, 1916, p.279.

Chapter 9

Missing
October 1914–May 1915

week later, Eve received a letter from General Lawford, written on a signal pad in the trenches the day after the battle:

Oct 31, 1914

I can't tell you how terribly sorry I am to say that the Welsh Fusiliers have practically disappeared. I expect you know how enormous their losses were lately both in officers and men- up to yesterday morning they were 5 officers and 450 others. Your husband, Dooner, Poole, and two boys were all left of the officers.[sic]

The night before last they held a line of trenches with cavalry on their right. About 10am very suddenly the Germans came on in force, drove back the cavalry out of their trenches and so took the Fusiliers in the flank. They were obliged to retire, but I believe the Germans got round and surrounded them, taking most of them prisoners. Only 56 men have come back and none of them can give a clear account of what really happened. The attack was so sudden we had no idea of anything serious happening until we saw men running back. I was only about 500 yards away at the time.

Ever since we began we have been up against much superior forces. We have not had a chance. Have fought every day & lost numbers of officers and men. The Fusiliers on three occasions have come in for the worst & hottest place. They have done splendidly on all occasions. Your husband has been marvellous – always ready to do all he could, & done it well under the most trying conditions. I hope that you will soon hear that he is a prisoner and all right. I am only too sorry that I can't tell you definitely how he is, and I am frightfully sorry to have to write you such bad

Hal's wife, Eve.

"A" Form.   Army Form C. 2121.

MESSAGES AND SIGNALS.   No. of Message

Prefix..........Code..........m.	Words	Charge	*This message is on a/c of:*	Recd. at..........m.
Office of Origin and Service Instructions.				Date..........
....	Sent			From..........
....	At..........m.		*Service.*	
....	To..........			
....	By..........		(Signature of "Franking Officer.")	By..........

TO   *Ven. Mrs Cadogan —*

| Sender's Number | Day of Month | In reply to Number | **AAA** |

I can't tell you how terribly sorry I am to say that — the Welsh Fusiliers have practically disappeared — I expect you know how enormous their losses were lately both in officers & men — up to yesterday morning they were 5 officers & 50 men. Your husband sooner. Poole & 2 others were all left of officers. The night before last they held a line of trenches with cavalry on their right. About 10 a.m. very suddenly the germans came on in force, drove back the cavalry one of their trenches and so took the Fusiliers in flank. They were obliged to retire. One I believe the germans got round & surrounded them — taking most of them as prisoners. only 56 men have come back. and none of them could give a clear account of what —

From   ....
Place   ....
Time   ....

The above may be forwarded as now corrected.   **(Z)**

....   *Censor.* | Signature of Addressor or person authorised to telegraph in his

* This line should be erased if not required.

Brigadier-General Lawford's letter to Eve Cadogan, dated 31 October 1914,
written on an Army message pad.

news. We must hope for the best. I know how terribly you will feel this, and he felt the losses to the regiment terribly. The whole Division is terribly reduced-all three brigades being in much the same state.

If I can find out any further details I will let you know at once, and I hope it will turn out that they are mostly prisoners. In any case you can feel he did splendidly.

Nov 1 – since writing above Captain Barker is killed – such a fine officer and splendid all round.

Much later, the official casualty figures for the battalion for 29 and 30 October were agreed as five officers and 270 other ranks killed, and four officers and fifty other ranks captured. From the time the battalion went into action on 19th, its casualties now numbered 1,260 out of a total of 1,350. As though to complete the tragic number of Royal Welsh casualties, Captain R. V. Barker, General Lawford's staff captain, was killed when the Brigade, little more than a battalion in strength, was being led in person by its brigadier-general. Before the end of the battle the general was left with four combatant regimental officers and some 700 men.

In 7 Division, between 14 October and 30 November, 366 out of 400 officers were killed, and 9,664 other ranks out of 12,000. In the same period, the total losses of the British Expeditionary Force were some 58,000. These losses are dwarfed by those of the Germans who lost an estimated 130,000 men.[1] Of the nine British regimental commanding officers, including Hal, killed in this period at First Ypres, six have no known graves and their names are inscribed on the Menin Gate. An illustration of the ferocity of First Ypres.[2]

Three weeks later General Lawford wrote again, plainly in reply to a letter from Eve, and after Walter Carlile had visited the Battalion:

Your husband's servant gave the sword to Mr Carlile, when he came to see the Battalion about 10 days ago. The sword had been left with his horse which was left behind as they were in the trenches all night before the attack.

Up to now Mr Carlile could not possibly go over the ground where the fight was because it is in the hands of the Germans.[3]

I am indeed sorry that not one of the men who came away can give any definite statement about your husband. All I can get from anyone is that they saw him in the trenches during the fight. I should certainly think that you should have heard by now, but he may be wounded and unable to write. You are very brave. I can only sincerely hope you may have good news soon. The uncertainty must be awful for you. I can only tell you that I felt the severe blow to my best battalion very deeply.

In mid-November Private Hugh Williams was interviewed at home in Rock Ferry, by a reporter from the *Liverpool Daily Post*. This was his story:

During the night of the 29th, I was sharing a trench with Private Morgan. He had been unable to sleep because of the cold as he did not have an overcoat. At 6am rations were issued. I opened a tin of bully beef, said Williams, and we said 'we'll have a bit of breakfast before they come.' We knew the Germans were coming- we could hear their maxims. I had just had a mouthful when I saw them coming in our rear and on our right flank. Many of them were directly behind us, and we opened fire. I am certain that I knocked twelve down. As soon as I pulled the trigger I saw my men fall, they were so close – only about 100 yards away. But they came on, right up to our fellows, firing point blank in their faces. The last I heard was Lieutenant Egerton ordering us to fix bayonets. The Germans were twenty yards off when I was wounded above the left eye by a ricocheting bullet, which glanced off. I could see our Colonel, who was about one hundred yards away, in tears, and then I saw our two Lieutenants being made prisoners.

After this my mate, Private Morgan, who had two South African ribbons on his breast, was shot right through the head by a German officer. His brains were scattered over the trench. I said to myself 'I'm the next one', so I lay down in the trench. I thought 'I may as well lie here as if I was dead'. The Germans jumped into the trench to take cover, and from there they kept firing. One of them picked a wounded German up and put him across my body, resting his head on my pack while he dressed his wounds. I was covered in blood. After that I lay in the trench for five hours. The overcoat, cap and pack of the wounded German, who had been taken away, were left behind, so I put the coat and cap on and walked to a Belgian house, about 150 yards away. I stopped there for five days, living on pears that grew close by. The big guns kept on firing the whole time.

This must have been very shortly before Hal was killed. He would have been utterly exhausted from lack of sleep, the constant shelling and foul weather over the three weeks since the Division had landed. He would have wept for the destruction of his Battalion, whose officers and men he had trained and who had been his responsibility, his friends and his life for so long. Their position was hopeless and he realised there was nothing he could do to improve the situation.

Among the letters forwarded to Eve in November was one which Hal would not have seen, from Captain John Smyth-Osbourne, now a prisoner of war at Crefeld in Germany:

28.10.14

I may only write you a few lines to say that Hindson, Barchard, Peppé, Bingham and myself are here – all unwounded, except myself who am slightly wounded in the leg. I am afraid I really cannot here describe how the incident occurred; we are all of course bitterly disappointed with our bad luck, but we were all well treated after our capture, and are being well treated now. We arrived here on 26th and have not seen the men since 23rd.

Everyone wishes to be remembered to you and to wish all the best of luck..

So much for 'bad luck', they were the lucky ones!

The fate of Claud Dooner, Hal's adjutant, was also unknown. Eve kept in close touch with his father, while she and Mary Coote, Hal's sister, pulled every string to discover their fate. On 21 November Colonel W. T. Dooner wrote:

> Ditton Place, Near Maidstone, Kent.
>
> This anxiety, and the impossibility of learning the truth about our Dear ones is almost too much to bear.
>
> I have just received a wire from a friend who heard there are some Welsh Fusiliers in the hospital at Manchester. A messenger of his has seen them and he wires: 'Soldiers in Manchester Hospital confirm Hall's story, saw Claud in hospital at Ypres'. In spite of this I can hardly credit it, as how could the dear boy have got back 4 miles to Ypres? If he had we should have heard long ago, and Sir A. Murray[4] sent his ADC to enquire and could get no information. So I place little reliance on this story... .
>
> All through I have tried to have great faith in our prayers ... I feel somehow Claud and your brave husband are together and alive.

In November the vicar of Carnarvon, the Reverend J. W. Wynne-Jones, who had recently lost his son serving with the 4th Battalion, received a letter from the 1st Battalion. 'The old 1st Battalion, got a severe shaking at Ypres ... The Commanding Officer and Adjutant were with the Battalion all through till the last day. They bore charmed lives, did splendid work, and were the talk of the Division. They simply laughed at the shells.'

At the end of November, Mary put a notice in the personal column of *The Times*:

> LIEUT-COLONEL H. O. S. CADOGAN,
> ROYAL WELCH FUSILIERS, MISSING, Oct. 30
> There are unconfirmed rumours of what happened. Should anyone have
> heard anything at all, will they most kindly WRITE to his sister,
> Lady Coote, West Park, Salisbury?

Eve with Edward, her son, based herself much of the time with Walter and Bee Carlile in their large house, Gayhurst. There she organized knitting sessions to add to the socks and mittens many well-wishers were sending to the Front. On 11 November she wrote to several papers, including the *Carnarvon & Denbigh Herald*:

> ... to thank all those who have been so generous in sending so many beautiful gifts for the 1st Battalion ... now at the Front. One parcel of gloves from Penarth bore the following message: 'Good luck to the lad whoever you are who wears these gloves. T. S. E. Penarth. I am too old, boys, or I would be with you." She

had been unable to acknowledge this as there was no address. The giver would like to know that the parcel was sent – message and all. Mrs Cadogan heard today from Private Horton who says: 'The fellows were all so pleased to get the warm mittens and scarves. We have had about two inches of snow'.

Eve had received a reply from Private Horton, one of Hal's orderlies:

In the Field, 22 Nov 14

I received your letter quite safe.

It was quite right what the General said, the Guards did give way. Myself and Sgt Thompson made it a practice of getting the Colonel and Lt Dooner's food up to their bomb proof trench every night. But this particular night when we went we learned that the Colonel was captured and about 250 men were missing. So I strongly believe the Colonel was captured. Well I sincerely hope nothing worse has happened to him. As I am sure he was one of the bravest officers we had. He never saw any fear and was always cheery. But I think we were in the hottest fire in the war, and luck always seemed against us.

I saw Mr Carlile and gave him the Colonel's sword, the Colonel's valise has been sent to the Base. Those other bags off the second horse are here but quite safe.

Major Gabbett got another slight wound in his back. But not a very serious one. I am servant to Major Gabbett now as his servant has been wounded. Our Battalion has been reorganized and is made up of army reserve men and special reserve. There are only about 40 of the old Battalion left.

The fellows were all pleased to get the mittens and scarves as it is so very cold. We have had about two inches of snow. I hope you will excuse this letter as it is written in an old cellar at a farm.

Goodbye, I remain your ever obedient Servant

Dick Gabbett, recovered from his wound and now back commanding the reformed 1st Battalion, also wrote: 'Could you send out more socks – the men want them very badly. There have been several cases of frost-bite. The doctors say the men ought to have more warm socks and gloves, as the mittens are not enough. I could only get 25 pairs today from the Government store instead of several hundred pairs.'

Towards Christmas, a further wave of letters arrived, many from Hal's regimental colleagues. Charles Dobell, now a brigadier-general commanding the allied forces capturing the Cameroons, wrote:

I fear from what I hear that you have little hope about Hal … He was such a splendid fellow – a fitting commander for a series of actions which even in the record of the 23rd has never been surpassed. He was one of my oldest friends in the Regiment and I need not tell you how fond I was of him. A fine man – a fine soldier. I can only hope that your boy will be like him & grow to be more and more comfort to you, although he cannot replace Hal in any way.

I only pray that the faint hope that Hal may be a prisoner may be realised.

It is difficult for me to write when you know all the things I would say about him so much better than I do. I and all his friends mourn his loss & feel very deeply & truly for you.[5]

Captain C. I. Stockwell, serving with 2nd Battalion, wrote:

Brig-Gen Sydney Lawford, commander 22 Brigade, 1914.

He and the Regiment did magnificently everyone says, and thoroughly upheld the great tradition of the Regt.

I went over and saw the 1st Batt. one day – they are about 5 miles away from us here and we were having a short rest from the trenches. Of course they are a perfectly fresh Battalion.

We had a pretty strenuous time close to where the 1st Batt are now- an awful lot of shelling for the first fortnight & constant night attacks. We were in those trenches 26 days without relief & it really got trying. This is like a rest camp after the other place tho' the shelling is bad. We get out for 8 days on the 27th having been in 24 days.

Eve also received a letter from Lieutenant Edmond Wodehouse written from his prison camp at Crefeld.

When I was taken prisoner a rumour came that Colonel Cadogan had been hit, but it was only from a private and both Poole and I very much doubted it, as rumours of that sort are more often untrue than true. It is quite probable, and I sincerely hope that he is either a prisoner or wounded in some other part of Germany … I did not actually see Colonel Cadogan at all on the 30th. When I last saw him the night before he was well and in good spirits. … I know that there are other prisoners at Torgau, Zena and Paderborne, but we can't find out any names, and I think it more than likely that he is at one of these places.

Meanwhile Captain Parker, the Quartermaster, and the only remaining officer from the Battalion, had kept in touch with the Secretary of the Dorset County Football Association. While stationed at Portland the year before, the Battalion had won the Dorset County Cup, the highest trophy the County could offer. Mr Frowde had visited the Battalion at Lyndhurst in October and again met many members of the Battalion Team who had sent good wishes to old football friends and supporters in Dorset. Parker had written to him from

Belgium on about 23 October:

> We have been in the thick of it with a vengeance, I cannot tell you details but we were told to hold a certain position at 'all costs'. We did our job, as the Royal Welsh Fusiliers always do, and the cost – ? We were 29 officers and 1,017 other ranks at that time, but when we mustered yesterday only 6 officers and 260 other ranks remain. We shall probably collect another 50 men, but no further officers. The German shell fire was awful, awful. The Colonel, Adjutant, and myself are well, but the battle is raging all along the line and on the flank. This is a rest for me for a few minutes in the trenches. Good luck, old friend. Our peckers are still up, and even our little lot can make itself felt yet.

On 19 November, this tough old soldier wrote again:

> Many thanks for the football, which came as near upsetting me as anything that has occurred out here, because there is not a single man of the old battalion left to use it. A couple of days ago a young officer[6] and 100 men came up to join us … All the other officers have gone. Thirty eight and about 1,200 men. We have had a pretty bad time of it….When we were ordered to hold our positions at all costs, what would you expect from the 1st Battalion Royal Welsh Fusiliers? They held the position, notwithstanding the damnable shell fire, which was really terrible day and night. The slaughter there was awful. The last to go – and I do not know their fate – were the Colonel, Adjutant, three young officers, and 250 men. I had been left on transport duty the night before. When I got back in the morning I was told that they were missing. There are now less than 100 men of the old battalion left. Yesterday Major Gabbett who had been wounded, returned with 100 and a new captain.[7]

The *Poole Herald* commented: It seems a pity that the gallant deeds performed by our valiant men, no matter from what country they come, should be hidden in obscurity, as they are at the present time.'

Just before Christmas 1914 Eve wrote to the *Morning Post* to complain that the sacrifices that 7 Division had made to hold the German onslaught were not appreciated at home. General Lawford wrote:

> France, 27 Dec 14
>
> I saw the letter in the *Morning Post* today. Most certainly – I have not the least objection, and I am only too glad that the splendid work of the Regiment should have had some recognition and be known to its many friends. It seems all wrong that 7th Div. should have received so little official notice. Perhaps this may be put right later, but it should be done while still in peoples' minds. An after thought is no use to anybody.
>
> You are brave, by the way you have taken the total absence of news. You have my sincere sympathy. If there is one person about whose safety I am longing to hear, it is your husband's. He was always ready to respond to any call at any moment, and gave his best.

The stirring reports which were now appearing in the newspapers inspired Major E. H. Clough-Taylor,[8] an elderly retired Royal Welshman to write:

> Firby Hall, York, December 27, 1914
>
> The reports which are now published of the splendid and stubborn valour of the Regiment give me an opportunity of sending you our most true sympathy in your great anxiety. But even sorrow must be mingled with pride at the immortal glory with which the Royal Welsh has again, as ever, surrounded itself. Nowhere does the spark which creates brotherhood, and devotion even to the jaws of Hell, flash so bright through all ranks as in the beloved Corps.
>
> If another name is be added to those of the Colonels at Waterloo and Alma, who cheerfully served to the last at the head of the Welsh Fusiliers – 'How can a man die better than facing fearful odds'.

On 24 December, General Capper's Order of 14 December was published in *The Times*. It contained the following tribute:

1ST BATTN, ROYAL WELSH FUSILIERS

On October 19 the battalion attacked Kleythoek with much gallantry and dash, and later on the same day acted with coolness and discipline under trying conditions.

On October 20 and 21 at Zonnebeke the battalion held the left of the line under very heavy enfilade artillery fire and enveloping flank attack of the enemy's infantry, until withdrawn by orders of the Brigadier. During these two days fighting this battalion lost three-quarters of its strength in officers and men.

On October 30 the battalion occupied the right of the divisional line. Owing to troops on their right being driven back the battalion became very exposed and was subjected to an enveloping attack by the enemy. The battalion, however, held on and lost nearly all its effectives, including the colonel rejoining the brigade. [sic]

This battalion has fought nobly and has carried out its best traditions by fighting on until completely overwhelmed. As a battalion it had, for the time being, ceased to exist.

22ND INFANTRY BRIGADE

This Brigade had very hard fighting and suffered specially severe losses. It speaks highly for the soldierly spirit of this Brigade that at the close of three weeks' continual fighting, and very weak in officers and men, it was able to make a gallant and successful counter-attack against the enemy at a critical moment, re-taking the enemy's trenches and capturing machine guns.

The Brigade at the close of the fighting before Ypres had only the Brigadier-General and four combatant regimental officers and a little over 700 other ranks left. It thus fought itself to a standstill. The 1st Battalion Royal Welsh Fusiliers had particularly distinguished itself for gallantry and devotion, and for holding out against the enemy until it practically ceased to exist.

General Lawford added his … sincere appreciation of the splendid behaviour of the 1st Battalion Royal Welsh Fusiliers on all occasions. I am proud to have had the honour of having the battalion in the Brigade under my command. The heavy losses both in officer and men bear witness to the efforts made by this battalion to uphold the honour of the Army and the Empire

In the New Year, Eve finally received a letter from Parker:

29-12-14

Please forgive me for not writing to you before, but I had nothing to say. Day after day I waited for news or to hear something of the Colonel or Adjutant. I was with them in their 'dug out' at about 8pm on the 30 October.[9] I was then sent back with the transport to fill up with rations for the following day. I heard nothing till the evening of the next day, the 31st (30th), when poor Barker[10] told me that only a few men of the 1st Batt(alion) were left, and they were scattered about all over the Brigade. I wanted to try and get them together, but Barker explained that it was impossible. He ordered me to take charge of the transport.

For days we wandered about being shelled from place to place. Then they commenced to take my transport to make up deficiencies in other units. I had nothing to do – all gone but myself. So when I was offered a job on the Divisional Staff I was only too glad to get it. I am still with General Capper as Camp Commandant.

I have seen Mr Carlile on several occasions[11] and I have given him all the details I could. I have written to him again today.

I do not know what to say to you about the Colonel. He was always the calmest man under fire in the whole Battalion. He was always thinking about the comfort of his men – Dooner too was the same. Personally I think both are prisoners, and I refuse to believe otherwise until I have clear evidence to the contrary. Please understand dear Mrs. Cadogan that this is only my own opinion. I have nothing to go on – no-one seems to be clear on what really happened when our remaining men where attacked. Story after story has been told to me, and when I have investigated it, the whole thing has crumpled away – the man who said he saw this or that, was proved not to be there at all at that time. Even now I do not know who is left that was with the Colonel and Adjutant on (29th–30th) Oct. Again and again men, who others were sure they saw wounded, have turned up. I do not believe anyone really knows what happened at that time.

I have nothing else to write. Of one thing only I am certain of, and that is the Colonel and Adjutant did their duty, and we who are still here must try and do ours in the best possible way. We are all passing through a bad time and have to make the best of it.

By May 1915 Eve still had no firm news, but suddenly on the 18th *The Western Mail* printed headlines:

COLONEL CADOGAN KILLED
HEROIC ACT IN A FIRESWEPT AREA

This stated that Hal was now officially reported killed in action. Two days later:

NEWS OF COLONEL CADOGAN.
NOW REPORTED NOT KILLED.

This said that he who was first of all officially reported wounded and missing, and on Monday night officially posted as killed, is now unofficially reported not killed. Presumably, the gallant Colonel is a prisoner of war in Germany.

On 22 May this was disputed by Eve who contacted *The Morning Post* to say that '… no such news has been received by her of her husband.' By the 25th, *The Times, Morning Post, The Scotsman* and others were printing his obituary and saying that he was now believed killed on 30 October 1914.

On 16 August Eve received the following telegram from Buckingham Palace: 'The King and Queen deeply regret the loss you and the Army have sustained by the reported death of your husband in the service of his country. Their Majesties truly ….' The rest is missing. Also one from the War Office: 'Lord Kitchener desires to express his sympathy on hearing of the death of Lieutenant Colonel H. O. S. Cadogan.'

Mary meanwhile, had contacted the German governess she and her sisters had had in the 1880s. She in turn enlisted the help of her old professor in approaching the *Jäger* battalion officers who had survived the battle. Sadly this yielded nothing. However, Lady Abinger, a friend of Mary's, wrote to the daughter of an old friend of hers, *Freifrau* von Pranckh, who had been widowed aged only twenty-two. In reply she wrote from Munich, probably via the American Embassy in Berlin: 'I have already written to my husband's regiment; perhaps one of the gentlemen might chance to know something about Colonel Cadogan, for my husband fell on October 31 1914 before Zandvoorde in a heavy fight against the English.' The time and the place agree totally. After corresponding with Eve, in her final letter Gisa Pranckh wrote:

1a Habsburger Strasse, München.
I am extremely sorry that I have not been able to find out anything about your husband. I have written to ask the Regiment, and from men and officers it is always the same answer, that at Zandvoorde everything was so difficult that they cannot remember, they have forgotten.

Nevertheless I shall go on trying, and hope to get to know something. I am frightfully sorry for you, and feel for you from my heart. With best greetings

On 30 October, the night before he was killed, her husband, *Oberleutnant* Freiherr von Pranckh, recorded in his diary that around Hal's battalion's position: '… the countless grey-clad corpses of German dead lay in drifts.' There were so many that the Germans had to dig mass graves for their dead as well as for the British dead.[12]

Some wounded soldiers were repatriated by September 1915, and among them was Corporal Sutton who, for five years, had been Hal's servant and who had been captured on 30 October. He was visited by Mary on 6 September in Wandsworth Hospital where he told her:

> When [the regiment on] the right gave way the Germans came up and enfiladed the RWF trenches. The Colonel shouted down not to leave the trenches. Sutton was hit by a bullet which went right through his throat. Then a private ran past him, wishing him luck. Sutton next noticed, 20 to 30 yards to his left…. Colonel and (Adjutant) in the trench, the Colonel nearest (me). I could see the side of his face- he was crouching forward. I could not see the wound, no blood on his face.

When Mary asked how he was 'crouching', not lying stretched out if desperately wounded, he said: 'The trench was very small, and shrapnel bursts the trenches, so you get packed in like. Both Colonel and Adjutant were perfectly still.' Sutton fainted from loss of blood, and '… on coming round, I think 2 or 3 hours after as it was getting evening, I looked and saw them in the same position.' He started crawling away when the Germans fired a machine gun at him and smashed his leg but he managed to crawl to what had been the HQ farm where he met Captain Robertson, the battalion's medical officer, and told him about the colonel. Robertson went out to search for him but he was later brought in by the Germans as a prisoner, with Sergeant Mills, who died as he was carried in on a stretcher.

Sutton was taken to Germany where his leg was amputated in March. He was sure that Dooner was dead, but he was not certain about Hal, but 'there were … no living men to the left of the Colonel. The Germans had got round both sides.' It worried Sutton that he had not managed to get to the colonel to take away his haversack and pocket book as he had given strict orders to do if he was killed, 'But the bullets was too thick.'

After much correspondence by Eve and Mary, some of the Royal Welshmen who had been captured on 30 October replied with eye-witness accounts, written on postcards censored by their German guards:

> Lager I, Munster, Sep 15
>
> Your Ladyship wrote with reference to Pte Currah, who at present is in Lager I and suffering from some sort of paralysis, he is unable to write in answer to your Ladyship's questions. He states when taken prisoner he was wounded

but able to walk. He was marched to where Colonel Cadogan was lying. The escort gave the water bottle to Pte Currah. It was full of water. He did not see the Colonel fall. He was only about 15 yards away. He did not see anyone bury the Colonel. Mr Dooner was not with the Colonel. The Colonel was lying on the ground in the open. …

Pte Currah thanks your Ladyship for the kind parcel of provisions. He has not seen Pte Trott for some time. Pte Currah was wounded in right arm. He is improving very slowly….

I beg to remain your humble Servant,
W. Roberts, Sergt.

Then Private G. Trott wrote to Mary:

Lager I, Munster, Sep 15

Received your letter on 20-9-15. Sorry to tell you that Colonel Cadogan is dead for I were fifty yards from him and also Pte Currah of the same regiment.

Sorry I could not get to him owing to leg being broken. Pte Currah is in hospital with me now and he read your letter and he states that he had Colonel Cadogan's water bottle which was taken of him. [sic] He also says that he were shot through the head just over the left eye. We could take you to the spot were it happened. Pleased to receive parcels from you.

Then Mary began a long correspondence with Currah, who had recovered sufficiently to write his own letters:

Pte J. H. Currah, N° 7911 Royal Welsh Fusiliers, Prisoner of War, Lager I

Hauspital [sic], 15/11/15, Lazerett Munster, Westphalia, Germany

Hoping you received the letter answering your questions which was written by Sgt Roberts of my Regiment who was anxious to answer it, as I had a doubt of my letter going through. I stated to him all I knew but he tells me he only answered the one about the water bottle which was given to me and a comrade by the Germans.

I did not see the Colonel hit, my comrade was running with him back to his trench. My back was turned towards him. My comrade then joined me and told me the Colonel was killed, also the Adjutant. My Colonel was still lying there when we were taken away. Myself and Pte Watson were the last two to see the Colonel. He was about 15 or 20 yards from his own trench which I was in. His orderlies were in one adjoining. The Adjutant and the Colonel together in the same trench as myself before they were killed …

I have had the misfortune to have a stroke or paralysis, I don't seem to be improving much

Hoping these particulars meet with your approval.

Sorry to say your parcel not arrived yet.

He wrote again on 29 November:

Hoping my few lines reach you safely. I send my utmost thanks for parcel which I received quite safe.

In answer to one of your questions, there was a gold double cased lever[13] also silver cased watch or compass. A leather pocket wallet and several papers ... Sorry to state I am not improving.

Sending you best wishes and compliments of the season.

Private John Currah.

In February 1916, Private Watson wrote from his POW Camp, Lager I, in reply to a letter from Mary:

I was the last man to see him alive. I was with him at the time that he was killed. We were running together to get in a trench, when he was shot clean through the forehead and died instantly. ... I was captured about an hour afterwards, but not before I was wounded myself.

I am pleased to say that I have absolutely recovered from my wound.

Hoping that this letter will find you in the best of health, as I am at present very well.

On 3 July 1916 Currah wrote a further eight pages from Chateau d'Oeux, whither he had been moved from Germany:[15]

... thanking you very much for the razor and brush, Lady ... I am the only man here of my Company who was with them in the Field the day of our misfortune. My company was holding some trenches on the left of a wood, when we were under very heavy shell fire. All at once the order came to commence rapid fire. We were all then unprepared, as we were receiving our rations and waiting for some tea to be brought. But all at once, after we had fired about 5 rounds rapid the order came, 'Retire'.[15] I was the only man left in the trench. I was some distance behind, running, when a shell dropped amongst them, killing several who were in the lead. Of course then as shells were dropping on my front, I changed my direction through the wood to my left front, which brought me out on the right of the wood. I could then see someone in khaki in a trench about 200 yards away. I doubled across the open, I was fortunate enough not to get hit. It was the Colonel and Adjutant standing up, and his three orderlies were undercover in a side trench, who were two L/Cpls and one Private.

Soon after that Private Watson came running in with the sad news that the CO was killed. I shouted to his orderlies and one, a L/Cpl, came to where myself and Watson was to look, and then he shouted 'Here they are.' He meant the Germans for they was all around us. Then we were helpless not knowing what to do. They were on top of our trench. They fired point blank at about two yards range several times at myself, Watson and the L/Cpl. who was killed instantly as he was hit twice in the stomach. The other two orderlies were not seen then, but they were seen afterwards and taken prisoner sometime before myself and Watson. I was wounded with one shot in the arm, and another shot hit Watson in the forearm … and onto my arm in the same place …

Lady, I hope you will excuse me for writing you this news, as I was afraid telling you too much while in Germany for fear of punishment …

Lady, I have just received some sad news from home, my one and only brother[17] was killed by shell fire on 11 April. He belonged to the Duke of Cornwall's Light Infantry. He was at one time in the Royal Welsh Fus. Mother claimed him out on account of his youth. I believe he was then only 15 years old.

Lady, I am sorry to let you know I've not received your Paper with photos of the English arrival. Lady we have heaps of books and Papers but writing material is very scarce.

There are several men who came with me here employed at light work, for which they receive [a] little pay which is very nice. I do wish I was strong enough so I could do something. We are allowed about 7 miles radius to walk but I dare not venture to go that far as I soon get tired for I am so weak in my left side. I have not had any treatment here yet for my paralysis. The doctor here says he will try electricity which will improve my strength. Private Priest as been sent to Lucerne for an operation.

I thank you very much for asking me to ask for any little thing I require. I should very much like a little tea and sugar as we only get a warm drink in the mornings, or a few English cigarettes …

Lady I will write again and let you know if I benefit from the new treatment.

He wrote again on 15 July:

I received your letter containing [money] order quite safe yesterday, for which I thank you very much indeed. I don't know what became of my late Colonel's waterbottle. I gave it to some of my comrades who were taken prisoners the same day as myself. We were then marching to Lille under German escort. There were one or two of the wounded prisoners who became faint, so I handed over the bottle because it contained water.

We had a very rough time with the German soldiers when they knew we were English. They took our hats and our putties and even took our buttons off our jackets. But our greatcoats had gone long before we reached Lille.

I am sorry to learn that you have had no tidings of the Colonel. But the Colonel's revolver and papers were given up to a German officer by the man who took them … The German soldier kept the watches and he was showing the other Germans what he'd got … One watch was gold and the other was a silver watch or a compass.

Lady I do know Sgt Evans very well as I was under him in the cook house at Lyndhurst.

I am pleased to let you know I have improved a great deal. I am now having electric treatment.

Lady, I was talking to a Colonel of the Grenadier Guards[17] this morning who says he knew Colonel Cadogan and the Adjutant quite well. He told me he is a friend of Capt Skaife who was with him in Germany. He was captured the day before me, on 29 October. …

And again on 29 July:

Thank you for your letter.

Lady I shall have no need for any more parcels as arrangements have been made, and Tea Rooms have been opened, for the benefit of the soldiers. We pay just a trifle and some Ladies have given us their services and wait on us. The Tea Rooms are open every day from 3 o'clock till 5. They supply writing material and there are different kinds of games too, so I am sure we all feel satisfied.

The second party of English prisoners from Germany has not arrived yet, but they are due any day now. I hope Pte Brown will get through and Pte Trott too who is a deserving case, as he was still in hospital when I left Germany.

He then goes on to give his mother's address in Birmingham.

Sometime in 1917 Currah was repatriated, and was in hospital in London where Mary and Eve went to see him in late October. They found him as honest and straightforward as he had appeared in his letters. In early November he was sent home at last, but not for long, for on 6 November, his mother, Mrs Causer, wrote to Mary:

I regret to say that my son, J. Currah, died this morning at 8 o'clock after a short illness, and culminating in a stroke.

You remember he was really ill when you saw him in London a week ago and has been in bed ever since. He suffered much. He had the comfort to know he died at home, but it is very hard to lose our boys- this is the second, and one in Germany as a prisoner of war.

It is remarkable that this was written on the very day he died. She wrote again on 24 November:

I am sending you a Memorial Card of my boy, and with it a cutting from *B'ham Daily Mail*.

I wish to thank you again for your kind letters you sent to him in Switzerland and Germany …

I have had so many letters of sympathy … I am lost myself.

Thanking you again,

The extract from the *Birmingham Daily Mail* explained why this gallant soldier had suddenly been paralyzed:

YARDLEY SOLDIER'S DEATH
INHUMAN TREATMENT WHILE A PRISONER OF WAR

Private John Henry Currah ... was buried at Yardley Cemetery with full military honours. He was an old soldier, joining the Army in 1903 and rejoining on the outbreak of war. ... while a prisoner he threatened a brutal German guard, and as a punishment had to stand immersed to the neck in a hogshead of cold water for six hours in winter time. It is believed that this inhuman treatment was a direct cause of the paralysis of the left side which attacked Private Currah. He was subsequently sent to Switzerland and repatriated later, his death following another stroke.

A brother is also a prisoner of war, while another brother was killed at Ypres in April 1916. A third is serving with the Colours.

Notes

1. *OHW*, pp 467–8.
2. Officers had metal identity discs. Soldiers were issued with cardboard ones which soon disintegrated.
3. Zandvoorde remained behind German lines until the end of the war.
4. Lieut-Gen Sir Archibald Murray, KCB,KCMG,CVO,DSO, Colonel The Royal Inniskilling Fusiliers, Chief of Staff to General French, was Claud Dooner's brother-in-law.
5. He clearly signs himself 'Douglas', perhaps this was how he was known to his friends.
6. 2nd Lieutenant F. R. Orme and 109 soldiers arrived in Ypres on 5 November and were thrust into the front line with the composite Battalion. The majority became casualties that day, including Orme, who was killed.
7.Captain J. R. Minshull-Ford, who became adjutant, as well as commanding A Company.
8. See Biographies.
9. He means 29 October.
10. Captain RV Barker was killed on 31 October.
11. Walter Carlile, who was too old to enlist, converted his Rolls-Royce into an ambulance which was used in France for some three years.
12. *Marching as to War*, p.59.
13. This gold pocket watch had been left to Hal by his father. He wore it every day.
14. In general repatriation was organized by the Red Cross, and they would also have administered the internment camp at Chateaux d'Oeux.
15. The shout 'retire' may well have been made by the Germans. They had used this ruse earlier in the battle against other regiments near Gheluvelt with the desired result. There is no evidence that any Royal Welsh officer gave this order, nor was one received from Brigade to that effect.
16. Currah had one brother and several half brothers.
17. Lieutenant-Colonel Earle, CO 1st Battalion Grenadier Guards, in the 20th Brigade.

Chapter 10

Epilogue

Living with my grandfather while unravelling the tale of his last frantic three weeks, I have often felt him at my elbow. I see him now, soaked and utterly exhausted but still indomitable, doing the round of the remains of his scattered Battalion that last morning, dressed in a soldier's greatcoat and his large frame easily carrying his rifle like a shot gun. He was a marksman himself, and may well have survived until the 30th because the overcoat would have concealed his collar and tie and his breeches – the 'thin legs' by which German snipers picked out British officers from afar. Whatever qualities he may have had, he most certainly did not lack robustness, top of the great Field Marshal Wavell's list of those qualities required of a military commander.

Lieutenant W. A. F. Kerrick was a section commander of 55 Field Company Royal Engineers, attached to 20 Brigade. On 16 October he was at Zandvoorde in support of 2nd Battalion Scots Guards. He may well have constructed the trenches in which Hal died on 30th. He ended the War as a Brigadier-General with a DSO and MC. In 1918 this experienced officer wrote:

> The papers are trying to give 7 Division the credit they deserve for that battle; but no-one will ever succeed in doing so. The facts can be stated of course – that for a week the infantry held a line five times too long against no-one knows how many times their number, and then when reinforcements came up held a divisional line with what remained of the men – only about 20% at the end, and were never broken as a whole, only forced back a little. The artillery support was negligible. What could the artillery do against the guns the Germans brought up? One watched a Battalion like the Grenadiers visibly shrinking day by day – men and officers utterly done – and yet carrying on exactly the same, the same punctiliousness about salutes, the same courtesy when you came up to see at night what you could do. You would see a man go to his post, stick his rifle against the parapet, and as he took his hand off the rifle fall into a dead sleep. Some men fell asleep as they fired. I meant the Grenadiers because they were the ones I saw most of, but they were all the same.

It was the lot of the BEF fighting at the First Battle of Ypres, to learn that there was not to be 'a quick path to victory' on the Western Front, because the 1914-18 technology of destruction vastly outstripped that of communication and mobility. Defenders could always reinforce a threatened sector more quickly than the attackers could advance across it.

But what of those we left along the way?

The story of Private Hugh Williams, who having survived by lying in the bottom of his trench, we left living in the Belgian house 150 yards from Zandvoorde, continued:

> Wearing my German coat and hat, I visited the deserted trenches to see if I could recognize any of the dead, before leaving the area. Taking my bearings from the position of the sun when it set, and knowing that in that direction lay the sea, I began to walk westwards, and after going about six miles I came to a house and stopped at the pump outside for a drink. A Belgian came out of the house, and saying 'coffee', beckoned me inside.
>
> He seemed frightened, as he must have taken me for a German, with my grey coat and hat. So I said `English`, and opened my coat and showed him my khaki clothes and putties. He was then most pressing, and took me inside, where I saw his wife and six daughters. He gave me some coffee and boiled bacon and a pipe and tobacco, and that night I slept there. Next day the peasant took me to a man- I think he was the British Consul- and that is where I got a civilian rigout. He gave me a shirt, socks, boots trousers, and jacket. I stayed there two days and all the time I could hear the big guns. Once some Germans stopped outside the house, and he took me out through the back door, saying that if they saw me I was to be his servant, but I must not speak.
>
> The next day a guide took me away, but I was not to open my mouth to anyone. I was supposed to be deaf and dumb. We passed hundreds of Germans on the road, but none of them spoke to us. On the following morning another man took me in hand, and we went along the canal to Sass Van Ghent and from there I got a train to Thalhousen. (Terneuzen)

Eventually Williams got to Flushing and then to Folkestone. He reported at Shorncliffe, whence he was sent to Wrexham Barracks. He was then sent on leave.

On 24 November, Eric Skaife's father, Dr F. Skaife, wrote to the *Sussex Daily News*:

> We have just received a letter from our son, Eric, … saying that he is wounded and a prisoner. Such universal sympathy has been shown to us in our sorrow at the reported loss of our two sons, that I shall feel much obliged if you will kindly publish part of the letter we have received telling us the good news that one of them has so far been preserved to us.

Hospital, Courtrai, Belgium. November 16, 1914.
I was wounded near Menin, Belgium, during an attack we made at that place
on 9 October. I was hit in the head by a rifle bullet when about 100 yards from
the German trenches. We did not know we were quite so close, as they were
hidden at this part by a tall thorn hedge. The trenches we could see were 300
yards to our left front. The attack did not succeed, and as the few men who
were with me were nearly all killed or wounded, I was, of course, taken
prisoner when the Germans ventured out. This was not for some time, and I
nearly got hit again several times. Their medical corps bandaged my head very
carefully and sent two men to help me to hospital at Menin. I was looked after
by Belgian sisters and a Belgian doctor very well, and was there three weeks.
Last Wednesday I was moved here. I expect to make another move towards
Germany tomorrow or soon. Write to me if it is possible. I think the American
Embassy has means of sending letters, but you might get Cox and Co. to find
out for you.

My right arm and right side of my face were paralyzed, but are getting right,
and the wound, which is on the left side, is healing up very well. The bullet
lodged in my great coat, which was rolled on my back, and I have succeeded
in retaining it so far. There has been continuous fighting ever since and I have
been within the sound of it all the time, which has been very tantalizing to us
wounded, as we are longing to get back to the 'show' and have hoped against
hope that somehow we might be retaken. The latter part of my stay at Menin
the fighting was only three miles away, or even less, and often we could hear
the rattle of the rifles and Maxim guns. I was, however, lucky to escape with
my life, but I do so wish I could have done more before getting hit.

On 21 December 1915/16 a letter appeared in the *Times* from one Emily
Fairey of Briansk, Gov, Orel, Russia.

In the island of Denholm, … are three English officers, prisoners, and it will be
a relief to their friends to know that they are alive and well. One of them is
called 'Skeff'. They made a doctor promise to tell of their fate to some British
subject in Russia. I at once wrote to our Ambassador in Petrograd….

Unfortunately the barracks at Denholm are very damp and cold, the food is
wretched and very scanty….: much money was taken from the prisoners to
send letters and telegrams but none were ever sent. All the prisoners are at the
mercy of a non-commissioned, drunken officer. He can shoot them when he
pleases.

Skaife learned both Russian and Welsh while a prisoner, and survived the
war to both command the 1st Battalion and later to become Colonel of the
Regiment.

Apart from the four Distinguished Conduct Medals, a battalion's ration
when an operation was not a victory, the only other decoration awarded to the
Battalion at First Ypres was the Military Cross awarded to Captain Parker, the
Quartermaster. This appeared in the first list of Military Crosses in 1915. A

full list of awards for First Ypres earned by members of the Battalion is at Annex D.

In March 1919 the certificates arrived for the two Mentions in Despatches which Hal had been awarded. One is from the Despatch of 14 January 1915 and the second from that of 31 May.

In May 1919, the bodies of Hal and Claud Dooner were found where they had been buried together on the battlefield by the Germans. The area had been behind the German lines since they were killed and they were re-interred in Hooge Cemetery on the Menin Road, beside that of Private 10936 Allen Davies, one of Hal's orderlies.

Determined to visit Ypres, Eve enlisted the help of Major-General Sir Francis Lloyd, Colonel of the Regiment, the Belgian Military Attaché and many others. Not unexpectedly she had difficulties in obtaining a passport and organising transport and accommodation in what was then a 'restricted area'. Finally she set off, armed with a letter from Brigadier-General Jack Seely, the Secretary of State for Air, to the Senior Naval Officer in Ostend:

> The bearer of this letter, Mrs Cadogan, a friend of my wife's, is going over to Belgium on a very sad quest. Her husband fell at Zandvoorde in command of his battalion, and for nearly 5 years she had no precise news. It has at last been found, for certain, that he was killed, and she is on her way to the place. All

Hal's original grave, showing the wooden German cross recovered by Eve and Walter Carlile in 1919.

Hal's memorial in Gayhurst Church. The section of the cross was taken from his original grave site.

Hal's grave in Hooge Cemetery, Menin Road, Ypres.

her friends have endeavoured to dissuade her from going, and I know that the official view, which I share, is that it is inadvisable, but Mrs Cadogan is bent on going, and I think perhaps the circumstances are exceptional. If you can help her at all, I shall be most grateful.

She visited Hooge and Zandvoorde, where there was nothing left standing. In the end, I believe she travelled with Walter Carlile, who had become a member of Major-General Ware's Unit of Missing Bureau. Together they brought back the wooden cross which marked the spot where his body was found and it now forms part of his memorial erected in Gayhurst Church by Walter and Blanche.

A later comment by Basil Liddle Hart leaves a final echo: '[The soldiers of the British Expeditionary Force] attained their end – in both senses. Ypres saw the supreme vindication of the final sacrifice of the old Regular Army. After the battle was over, little survived, save the memory of its spirit.'

Postscript

In 1915, Eve rented a small house, Friars Oak, in Beaulieu, on the Montagu estate. Lord Montagu later allowed Eve to buy a nineteen-acre plot of land near Buckler's Hard on which she built a house, Little Salterns. Edward was brought up there and Eve remained there until she died in 1965. The house was sold by the family in 1968.

Hal's son was commissioned from the Royal Military College Sandhurst in 1927, and joined the 1st Battalion in Quetta. On the Battalion's return from India, he was a member of the representative party which visited Buckingham Palace in 1931; HM King George V being Colonel in Chief of the Regiment. Hal's old friend Lieutenant-General Sir Charles Dobell was Colonel of the Regiment, and presented Edward to the King, who said at once: 'I remember your father well. When I asked him should the Royal Welsh become the Welsh Guards, he replied "On no account!" And he was quite right.' This conversation no doubt took place in 1913 when the 1st Battalion was carrying out Public Duties at Windsor. The Welsh Guards was formed two years later.

Edward had an excellent eye. Apart from playing cricket for Hampshire and the Army in the 1930s, he was a superb shot with both rifle and shotgun. As adjutant of the 6th (Anglesey & Caernarvon) Battalion of the Royal Welch he co-ordinated the 250th Anniversary celebrations in Caernarfon in 1939, before they mobilized. In 1942, he commanded 164 Officer Cadet Training Unit in Barmouth – it later moved to Eaton Hall, Chester. Then, in 1943, he was given command of the 6th Battalion which he took to Nomandy in June 1944, but was shot through the neck in late July during

Lt-Col Edward Cadogan, Hal's son.

Henry Cadogan, Hal's grandson, who commanded the 3rd Battalion.

Oliver Cadogan, Hal's grandson, who served in the RWF during the 1960s

the battle for Caen, an injury which put him out for the rest of the war and after which he was never fully fit. Nevertheless, he was GSO1 of 4 Division in Greece in 1946–7 before commanding the 1st Battalion in Germany for three years. The highlight of his tour was in April 1949 when the Battalion was flown into Berlin during the Airlift.

After a tour as chief instructor at the Senior Officers' School he became military secretary to General Sir Charles Keightley in the Middle East. This was over the Suez operation for which he was awarded the CBE.

After he retired, he had a series of jobs, the last being Steward to the Verderers of the New Forest. This he found hugely rewarding, being a considerable naturalist who knew the Forest and its people very well.

Two of Edward's sons, Henry (the editor of these letters) and Oliver, also served in the Royal Welch Fusiliers, for forty-four and three years respectively. Added to Edward's thirty-three and Hal's twenty-seven, the total becomes 107 years, which must be some sort of a record.

Appendices

Appendix 1

Biographies

ACKLAND-ALLEN, Hugh Thomas, son of Charles Ackland-Allen, JP, of St Hilary Manor, Cowbridge, Glam. Ed: Wellington, 2Lt 1RWF, 3 Sep 1913. KiA Zonnebeke 23 Oct 1914.

ALSTON, Llewellyn A. A., B: 21 Dec 1890, son of Arthur Alston, Whitley Lodge, Glos. Ed: Cheltenham. Via Sp Res Bn RWF, 2Lt 1RWF, 4 Dec 1912. Wounded Zonnebeke, 20 Oct 1914. Later CO 1RWF in Italy 1918, DSO, MC, MiD twice. CO Regimental Depot 1930–2. CO 1RWF 1937–9. Comd Inf Bde & Area Comd Home Forces until 1946. Retd. CBE, 1945. Officer American Legion of Merit. Col RWF 1 Jan 1947–23 Jun 1948. D: 18 Mar 1968.

ANWYL, Maurice I. H., B: 22 Aug 1889, son of R. A. C. Anwyl of Llugwy, Merioneth. Ed: Wellington and RMC. 2Lt 1RWF, 6 Nov 1909. Capt, 27 Oct 1914. On establishment 1RWF until 19 June 1918. Retd, 1923.

ARCHDALE, Hugh James, B: 15 Jan 1854, son of Capt M. E. Archdale, of Castle Archdale, Fermanagh. Via Fermanagh Militia. Lt RWF, 11 Feb 1875. Served Sudan Expedition 1884–5. Capt 1RWF, Mar 1885, Burma 1886–7. With 2RWF Crete 1897–8. CO 2 Lincolns, 6 Oct 1900 in Anglo-Boer War. Brevet Col 10 Feb 1904. Retd 1911. Recalled for Great War. Bde Comd 1914–16, CMG. M: 1894, Helen Trevor, d of Capt Boscawen Trevor Griffith Boscawen of Trevalyn Hall, Rossett (formerly RWF). D: 31 Aug 1921.

BANCROFT, Charles Edward, B: 20 Oct 1863. Lt The Duke of Cornwall's Light Infantry, 25 Aug 1883, transferred to RWF, 24 Oct same year. Capt 2RWF, 21 Jan 1893. Half-pay, 7 Sep 1896. Returned to full pay RWF, 8 Jun 1898. Retd. Dec 1902. M: Ellis Maude, d of the Hon H. Moses, a member of the Legislative Council of New South Wales (see J. A. Higgon below). D: 6 Oct 1906. His widow married Sir Horace W. McMahon (q.v.) in 1911.

BARCHARD, David Maxwell, B: 3 Nov 1891, son of H. G. Barchard of Buxton, Derbyshire. Ed: Uppingham and RMC. 2Lt 1RWF, 11 Oct 1911. Lt, 17 Feb 1914. POW Zonnebeke, 20 Oct 1914. Capt, 8 Oct 1915. MiD for conduct as POW. Adjt 3(Res) Bn RWF 1919–Aug 1922. Adjt, 2RWF Feb 1923–Feb 1926. Maj, 5 Dec 1927. Supt of PT, Western Comd, Feb 1927–Oct 1929. Local Lt-Col, CO Nigeria Regt Bn, Oct 1930–Mar 1934. Lt-Col, CO 2 RWF, 1 Aug 1936–10 Sep 1939. Comd E African Bde. Retd, 1945. Ran Banda Hotel, Nairobi. Married 1919. D: Nairobi, 10 Mar 1954.

BARKER, Richard Vincent, B: 13 Jun 1880, son of Rev Frederick Barker. Ed: Winchester and New College, Oxford. 2Lt 4 (Militia) Bn RWF, 19 Apr 1900. 2Lt 1RWF, 5 Jan 1901. Anglo-Boer War. Adjt 1RWF, Jul 1904–Jan 1909. Capt, 9 Sep 1911. West African Frontier Force, April 1909–April 1912. With 1RWF in Dublin, Malta, Lyndhurst. Staff Capt 22 Bde (in which was 1RWF), Oct 1914. KiA, 31 Oct 1914, near Zandvoorde.

BARTTELOT, George Frederick. B: 13 June 1865, son of Brian Barttelot Esq of Bramblehurst, Sussex. 2Lt 1RWF 7 Feb 1885. Burma 1886–7; invalided home due 'to disease'. Capt 16 May 1894.

Anglo-Boer War, wounded 7 Aug 1900. MiD. Maj 25 Oct 1902. Retd 26 July 1911. During First World War employed in Officers' Records, Infantry Records Office.

BERESFORD (-Ash), William Randal Hamilton, B: 19 July 1859, son of John Barré Beresford of Learmont Park, Co. Londonderry. JP, DL, and his wife Caroline, only child and heiress of William and Lady Elizabeth Hamilton Ash of Ashbrook, Co. Londonderry. Ed: Eton. 2Lt Londonderry Militia, 13 Feb 1878. 2Lt 1RWF, 6 Aug 1880. Captain, 9 Dec 1885. Burma 1885–6. MiD. Adjutant 1RWF, 23 April 1890–April 1894. Hazara 1891. DAAG, May 1896. Major, 24 March 1897. Second Boer War 1899. CO 1RWF 12 May 1904–13 May 1908. Brevet Colonel 12 May 1907. Retired. M: 23 October 1886 Lady Florence Browne, daughter of 5th Marquess of Sligo. On death of his mother in 1901, assumed additional surname of Ash by royal licence. DL Londonderry, HS 1912. Recalled in First World War. CO 10th (Service) Bn RWF until wounded at Ypres in December 1915. Recovered and became CO 1st Bn The Welsh Regt until he retired in 1917 (aged 58!). Keen cricketer, fine shot. Member of General Synod of the Church of Ireland. D: 8 March 1938. One son (Douglas), major RF (Retd). Family still living at Ashbrook when 1 RWF served in Londonderry in 1971–3.

BERNERS, Ralph Abercrombie, B: 14 Jun 1871, son of C. H. Berners, Woolverstone Park, Ipswich, JP DL, HS, and Mary, d of Sir Ralph Anstruther, Bart of Fife (her brother, Lt Henry Anstruther, KiA at Alma). Ed: Eton & RMC. 2Lt 1RWF, 29 Oct 1890. Hazara 1891. With 2RWF Crete, 1897–8. Maj, Jul 1908. CO 1RWF, May–Sep 1915. CO 9 (Service) Bn RWF, Dec 1915–Nov 1916. DSO, MiD 3 times. Retd 1920. JP Dorset. M: 1898 Laura, d of Sir Robert Laffan, KCMG, late RE. Lived Bourton, Dorset. D 25 Feb 1949.

BERTIE, Hon Reginald Henry, B 26 May 1856, 6th son of Earl of Abingdon, DCL, High Steward of Oxford and Abingdon, Ld Lt of Berks. Ed: Eton. 2Lt 2RWF, 21 Sep 1874. Adjt 2RWF and 3 (Militia) Bn RWF, 1878–90. With 2RWF in Crete, 1897–8. CO 2RWF, 1899–Aug 1903. Peking 1900, CB. Brevet Col, Aug 1903. Retd, 1904. D: 15 Jun 1950.

BEST, William, B: 24 Jun 1874, son of J. C. Best of Vivod, Llangollen. Ed: Eton & RMC. 2Lt 1RWF, 21 Sep 1894. Anglo-Boer War. Resigned, 6 Dec 1902. M: 1903. D: 19 Apr 1950.

BINGHAM, the Hon George Roderick Bentinck, B: 10 May 1894, son of 5th Lord Clanmorris of Newbrook, Co. Mayo. Ed: Cheltenham & RMC. 2Lt 1RWF, 8 Aug 1914. Wounded and POW Zonnebeke, 21 Oct 1914. With 1RWF in Lucknow & Waziristan 1919–21. Adjt 4RWF (TA), Feb 1923. Retd, 31 Aug 1924. In Second World War reached rank of Sqn Ldr in RAFVR. D: 10 Dec 1972.

BLOOD, Bindon, B: 1842. Descended from Col Blood who stole the Crown Jewels in reign of Charles II. Ed: Queen's Coll, Galway and Indian Military Seminary. 2Lt RE, 1860. Zulu War 1879. 2nd Afghan War 1880. Tel el Kebir 1882. Chitral 1896. Malakand Field Force 1896–8. Maj-Gen 1898. GOC Punjab 1901–07. Gen 1906. GCB. D: 1940.

BLYTH, Sidney Beckwith, B: 15 Jan 1846. Ensign RWF, 1 Dec 1865. Adjt 4 (Militia) Bn, Sep 1884–Aug 1889. CO 2RWF, 1891–95. Led 2RWF in march through Wales in 1892, which was a great success because of the links he had made during his tour as adjt. Retd.

BRAITHWAITE, William Garnett, B: 21 Oct 1870, son of W. G. W. Braithwaite of Plumtree Hall, Westmorland, JP. Ed: Marlborough & RMC. 2Lt 1RWF, 21 May 1891. Adjt 1RWF, 2 Mar 1898–5 May 1900. Capt, 19 Jul 1899. Anglo-Boer War. Brigade-Major 6 Bde. DSO, MiD twice. Coy Comd then Adjt RMC, Jan 1906–Jan 1910. Maj, 4 May 1910. psc. Served with NZ forces in Great War, Bde Comd by 1918. CMG, CB, MiD (8 times). Comd Alexandria Brigade, 1921–25. Retd. A delightful character, with the nickname in the Regiment of 'The Alderman'. D: 15 Oct 1937. Son, G. E. Braithwaite, commanded 1RWF in Burma during Second World War.

BRENNAN, John Henry, B: 1869, son of T. C. Brennan of Montreal Canada. 3 (Res) Bn RWF. Served with 1 RWF in Malta and the UK as a Capt, aged 45. KiA near Kleythoek, Roulers–Menin road, 19 Oct 1914. Name on Menin Gate Memorial.

BRUXNER-RANDALL, James Gerald, B: 7 Apr 1890, son of Col R. G. Bruxner-Randall, JP. Ed: Winchester & RMC. 2Lt 1RWF, 9 Mar 1910. Nigeria Regiment West African Frontier Force, 14 Jan 1914. CO 1RWF, 18 May 1933–18 May 1937. Col 18 May 1936. Comd 159 (Welsh Border) Bde, 1937–41, Comdt RMC Sandhurst , 1941–3. Comd 57 (Naples) Area, 1943–4. CBE. Retd, 1946. D: 1986, aged 96. His son, P. D. Bruxner-Randall, served RWF 1946–64.

BULWER, Edward Earle Gascoigne, B: 22 Dec 1829 at Norwich, nephew of Lord Lytton. Ed: privately and at Cambridge Univ. 2Lt RWF, 21 Aug 1849 by purchase. Fought with 1RWF at Alma, Inkerman and Sebastopol. Capt, 21 Sep 1854. Indian Mutiny, was present at the capture of Lucknow. Commanded a Column in Oudh, 1858. MiD. Brevet Lt-Col, Apr 1859. He made his name as AAG Northern District, 1870–73. War Office 1873–Mar 1879. Maj-Gen, Comd Chatham District. Inspector Gen of Recruiting 1880–6. KCB. Lt-Gen, 21 Jan 1887. Lt-Governor of Guernsey 1889–94. Gen, 1 Apr 1893. Col RWF, Mar 1898–Dec 1910. GCB, 1905. M: Isabella, d of Sir J.Jacob Buxton, Bart. D: 8 Dec 1910.

CARLILE, William Walter, B: 15 Jan 1862, son of James W. Carlile, of Ponsbourne Manor, Herts. Ed: Harrow and Clare Coll, Cambs. James bought Gayhurst House, Bucks, a large and beautiful Elizabethan mansion, in 1882. Walter inherited it in 1909, but had lived there since 1882. JP, 1888. After being defeated in the 1892 General Election, he won the seat of North Bucks in 1895 for the Conservatives and remained an MP until 1905 when he did not seek re-election. DL Bucks, 1897. Although for most of his electioneering he was transported by a coach and four, he was one of the first MPs to drive a car to the House of Commons. M: 1st, 1885, Blanche Anne Cadogan (d 1939, Hal Cadogan's second sister); 2nd, 1940 (Catherine) Elizabeth (Mary) Field, (daughter of Hal Cadogan's youngest sister, Frances, & therefore his niece by marriage). In the Great War he was too old for active service, but went as a chauffeur, with his Rolls Royce fitted out as an ambulance, in No. 2 Motor Ambulance Unit of the British Red Cross Society. At the end of the war he served in General Ware's 'Unit of Missing Bureau'. OBE, 1923. Baronet, 1928, for 'Political and Public Services'. He played an active part in public affairs in Buckinghamshire for more than forty years, and was an alderman on the county council. He was probably Hal Cadogan's greatest friend. He was a great sportsman and a generous man, particularly to all on his estate at Gayhurst and Stoke Goldington. He sold Gayhurst to Lord Hesketh. D: Dec 1949.

CAPPER, Thompson. B: 20 Oct 1863, son of William Copeland of the Bengal Civil Service. His older brother was Maj-Gen Sir John Capper. Ed Haileybury and RMC. 2Lt E. Lancashire Regt, 9 Sept 1882. Capt, 22 Apr1891. Chitral Relief Expedition 1895. Staff Coll Camberley, 1896–7. Served with Egyption Army in Sudan Dec 1897–July 1899, being present at battles of Atbara and Omdurman. Brevt Maj, 16 Nov1898. 2nd Boer War, Nov 1899 as DAAG of Natal Army. Relief of Ladysmith and advance into Transvaal. . Brevt Lt-Col, 29 Nov 1900. Comd a mobile column July 1901–May 1902 in Cape Colony. DSO. Professor then DAAG at Staff College, Dec 1902–Dec 1905. Brevet Col, Dec 1904. First Commandant of Quetta Staff Col, Mar 1906–Jan 1911. Brig-Gen ,May 1906. Expert on Russo-Japanese War. CB, 1910. Comd 13th Inf Bde, Dublin, 19 Feb 1911. Inspector of Inf, Feb 1914. Comd 7th Div, 27 Aug 1914 as Maj-Gen. Covered Belgian retreat to River Yser and 1st Battle of Ypres. KCMG. Wounded, 1915. Although selected to comd a corps, received permission to remain with 7th Div till after Battle of Loos, Sep 1915. He was forward in the trenches when hit by a sniper, and died next day, 26 Sep 1915. He had been true to the priciples he had set out in one of his lectures in 1908: "That wars could not be won unless the individuals composing an army set out to fight with the determined spirit that they will conquer, or they will die in the attempt to do so." (Note. Capper MSS II/4/16).

CAVAN, Field Marshal Frederick Rudolph, 10th Earl of Cavan, KP, GCB, GCMG, GCVO, GBE, B: 16 Oct 1865, son of 9th Earl, of Wheathampstead, Herts. Ed: Eton. 2Lt Grenadier Guards, 1885. Anglo-Boer War, 1900.CO 2Grenadier Guards, 1908. Col, 1911. Half-pay, 1912. Reserve, 1913. Recalled. Bde Comd TA Bde, then 4 Guards Bde, 17 Sep 1914 at 1st Ypres & Festubert May 1915. Maj-Gen, GOC 50th (Northumbrian) Div, Jun 1915, GOC Guards Div, Aug 1915, at Loos. Lt-Gen, Comd XIV Corps, Jan 1916 at Somme & 3rd Ypres. With his Corps to Italy, Oct 1917. Succeeded Gen Plumer as Comd British Forces in Italy, Mar 1918. Gen, 1921. GOC Aldershot, 1922. Succeeded Sir Henry Wilson as CIGS, 1922–6. Col Irish Guards and Beds & Herts Regt. Field Marshal, 1931. M: 1st Caroline Crawley, 2nd Lady Hester Mulholland, 2 daughters. D: 28 Aug 1946. He was succeeded by the Ven the Hon H. E. S. S. Lambart, Archdeacon of Salop, his youngest (surviving) brother, E. H. Cadogan's father-in-law.

CHANCE, Guy Ogden de Peyster, B: 28 Feb 1892, of the Chance family of Great Alne Hall, Warwickshire. Ed: Eton. 2Lt 1RWF, 20 Sep 1911. Lt, 19 Apr 1913. KiA, 19 Oct 1914 on the Menin–Roulers road in 1st Battle of Ypres.

CHILDE-FREEMAN, John Arthur, B: 17 Aug 1890. Ed: Wellington. 2Lt 2RWF, 9 Mar 1910. Lt, 14 Aug 1911. Great War. MC, 1915, KiA at Loos, 29 Sep 1915.

CLEGG-HILL, Hon Charles Rowland, B: 5 May 1876, son of Viscount Hill, DL. Ed: Radley. Via 4 (Militia) Bn RWF. 2Lt 1RWF, 9 Nov 1896. Anglo-Boer War. DSO & MiD. Res of Officers, 6 Nov 1912. Recalled, 1914. With 2RWF, Béthune, GSO2, MiD (3 times), Bt Lt-Col, 3 June 1919. Retd. Succeeded brother to become 6th Viscount Hill, JP, DL (Salop). D: 3 May 1957.

CLOUGH-TAYLOR, Edward Harrison, B: 1849, son of E. Clough-Taylor, DL, JP, of Firby Hall, East Yorks. Ed: Harrow. 2Lt RWF, 18 Apr 1868. Capt, 1880. ADC to Viceroy of India, The Marquis of Ripon until 1884. Maj, 1885. Retd, 1886. JP East Yorks, 1898. On Reserve until recalled to comd RWF details 1900–01. M: 1st, 1880, Lady Elizabeth, daughter of 8th Duke of Argyll, (d 1896), 2nd, 1898, Lady Mary, daughter of Earl of Castle Stewart. One of his two sons, W. S. A. Clough Taylor, b 1905, was commissioned RWF in 1928. He was Sen Maj to E. H. Cadogan, Hal Cadogan's son, when he was CO 1 RWF in Dusseldorf and Berlin in 1948–9.

COLLETON, Sir Robert A. W., Bart, B: 31 Aug 1854 at Cape of Good Hope, son of Sir R. A. F. G. Colleton, 8th Bart, Barrack Master at Buttevant, Co Cork. Succeeded father as 9th Bart, Oct 1866. Via Militia. Lt 96th Foot, 2 Dec 1874. To 1RWF, 23 Jan 1875. Before sailing to India from Portsmouth in Aug 1880, he carried the old Queen's Colour onto the Royal Yacht for safekeeping by HRH The Prince of Wales, who presented new Colours. The old Colour was that carried by Sgt Luke O'Connor at Alma when he won the VC. Capt, Mar 1885. Hazara, 1891 (BM to 2 Bde), MiD. Maj, 1892. To 2RWF, 1898, Crete and Hong Kong. When Col Thorold was KiA in South Africa on 12 May 1900, he succeeded him as CO 1RWF, 24 Jun. CB, MiD 3 times. Brevet Col, Feb 1904. O-i-c Inf Records, Shrewsbury, 1906–9. OC Pretoria District, South Africa until 31 Aug 1911. Retd. Hon Brig-Gen. M: Aug 1880, 2 sons and 6 daughters but both sons predeceased him, so when he died on 1 Sep 1938, the baronetcy became extinct.

COOPER, August Frederic, B: 25 Jan 1861. Ed: Clifton. 2Lt 1RWF, 11 Aug 1880; Capt, 17 Jul 1889; Hazara 1891; Adjt 4 (Militia) Bn 1894–9. To Res of Officers (Maj), 5 Oct 1898.

COTTRILL. Joseph (Joe), B: 10 Oct 1870 in Manchester. Enlisted 1886 – number 2251. Joined 1RWF in India as a boy. Sgt Anglo-Boer War. Served with 1RWF 1899–1901, wounded and awarded DCM at Naauwpoort. LS&GC medal 1908. QMS 1RWF by 1911, including 1RWF detachment at coronation of King George V. Served Malta, Lyndhurst and Belgium, 1914. 2Lt 2RWF, 1914; Lt & QM; Temp Capt 20 May 1915. DSO 14 Jan 1916. Invalided out with the rank of captain 14 Nov 1918. Secretary Caernarvon & Anglesey T.A. 1919. Attended the unveiling of 7 Div Memorial, Ypres 1 Oct 1924. D: 13 Jan 1925, buried Llanbeblig, Caernarfon.

COURAGE, John Hubert, B: 28 Dec 1891, son of H. Courage, chairman of Courage Brewery, of Kirkby Fleetham Hall, Northallerton, North Yorks. Ed: Wellington & RMC. 2Lt 1RWF, 11 Oct 1911. Served Dublin, Portland, Malta, Lyndhurst. Won Army High Jump, 1913. Wounded and POW Zonnebeke, 21 Oct 1914. Retd, 1921. In Second World War he served as a Lt-Col in Aux Mil Pioneer Corps in BEF, Egypt and Western Desert. Survived the sinking of the *Lancastria* off St Nazaire in June 1940 to be taken prisoner in Greece in 1941. MiD. Chairman of Courage Brewery 1947–59. Great sportsman, and farmed 1,000 acres in Yorkshire. D: 28 Apr 1967.

CREAGH, VC, GCB, GCSI, Gen Sir Garrett O'Moore, B: 1848. Commissioned 95th Regt, 1866. Transferred to the Indian Army where he served for the remainder of his career except for the period when he commanded a brigade in China, 1900–01. Afghan War, 1879-80, VC. Political Resident & GOC Aden. GOC BEF, China 1901. KCB, 1902. Gen, 1907. C-in-C India, 1909–14 (in succession to Lord Kitchener). Co-author (with H. M. Humphris) of *The VC and DSO* (1924). D: 1923.

CREEK, Edward S., B: 26 Nov 1842. Ensign 1RWF, 23 Jul 1861. Capt, May 1871. BM Bermuda 1876–8, DAA & QMG Dublin Dist, 1878–81. Maj, 1 Jul 1881. psc. DAA & QMG Northern Dist, Mar 1885–May 1886. Lt-Col, 26 May 1886. To Burma with 1RWF, 1886–7 (MiD). CO 1RWF, 1 July 1887–Jan 1890, when he changed with CO 2RWF (R. F. Williamson) for health reasons, 'At no expense to the War Office'. AAG NW Dist, 1892. OC Regtl Dist at Wrexham, 1897–9. Retired.

DELMÉ-RADCLIFFE, Henry, B: 30 March 1866. Lt 1RWF, Aug 1885. Burma, 1886–7. Capt, 1 Nov 1894. Anglo-Boer War (MiD 3 times). Maj, May 1904. Lt-Col, CO 2RWF, 21 Aug 1911. To France 11 Aug 1914. Evacuated sick, 26 Oct 1914. CO 12 (Res) Bn RWF, April 1915, (MiD). Retired, 24 Apr 1920. D: 14 Mar 1947.

DICKSON, George Frederick Hayes, B: 25 Aug 1873, son of A. B. Dickson, JP, of Haverthwaite, Ulverston, Lancs. Ed: Eton. Via 3 (Militia) Bn RWF. 2Lt 2RWF, 2 Jun 1894. Lt, 7 Sep 1896. Crete 1897–8. With 1RWF in South Africa 1899–1900. To 2RWF Hong Kong, Jul 1900, then India. Maj, 19 Oct 1912. Retired, 19 Apr 1913. M: 1913 Grace, d of Thomas Robertson of New South Wales, by whom he had 2 sons, both RWF (George, DSO, KiA Germany 1945, and John, adjt to Hal Cadogan's son, E. H. Cadogan, when he was CO 1RWF in Hubblerath and Berlin 1948–50. CO 1RWF, 1960–2. Retired as a brigadier). Recalled 5 Aug 1914. 2ic 2RWF, severely wounded at Festubert, 1 May 1915. Temp Lt-Col, 1916. MiD. Retired, 2 Mar 1919, to Ulverston. D: Dec 1957.

DOBELL, Charles Macpherson, B: 22 June 1869, son of R. R. Dobell of Quebec. Ed: Charterhouse and RMC Kingston, Canada. 2Lt 1RWF, 22 Aug 1890. Hazara, 1891. Adjt 2RWF, 1896–Nov 1900. Capt, 22 Feb 1899. Brevet Maj, 8 Mar 1899. When Anglo-Boer War began he was on leave in England, and successfully applied to serve there. CO 2 Bn Mounted Infantry till late 1900. DSO & MiD. Rejoined 2RWF in Peking. Active service in West Africa, Jan 1904–Oct 1906 (MiD twice, Brevet Lt-Col). psc 1907. GSO3 WO, 1907–08. GSO2, 1909–11. Brevet Col and ADC to HM King 1910. Coy Comd 1 RWF in Ireland, 1911–12. CO Bedfords, May 1912. Brig-Gen, Inspector-Gen West African Frontier Force, Sep 1913. Comd allied forces in capture of the Cameroons. KCB & CMG. Maj-Gen, Jun 1915. Western Frontier Force, Egypt, June–Oct 1916. Lt-Gen, Sep 1916. Comd at 1st & 2nd Battles of Gaza. GOC 2 (Rawalpindi) Div, India, 6 Aug 1917. 3rd Afghan War, 1919 (MiD twice). GOC Northern Army India, 1920–3. Retired. M: 1908 Elizabeth (Elsie), daughter of Maj Meyrick Bankes, and widow of Capt F. L. Campbell, RN. Col RWF, 1926–38. D: Oct 1954.

DOONER, Alfred Edwin Claud Toke, B: 3 Apr 1892, third son of Col. W. T. Dooner CBE, late R. Inniskilling Fus. of Ditton Place, Maidstone, by his wife, Augusta. Ed: King's Sch. Rochester, then scholarship to Tonbridge, passed third into RMC. Drill Prize. 2Lt 1RWF, 20 Sep 1911. Lt, 4 Sep 1912. 1st Class Interpreter in German, Jan 1912. Succeeded E. O. Skaife as Adjt 1RWF, 26 Jul 1914, (probably youngest in the army). Served Dublin, Portland, & Malta. Temp Capt, Oct 1914. KiA with Lt-Col H. O. S. Cadogan at Zandvoorde, 30 Oct 1914. MiD 1915. Memorial in Rochester Cathedral. Buried in Hooge Cemetery next to Hal Cadogan.

DOUGHTY-WYLIE, Charles Hotham Montagu, B: 23 Jul 1868, son of H. M. Doughty, of Theberton Hall, Leiston, Suffolk, by his wife, Edith, daughter of D. Cameron, Chief Justice of Vancouver Island. Ed: Winchester. 2Lt 1RWF 21 Sep 1889. Hazara 1891, severely wounded in knee. Lt 23 Sep 1891. Chitral Relief Force, 1895. Capt, 9 Sep 1896. With Egyptian Army on Nile Expeditions of 1898 & 99 (MiD on each expedition). With 2 RWF in Crete, 1897–8. Anglo-Boer War attached to Mounted Infantry, wounded. 2RWF in Hong Kong, 1900. OC B Coy to Tientsin in China after suppression of Boxer Rebellion. From Jan 1903–June 1904 a Special Service Officer with Somaliland Frontier Force, East Africa. Seconded for duty with the Foreign Office, 26 Sep 1906–3 Dec 1909 as vice-consul in Mersyn and Konia. Maj, 21 Aug 1907. During the mass slaughter of the Armenians, displayed outstanding bravery and saved hundreds of lives by facing hostile crowds alone on horseback. CMG. Consul in Addis Ababa, 4 Dec 1909. British Representative, and then President of International Commission for the Southern Frontier of Albania, 29 Aug–31 Dec 1913. CB. Lt-Col, 1915 on staff of Gen Sir Ian Hamilton for the Gallipoli Campaign. After the *River Clyde* landings on 'V' Beach he saved a desperate situation by organising and leading a charge on Sedd-el-Bahr Fort and capture of Hill 141, but was killed in the moment of success on 26 Apr 1915. VC. He was buried where he fell, in the only isolated war grave in the Gallipoli peninsula. M: 1904 Lilian Wylie, Westcliffe Hall, Hants, the widow of Lt Henry Adams-Wylie of the Indian Medical Service. Adopted surname 'Wylie' on marriage.

DUNN, Robert Henry William, B: 23 Nov 1857, son of Maj-Gen William Dunn. Ed: Eton. 2Lt 35th Foot, 1876. To 1RWF, 1 May 1878. Lt. Burma 1885–6. Adjt 1RWF, 9 Oct 1885–22 Jan 1890. Maj, 4 Mar 1896. Retired, 24 Mar 1897. Reserve of Officers. Brigade-Major Welsh Border Bde, 1897–1906. Lt-Col (& temp Col), 1 Jun 1908 while commanding North Wales TA Bde, until July 1912. Brig-Gen, 27 Oct 1914. D: 8 Jan 1917.

EDWARDS, Henry Herbert, B: 15 Jul 1854. 2Lt 96th Foot, 28 Feb 1874. Lt RWF, 13 May 1874. Capt, 16 Aug 1882. Maj, 21 April 1886. Adjt 9 KRRC (Militia) Bn, 1 Jul 1884–30 Jun 1889. Retired, 18 Mar 1892. Hon Corps of Gentlemen at Arms. D: 21 Apr 1895.

EGERTON, Rowland le Belward, B: 4 Apr 1895, younger twin son of Sir Philip Grey Egerton, 12th Bart, DL, JP, of Oulton Park, Cheshire. Ed: Wellington & RMC. 2Lt 1RWF, 8 Aug 1914. Joined at Lyndhurst. Sailed day after main body of 1RWF left Southampton, with men who had been on local leave. Landed Zeebrugge, 7 Oct 1914 (same day as main body). KiA Zandvoorde, 30 Oct 1914, within an hour of Hal Cadogan, his CO.

ENGLEHEART, Evelyn Linzee, B: 26 Jun 1862, son of Sir John Engleheart. KCB, Private Sec to Duke of Newcastle, Sec of State for the Colonies. Ed: Charterhouse & RMC. Lt RWF, 9 Sep 1882. Capt, 6 Apr 1891. Adjt, 2RWF Jan 1893–30 Jun 1896. Maj, 30 Jun 1899. DAAG at WO 1900–02 & Malta 1902–05. Invalided, half-pay. Retired, 14 Mar 1906. Staff Capt WO, 1914. Brevet Lt-Col 1918. CBE & MiD (twice). D: 4 Feb 1943.

EVANS, Ernest Riddle, B: 19 Oct 1851. Col, DSOLt RWF, 28 Feb 1874. Capt, 24 Dec 1881. Maj, Dec 1885. Special Service as Signals Officer in South Africa 1879–80, and in Transvaal Campaign. Staff Coll, 1886. With 1 RWF in Burma, 1886. Hazara, 1891. During advance on Durband he contracted pneumonia and died in hospital at Palosi, 5 Apr 1881.

EVANS, John Meredith Jones, B: 24 Mar 1894, son of Owen L. J. Evans of Broom Hall Pwllheli, JP, DL, MA, (formerly Lt-Col & Hon Col 4 (Militia) Bn RWF.) 2Lt 1RWF, 5 Feb 1913. Lt, 20 Jun 1914. Wounded at Zonnebeke, 21 Oct 1914. Adjt, 24 June–24 Sep 1915, wounded Loos. Capt, 17 Dec 1915. MC & MiD, French War Cross. Brevet-Maj, 3 Jun 1919. WO Staff, 1917–22. Retired, 1 Oct 1927. Recalled during the Second World War, and became Deputy Military Secretary (DMS) at WO. Also DMS to C-in-C Middle East. CBE. Retired as Hon Brig, 9 Aug 1945. D: 20 Jul 1957, at Churt, Surrey. His obituary in *The Times* (1 Aug 1957) described his many qualities 'Shrewd, *sans peur et sans reproche*, completely sincere, imperturbable, incapable of a mean thought or action…'

EVERITT, Sydney George, B: 21 Jul 1860, son of George A. Everitt, FRGS, JP, of Knowle Hall, Warwick. (Consul at Birmingham for Belgium and Hanover, K of Order of Hanover). Ed: Harrow & RMC. 2Lt 1st Foot, 22 Jan 1881, transferred 2RWF, 12 Mar 1881. Capt, 2 July 1890. Maj, 22 Feb 1899. Served with 2RWF in Wales, Ireland, England, Malta, Crete, Egypt, India, Hong Kong & Peking. Commanded the Brit Legation Guard in Peking. Retired to Reserve of Officers, 4 Feb 1903. Lord of the Manors of Knowle, Nuthurst and Kinwalsey. JP. D: 1932.

FIRMAN, Robert Bertram, B: 18 Sep 1859, son of H. B. Firman of Brayton, Selby. Via West Yorks Militia, 2Lt 2RWF, 11 Oct 1879. Nile Expedition, 1884–5. To 1RWF. Capt, 21 Apr 1886. Burma, 1886. Invalided home, 27 Sep 1893. Transferred to Middlesex Regt Reserve of Officers, 1895. Anglo-Boer War joined Imperial Yeomanry, 7 Feb 1900. CO 11 Bn Imp Yeo. DSO, 29 Nov 1900. Retired, 29 Sep 1902. Had nickname of 'Milly' in RWF. Keen horseman. D: 25 Oct 1936.

FITZROY, Charles Alfred Euston, B: 4 June 1892, son of Revd Lord Charles Fitzroy of Thetford, Suffolk, Chaplain to Queen Victoria and Hon Chaplain to King Edward VII and King george V (fourth son of the Duke of Grafton). Ed: Wellington and RMC. 2Lt 2RWF 20 Sep 1911, Lt 27 Dec 1912, Capt 1 Oct 1915, ADC to Gov-Gen and High Commissioner of South Africa. Retd 13 Jan 1931. M: firstly 24 Jun 1918, Lady Doreen Buxton, d. of first Earl of Buxton, PC, GCMG (she died 1923); secondly Lucy, d. of Sir George Barnes, KCB, KCSI (she died 1943); thirdly Rita, widow of Lt-Cmdr J. T. Currie, RN. Succeeded to the dukedom of Grafton on death of 9th Duke on 4 Aug 1936. DL and JP Suffolk. D: 11 Nov 1970.

FLOWER, Oswald Swift, B 27 Apr 1871, son of E. F. of Stratford-upon-Avon, JP. Ed: Wellington & Jesus Coll Cambridge. Via 4 (Militia) Bn R Warwick, 18 Jan 1890. 2Lt 2RWF, 19 Oct 1892. Crete, 1897–8. Peking, 1900. MiD. Adjt 1(Vol) Bn RWF & 4RWF TA, 1904–08. Reserve of Officers, 4 May 1912. Recalled 1914. Brigade-Major raising RWF Service Bns, 13 July 1915. CO 13th Service Bn RWF. D: of wounds, 12 July 1916, after capture of Mametz Wood.

FORD, Harry Burroughes, B: 6 Jan 1868. 2LT 1 RWF 14 Mar 1888. To Indian Staff Corps as Lt 4 Apr 1890. Served on 2nd Miranzai expedition 1891, Waziristan 1894–5, Malakand Field Force as staff officer 1897, wounded. Capt 14 Mar 1899; wing officer, Bengal Native Infantry; Maj 14 Mar 1906; OC Mounted Infantry School, India, 2 Feb 1909–2 Feb 1910; Lt-Col 14 Mar 1914.

GABBETT, Richard Edward Philip, B: 14 Apr 1869, son of Windham Gabbett of Mount Rivers, Limerick. Via 5 (Militia) Bn R Irish Rifles. 2Lt 2RWF, 10 Oct 1891. Lt, 20 Jun 1894. Employed Niger Coast Protectorate, Feb 1897–May 1900. MiD. Capt, 19 Jul 1899. 1RWF South Africa, wounded (lost eye). Aro Expedition, Southern Nigeria, Oct 1901–May 1902. MiD. Brevet-Maj.

Adjt 3 (Militia) Bn RWF, Sep 1904–Sep 1908. Adjt 1RWF Jan 1909–Jul 1911. 2ic 1RWF, 1913–14. Wounded near Roulers–Menin road, 19 Oct 1914. MiD. CO 1RWF, 9 Nov 1914 after death of Hal Cadogan. KiA at Festubert, 15 May 1915.

GAMBIER-PARRY, Michael Denman, B: 21 Aug 1891, son of S. Gambier-Parry, JP of Downham House, Billericay, Essex, by his wife, Grace, d of Rt Hon Sir George Denman PC, Judge of the High Court. Ed: Eton and RMC. 2Lt 1RWF, 15 Mar 1911. Lt, 28 Aug 1911. Adjt 3 (Militia) Bn RWF, 1911–14 & 8 (Service) Bn until Nov 1915. Served in Gallipoli, Egypt, Mesopotamia. MC, MiD (6 times). CO 8 RWF, Feb 1917–Jan 1919. Staff Coll, 1924. Transferred to Royal Tank Regt, 1924. Maj, 1925. Brevet Lt-Col 1929. Brig Comd Malaya, 1938–40. Served Egypt, Crete, Greece, Libya. Maj-Gen 1940. GOC 2 Armd Div, 1941. POW Italy, 194–3 (with Generals O'Connor & Neame, VC.) Repatriated and retired, 1944. DL Wilts, 1952–4. Member of Council of Royal College of Music, 1951, Fellow, 1961. D: 30 Apr 1976.

GARNETT, William Brooksbank, B: 31 July 1875. Ed: Charterhouse. Via 24 Midx (PO) Vol Rifles, 2 Jan 1895. 2Lt 1RWF, 5 May 1900. Anglo-Boer War. To 2RWF in China, 20 Feb 1901, & to India. 1RWF Lt, 28 May 1908. Capt, 11 April 1911. Comd Guard of Honour at Carnarfon at Investiture of Prince of Wales, 1911. Great War, CO 20th (Public Schools) Bn RF, 20 Aug 1916–18 Feb 1917. 2RWF, Feb 1917–6 May 1918. Comd 121 Inf Bde, 6 May–19 Sep 1918. DSO, MiD (4 times). Retired, 1927. Secretary Flint and Denbigh TA, Association, 1927–36. Hon Freeman City of London. HS Tyrone & Officer of Ulster Home Guard in Second World War. D: 17 Aug 1946.

GOUGH, Alan Percy George, B: 13 Sep 1863, son of Gen Sir John Bloomfield Gough, GCB by his third wife, Elizabeth Arbuthnot of Elderslie, Surrey. Ed: Wellington & RMC. Lt 1RWF, 9 Sep 1882. Capt, 15 June 1892. Burma, 1885–7, MiD (twice). ADC to Maj–Gen Sir Charles Gough, in Bengal 1887–90. Maj, 25 Jul 1900. Anglo-Boer War, wounded, DSO, MiD (twice). Retired, 25 Oct 1902. DL & JP Carnarfonshire. Recalled Great War, employed on staff. AAG at WO, 14 Jul 1917, CMG, CBE, MiD. Chairman Carnarfon TA. M: Mary Georgina d of F. Lloyd Edwards of Nanhoron, Pwllheli. D: 17 Aug 1930.

GRANT-THOROLD, Richard Stanley, B: 9 Aug 1868, son of A. W. T. Grant-Thorold, Weelsby House, Lincs. Ed: Eton & RMC. 2Lt RWF, 11 Feb 1888. Resigned, 1891. Great War Maj, RF, DSO, wounded, MiD. CO 18 Bn Welch Regt. M: aged 77, lived in France. D: 2 Apr 1953.

GRIFFITH, Henry Woolgar, B: 6 Oct 1848, son of G. W. Griffith, JP, of Pantgwyn, Cardiganshire. Ensign 21st Foot, 2 Mar 1866. Transferred to RWF, 30 Mar 1866. Capt, 1879. ADC to Brig-Gen, Belfast District, 1880–1. ADC to Maj-Gen Cork Dist, Oct 1881–4. ADC to Brig-Gen Aldershot, Apr 1884–5. Maj, 21 Jun 1885. Assistant Military Secretary to GOC South Africa, Lt-Gen Henry D'Oyley Torrens, CB, (QV), 5 Nov 1885–22 Jan 1888. Hal Cadogan was posted to his company on joining 1 RWF in 1889, in Dilkusha, Lucknow. CO 1RWF, 2 Apr 1895–4 Mar 1896. Retired. M: Victoria Alma, d of Capt F. Sayer, RWF. She died at Muri, India, 1891 (see Hal Cadogan's letter of 26 Jul 1891.) In 1893, he married, secondly, Georgina Frances, d of Lt-Col D. C. Butts, Madras Engineers, and widow of Lt-Gen Sir H D'Oyley Torrens, KCB, KCMG, Governor of Malta 1888–9, his previous superior. D: Bath 24 Aug 1922.

GWYNNE, James Hugh, B: 6 Feb 1863, son of E. R. X. B. Gwynne of Llandetty, Brecon. Ed: Eton & RMC. Lt SWB Militia, July 1881. 2Lt 1RWF, 12 Nov 1884. Burma 1885–6, wounded, MID. Hazara, 1891. M: 26 Feb 1890, d of CO Cameronians. To 2RWF, Crete, 1897–8. Pekin, 1900 (MID). Brevet-Maj. Retired, 8 Aug 1906. D: riding accident, 5 Mar 1910.

HALL, William Charles, B: 10 May 1866. Ed: Wellington. Lt 1RWF, 4 Nov 1885. Hazara, 1891. Capt, 16 Sep 1895. To Reserve List, 1899. In Great Wat, CO 5 The King's Own (R Lancaster R). D: 27 Oct 1917.

HARDIE, Herbert Reginald, B: 7 Jan 1891. 2Lt 1RWF, 19 Jan 1912. Placed on half-pay 15 Sep 1915.

HARRIS-ST JOHN, Wilfred, B: 25 June 1878, son of C. E. Harris, JP, of Hook, Hants and Borough Court, Winchfield, Hants, barrister, and his wife Jessie, dau of Harris-St John, JP, of Westcourt, Finchampstead, Berks. His father took the additional name of St John 39 Mar 1907. Ed: Winchester. 2Lt 1RWF, 7 May 1898. Anglo-Boer War. Adjt 1RWF, Sep 1904–July 1905. Capt, 1 May 1906. Adjt 6 (Caerns & Anglesey) Bn RWF (TF), May 1910–May 1914. To 1RWF. Probably a company commander. Wounded, 20 Oct 1914, at Zonnebeke. GSO III, substantive Maj, 1 Sep 1915. Wounded & DSO 1918. M: 1910, Hilda, d of F. G. Chinnock of Dinorben Court, Fleet. Retired, 3 Dec 1919.

HAY, Archibald, B: 9 Aug 1872, son of Gen Sir R. J. Hay, KCB, Col Comdt RA. Ed: Charterhouse & RMC. 2Lt 2RWF, 13 Jul 1892. Crete 1897–8. Pekin, 1900. To 1RWF, South Africa 1901. Maj, 21 Aug 1911. In India with 2RWF, and commanded 2RWF for their return to UK and reunion with 1RWF in Malta in March 1914. CO 8 (Service) Bn RWF in Gallipoli and Mesopotamia. KiA, 3 Feb 1917 in Battle of Kut. His medals in Regimental Museum are unique being the only group to have Peking 1900 and the Queen's South Africa medals.

HIGGON, John Arthur, B: 12 Nov 1873, eldest son of John Higgon of Scolton, Pembrokeshire. Ed: Wellington and RMC. 2Lt 2 RWF, 10 Oct 1894. Lt, 7 Nov 1896. With 2 RWF Crete, 1897–8 and, after the suppression of the Boxers, appointed staff captain in Wei-Hai-Wei, 1902. Capt, 14 Mar 1803. Retired, 4 Dec 1909. Capt in the Pembrokeshire Yeomanry, 8 Mar 1910. M: 27 Jun 1900, Lurnine May, d of Hon H. Moses, a member of the Legislative Council of New South Wales (see also C. E. Bancroft above and Sir H. W. McMahon below). Maj in Pembrokeshire Yeomanry, he was attached to the Australian Infantry when KiA, 19 July 1916.

HINDSON, Richard Eldred, B: 17 Jul 1892, son of Rev J. H. Hindson, Bradwell Hall, Sandbach, Cheshire. Ed: Winchester. 2Lt 1RWF, 20 Sep 1911. Lt, 18 Dec 1912. POW, 22 Oct 1914 at Broodseinde, Ypres. Capt, 1 Oct 1915. Escaped several times, recaptured (MiD). Served Murmansk, 1919 (MiD twice). Maj, 26 Oct 1927. CO 2RWF in Hong Kong, 1 Jan 1935–1 Aug 1936 when he retired from the effects of being POW in the Great War. Secretary Flint & Denbigh TA Association 1937–42. Reserve of Officers War Office until 1957. D: 15 Sep 1966. He took the well-known photographs of officers and sergeants at Lyndhurst in Oct 1914, which is why he does not appear in them.

HOLMES, William George, B: 20 Aug 1892, son of Dr R. Holmes of Aberdeen. Ed: Gresham's, Holt and RMC. 2Lt 2RWF, 11 Oct 1911; Lt, 15 Feb 1914; Capt, 1 Oct 1915; Temp Maj 30 May 1916; A/Lt Col CO 1RWF 16 Sep 1916–18, in France, Belgium and Italy. Wounded twice. DSO and Bar; MiD four times. Brevet Maj 1 Jan 1918; Brevet Lt-Col 1 Jan 1919. After war reverted to adjt 1RWF. Waziristan 1919–21 and 1921–24. Sub Lt Col 22 Apr 1929; CO 2 E.Lancs Regt until 1933; GSO1 N. Ireland until 1935; Comd 8 Inf Bde until 1937. CB. Maj Gen 1938; Comd 42 E.Lancs Div with BEF in 1940. MiD twice. Lt Gen 1940; Comd 10 Corps during withdrawal to El Alamein 1942. Director-Gen of transport at War Office 1942–3; GOC 9Army (Levant) until 1945 when he retd. KBE, 1944. M: Yvonne, dau of Georges de Bourbon, 1930. Lived Santa Cruz, Arizona. D: Tucson, Arizona, 6 Jan 1969.

HOSKYNS, Edwyn Cecil Leigh, B: 22 Sep 1890, son of Leigh Hoskyns, BA, JP, barrister, of Cotefield, Banbury, Oxon. Ed: Eton. 2Lt 1RWF, 20 Sep 1911. KiA, 19 Oct 1914 near the Menin–Roulers road in 1st Battle of Ypres.

IGGULDEN, Herbert Augustus, B 26 Nov 1861, son of Rev W. H. Iggulden. Ed: Victoria College, Jersey. 2Lt Channel Islands Militia, 27 Mar 1880. Lt Derbyshire Regt, 28 Jan 1882. Capt, 1 May 1890. With Sherwood Foresters on Egyptian (1882) and Sikkim (1888) Expeditions. Tirah Expedition, 1897–8. Maj, 11 Jun 1902. Marched to Lhasa, Tibet, Nov 1904 with Younghusband. DAA & QMG 1 Div Aldershot, Nov 1905–May 1908. CO 1 RWF, 12 May 1908–12 May 1912. Succeeded by Hal Cadogan. Brevet-Col, 11 Aug 1909. AQMG India, 5 Oct 1912–10 Nov 1914. In Great War, Bde Comd, India. CIE, 1918. Retired. D: 8 May 1937.

JOHNSON, Robert Ingelow Bradshaw, B: 13 Nov 1874. Ed: St. Paul's School, Sydney and Sydney Univ. 2Lt Loyal N. Lancs R, 6 June 1896. To 2 RWF, 29 July 1896 in Malta. Crete 1897–8. Peking, 1900. To Meerut, India with 2RWF, 1902. Burma, 1909. Retired, 1913. In Great War company commander 8 (Service) Bn. CO Welsh Pioneer Bn in Mesopotamia. Wounded. In 1918, Bde Comd, France (DSO). Retired, 1919. Leased Manor House, Wroughton, Wilts and trained horses. Returned to Australia 1932. Killed at a level crossing in New Zealand, 16 Oct 1955. His son Col J. R. Johnson was CO 1RWF, 1951–4.

JONES, Stanley, b 26 Oct 1880, eldest son of Gen Sir H. S. Jones, KCB. Ed Cowley Coll, Oxford & Hanover. Spoke German, French, Hindustani & Hausa. 2Lt 1RWF 5 Jan 1901. Capt 21 Aug 1911. Coy Comd 1 RWF from 21 Aug 1911. Wounded 20 Oct 1914 at Broodseinde. KIA Festubert 16 May 1915.

JONES-VAUGHAN, Evan Nanney. B: 5 Sep 1885. Son of Maj-Gen H. T. Jones-Vaughan, JP, of Tyddyn, Rhydyclafdy, Pwllheli, Caernarfonshire. Ed: Wellington and RMC. 2Lt 2RWF 22 Feb 1905; Lt 4 Dec 1909; Capt 19 Apr 1913. To France with 2RWF. KiA, Neuve Chapelle, 26 Oct 1914.

KINGTON, William Miles, B: 25 April 1876, son of Col W. M. N. Kington, 4 Hussars. Ed: Glenalmond & RMC. 2Lt 2RWF, 5 Sep 1896. In Aglo-Boer War Bde Signals Officer and with Mounted Inf. DSO & MiD (4 times). Capt, 20 Apr 1906. Adjt TA, 1906–10. OC B Coy 1RWF, 1912 (from Hal Cadogan). KiA, 21 Oct at Broodseinde. M: 1908 Edith, d of F. W. Soames of Brynestyn, Wrexham & sister of F. E. Soames (RWF). Excellent cricketer, superb musician – conducted the massed bands at the Delhi Durbar in 1903.

LAWFORD, Sydney Turing Barlow. B: 16 Nov 1865, son of Thomas Acland Lawford. Ed: Wellington and RMC (same year as Douglas Haig). 2Lt RF, 1885. 2nd Boer War. Commandant Mounted Inf School, Longmoor. Comd Essex Inf Bde. Cmd 22nd Inf Bde, Sep 1914 including 1RWF at 1st Battle of Ypres. CB, 1915. Comd 41st Div on Western Front. KCB, 1918. GOC Kagire distruct (India) 1920–3, as Lt-Gen. Retd, 1926. M: May Somerville, one son, Peter, born 1923. In 1938 went to Florida, and later to Hollywood where his son was an actor. Peter later married Patricia, sister of the future President John F. Kennedy. Sir Sydney played the part of a general in the British Army in a Hollywood film, and took other minor parts. D: 15 Feb 1953.

LAYTON, Edward. B: 21 Mar 1857 (possibly 27 Nov 1851). 2Lt 1RWF from TSM 8th Hussars, 21 May 1887 after 10 years, 61 days in the ranks. Lt 2 July 1887; Adjt Ghazipur Volunteer Rifle Corps 6 May 18889–5 May 1894. On 20 Jun 1894 to 1 S.Staffs as Capt and Adjt in Anglo-Boer War. Adjt 2 W.Yorks, 30 Nov 1900–14 Aug 1901; DAQMG Natal. Retd 21 Mar 1905. MiD; DSO. Assistant to Col-i-C, Records at Lichfield. D: 15 Oct 1913.

LEIGHTON, Charles Arthur Baldwin Knyvett, B: 9 Nov 1854, son of Revd F. K. Leighton, DD, formerly fellow and warden of All Souls Coll, Oxford & canon of Westminster. 2Lt RWF, 12 Nov 1873. Capt, 1 Jan 1881. Maj, 21 Oct 1885. M: 17 Apr 1879, Agatha Georgina, d of Lt-Gen E. A. Somerset, CB. With 1RWF Lucknow. Hal Cadogan was in his company (letter 19 May 1889 refers). D: Naini Tal, North West Province, 18 May 1889.

LLOYD, George William David Bowen, B: 6 Nov 1866, son of C. Lloyd, JP, of Brunant, Carmarthenshire. Ed: Privately and at St Peter's Coll, Camb & RMC. 2Lt RWF, 11 Feb 1888, Capt, 8 May 1896. Adjt 3rd (Militia) Bn RWF, 15 Aug 1896–11 Mar 1901. Maj, 8 Aug 1896. In Anglo-Boer War was a special-service officer attached to 8th Bn Mounted Infantry. Hal Cadogan was preferred to him as CO 1RWF in May 1912. Retired, 18 Jun 1913. Recalled 1914. CO 11 (Service) Bn RWF, 23 Feb1915–23 Mar 1916 in France and Salonika. Invalided home. OBE. Retired, 1920. Married, 1891 Lilian, d of D. G. Lloyd Owen, JP, FRCS, Birmingham. Lived at Brunant and Harlech. JP. D: 16 Nov 1926.

LLOYD, Meyricke Entwistle, B: 13 May 1880, son of Henry Lloyd, JP, of Pitsford Hall, Northants, & Dolobran Isa, Montgomeryshire. Ed: Eton. 2Lt 3 (Militia) Bn, Northants Regt, 18 May 1899. 2Lt RWF, 30 Jun 1900. Capt, 11 Apr 1911. M: 1 Oct 1912. Serving with 3 (Res) Bn RWF in early 1914. Joined 1RWF at Lyndhurst, 19 Sep 1914. KiA, 23 Oct 1914 near Zonnebeke in 1st Battle of Ypres.

LOCK, John Lock, B: 15 July 1862. 2Lt RWF, 9 Sep 1882. Capt, 2 Apr 1891. Retired, 19 Jul 1899. 3rd (Militia) Bn RWF until Sep 1908. D: 20 Jan 1944.

LOVETT, Richard Gordon Beresford, B: 17 Apr 1870, 5th son of Revd Robert Lovett, rector of Caundle Bishop, Dorset. Ed: Sherborne. 2Lt 1RWF, 4 Mar 1891. Employed in Army Pay Dept, 15 Sep 1898–19 Sep 1899. Mortally wounded at Rooidam, 5 May 1900, Anglo-Boer War.

LYLE, Hugh Thomas, B: 24 Apr 1858, son of Revd John Lyle of Knocktarna, Coleraine, Co. Londonderry. Ed: Uppingham. 2Lt 2RWF, 22 Jan 1879. To 1RWF, 6 Aug 1880 in India. Lt, 13 Apr 1881. Capt, 6 Dec 1885. Burma, 1885–6, severely wounded. MiD, DSO, 25 Nov 1887. Married in India, 24 Jun 1886, Alice Fanny, dau of Sir Warren Hastings D'Oyly, ICS, 10th Bart, of Shottisham, Norfolk (their son, Maj Hugh D'Oyly Lyle, served RWF, 1914–33). To 2RWF in Malta, 6 Nov 1896. CO a Provisional Bn, 12 June–20 Aug 1900 for operations at Wittebergen, South Africa. Rejoined 1RWF in South Africa, 24 Aug 1900 as senior major. Fought at Friederichstadt and in Orange River Colony. MiD (twice). Brevet Lt-Col 29, Nov 1900. CO 2RWF, 21 Aug 1903–07. Brevet Col, 10 Apr 1905. Retired, 2 Nov 1907. In 1909 commanded E. Territorial Force Brigade. CO 8th Bn R Irish Rifles, Sep 1914–Sep 1915 and 17th Res Bn, Nov 1915–9 May 1918. CBE. Retired. DL Londonderry. D: Knocktarna, 24 Jan 1942, aged eighty-three.

McMAHON, Sir Horace Westropp, 5th Bart, B: 28 Oct 1863, son of Gen Sir Thomas McMahon, 3rd Bart. Lt 3 (Militia) Bn R Warwick R, Feb 1884. To 2RWF, 16 Dec 1885. Capt, 2 April 1895. Volunteered for Mounted Inf in Matabeleland 1896. Wounded, DSO & MID. With 2RWF in Crete, 1897–8. Maj, 8 Mar 1899. Anglo-Boer War on Mounted Inf Staff. Returned to 2RWF, 1901, Peking, commanded Legation Guard. Asst Comdt Mounted Inf School, Longmoor, 15 Jul 1905–28 Sep 1907, when he retired. M: 3 May 1911, Ellie d of Hon H. Moses (Member of Legislative Council NSW), widow of his old friend and brother officer Capt C. E. Bancroft (q.v.). In Great War, Lt-Col, raised 9 RWF. Failed medical, spent war on staff in France. OBE, French *Croix de Guerre*. D: 9 July 1932. His widow remained a close friend of Eve, Hal Cadogan's widow, for the rest of their lives.

MAINWARING, Rowland Broughton, B: 11 Sep 1850, son of Revd C. H. Mainwaring and his wife, d of Sir H. Delves Broughton, Bt, of Doddington Hall. Ed: Marlborough. 2Lt 2RWF, 30 Dec 1871. Ashanti 1873–4. Maj, 10 Oct 1885. To 1RWF Burma, 1885–6. Hazara, 1891. 2RWF, 1 Jul 1895. Crete, 1897–8. CMG. In Anglo-Boer War, Comdt Depot in South Africa. CO Depot, Wrexham. Retired, 20 Sep 1905. Wrote a history of RWF. Lived Bembridge, Isle of Wight. D: 22 Nov 1926.

MANTELL, Patrick Rivers, B: 28 Dec 1862, son of Col R. Mantell, Indian Med Service. Lt 1RWF,

20 Oct 1883. Burma, 1885–7. Hazara, 1891. Capt, 13 Jul 1892. Anglo-Boer War, DSO, MiD (twice). Maj, 26 Oct 1900. CO 2RWF, 21 Aug 1907–20 Aug 1911. Retired, 1912. D: 9 Jan 1936.

MARTIN, Claude, B: 5 Jan 1735 Lyons, France. Arrived in India aged seventeen. Captured by British at Pondicherry 1776. Later joined British East India Co. Lived in Lucknow and also served Nawabs of Avadh. Amassed a fortune trading in indigo the bulk of which he left to found schools in Lucknow, Calcutta and Lyons. Retired as major-general. Built the Palace of Constantia, now La Martiniere College, and a most elegant town house, later 'The Club', now a government building. D: Lucknow 13 Sept 1800. Buried in basement at Constantia … 'in order to prevent the building … being appropriated by the Mussalmans' [Sidney Hay, *Historic Lucknow*].

MILFORD, Charles Henry, B: 7 Jan 1853. 2Lt R. Glamorgan Militia 19 Nov 1873; Lt 1RWF 20 Nov 1875. To 1RWF in Calcutta 1883. Capt 10 Apr 1885. With 2RWF on march through north Wales 1892. Retd 23 Dec 1894. D: 26 Oct 1899. Memorial St Giles Church, Wrexham.

MINSHULL- FORD, John Randle, B: 12 May 1881. Ed: Haileybury & RMC. 2Lt 2RWF, 11 Aug 1900. Interpreter French. Adjt 4 (Denbigh) Bn RWF, TA 21 Nov 1912–16 Apr 1915. Brigade-Major, France, Jun–Oct 1915. CO 1RWF, 1 Oct 1915–3 Feb 1916. Brig-Gen, 1916–19. Wounded 4 times, DSO MC MiD (6 times). Bde Comd Rhine Army, Sept–Dec 1919. CO 4 S Staffords, Mar 1920–1. Brevet Col, Jul 1926. Bde Comd 5 Bde (Aldershot), 1930–2. ADC. Maj-Gen Comd 44 (Home Counties) Div, Jan 1932. CB. Retired, 1938. Col RWF, 26 Oct 1938–3 Mar 1942. Lt-Governor Guernsey, 1940 (escaped just before German occupation). M: Dorothy, d of Sir J. Harmood-Banner, Bart, MP, by whom he had a son and a daughter, Anne, (who married Lt-Col Lord Wynford, MBE, DL, RWF). D: 1 April 1948.

MONRO, Gen Sir Charles Monro, Bart, GCB, GCSI, GCMG, B: 15 Jun 1860. 2Lt Queens R. Regt, 1879. Malakand Field Force & Tirah Expeditionary Force. Anglo-Boer War, 1899–1900. Brevet Lt-Col. Comdt School of Musketry, Hythe 1903–07. Introduced concept of fire and movement and need for rapid, aimed fire. Maj-Gen GOC 2Div in BEF, 1914. Lt-Gen, Comd 1 Corps, Dec 1914. Gen, Comd 3rd Army, Jul 1915. CinC Mediterranean, Oct 1915. Successfully organised withdrawal from Gallipoli. Returned to France, 1st Army, Jan 1916. CinC India, Oct 1916. Baronet, 1921. Governor Gibraltar, 1923–8. Col Queens R. Regt. M: Mary, daughter of 2nd Lord O'Hagan. D: 1929.

MORRIS, Frederick, B: 20 Dec 1854, son of F. Morris, RN, 3rd son of Sir John Morris, 2nd Bart of Clasemont, Glam. Lt Warwickshire Militia, 23 Nov 1872. Lt 1RWF, 2 Dec 1874. Capt, 1 Jul 1884. M: 1884. Burma, 1885–7. Hazar,a 1891. Maj, 1 Jul 1891. Senior major 2RWF, 26 Jun 1896. Crete, 1897–8. Peking, 1900. OC A, C & E Coys, embarked HMS *Terrible* for relief of Tientsin, 16 Jun 1900. After landing at Taku, the train was derailed on 22 June and he was first member of RWF to be injured. Retired, 16 Jan 1901. Secretary to the Club of Western India, Poona. D: 3 Jan 1915 at Maymyo, Burma.

MOSTYN, Pyers George Joseph, B: 28 Sep 1893, son of G. T. B. Mostyn, formerly Lt HLI, and his wife, Augusta, dau of Capt W. G. Walmesley, formerly 17th Lancers. Ed: Stonyhurst and RMC. 2Lt 2RWF 22 Jan 1913; Lt 3 Jun 1914; Temp Capt 23 Mar 1915. MC, MiD twice. Wounded twice. Succeeded cousin as 11th Baron Mostyn of Talacre, Flintshire in 1917. Retd 1920. M: Margery 1927, dau of A. S. Marks of Sydney, New South Wales. D: Kenya 28 Feb 1937 as a result of a riding accident. Times obituary described him as 'one of the pioneers of flight to S. Africa'.

MOSTYN, The Hon Savage Lloyd, B: 27 Mar 1835, 3rd son of 2nd Lord Mostyn. 2Lt 1RWF, 13 May 1853. Crimea (Redan). Indian Mutiny. Maj, 29 Mar 1864. CO 2RWF, 1 Sep 1869–9 Aug 1880. Ashanti, 1873–4. CB, MiD (3 times). Comd 23rd Regtl Dist, 1880 –5. Maj-Gen, 1885. Retired, 1890. Col Devonshire Regt, 1907–9 Dec 1910. KCB. Colonel RWF, 1910–14. D: 2 Jun 1914.

NAYLOR, Rowland Edmund, B: 25 Apr 1894, fourth son of John and Magdalene Naylor, of Leighton Hall, Welshpool and Elmwood, Woolton, Liverpool. Ed: Eton (Cricket XI 1912 & 13 (capt)) and RMC. 2Lt 1RWF, 12 Aug 1914. Wounded near Kleythoek, Roulers–Menin road, 19 Oct 1914. Returned to 1RWF. KiA Festubert, 16 May 1916.

NORMAN, Compton, B: 7 Oct 1843. 2Lt RWF, 2 Sep 1862. Capt, 1 Jun 1874. Maj, 24 Dec, 1881. Adjt 2 (Vol) Bn RWF, 2 Jul 1883–14 Sep 1887. CO 1RWF, 2 April 1891–1 Apr 1895. Hazara, 1891. MiD. Retired, 1895. Father of Brig C. C. Norman, RWF.

NORMAN, Compton Cardew, B: 14 Dec 1877, son of Col C. Norman, RWF. Militia. 2Lt 1RWF, 4 Jan 1899. Anglo-Boer War 1899–1902. Wounded. Capt, 17 Nov 1906. Adjt 2RWF, April 1911–Oct 1913. Lt-Col CO 15 RWF, 19 Sep 1916. CO 7 DLI, 28 Jan 1918. CO 17 RWF, 5 Jul 1918. CO 53 Bn Welch Regt, 10 April 1919. CMG, DSO. CO 2RWF, 30 Oct 1920–12 May 1924. Comd 158 (RW) Inf Bde 1927–9. Comdt Nigeria Regt 1929–30. Inspector Gen RWAFF & KAR, 1930–6. Retired. CBE. D: 15 Feb 1955.

O'CONNOR, Luke, B: 21 Feb 1831 in Roscommon, one of six children. In 1839 the family emigrated to Canada. Parents & one sister died, family returned UK. Luke went to an uncle who owned shop in Boyle. Ran away & enlisted as a private in 1RWF, 1849. Corporal, May 1850. Sergeant, 1851. Colour Sergeant, 1854. Crimea. Wounded, saved Queen's Colour at Alma, VC & commissioned. Sebastopol, wounded again at Redan. VC from Queen Victoria in Hyde Park, June 1857. Served Indian Mutiny. Capt, 24 Aug 1858. Brevet-Maj, July 1872. With 2RWF in Ashanti 1873–4. Brevet Lt–Col, 1 Apr 1874. Maj, 19 Aug 1874 & Lt-Col, 21 Jun 1880, on becoming CO 2RWF. Brevet-Col, 19 Aug 1879. Half-pay, 21 Jun 1885. Col, 1886 and allowed a Distinguished Service Award. Retired, 2 Mar 1887, with honorary rank of major-general. CB, 1906. KCB, 1913. Col RWF, 3 June 1914–1 Feb 1915. D: 1 Feb 1915, HM King was represented at his requiem mass, and he was buried at St Mary's Cemetery, Kensal Green.

OWEN, Charles Samuel, B: 23 Jan 1879, son of G. H. Owen of Ymwlch Fawr, Carnarfonshire. Ed: Cheltenham & RMC. 2Lt 2RWF, 11 Feb 1899. Peking 1900, Capt, 17 Nov 1906, Adjt 2RWF, Oct 1913–Dec 1915. Maj, 1 Sep 1915. CO 6 Royal West Kent Regt, 17 Dec 1915–27 Nov 1916. Comd 39 Inf Bde, 28 Nov 1916–16 April 1919. DSO (1915), CMG (1918), MiD (8 times), *Croix de Guerre*. CO 1RWF 10 Sep 1921–10 Sep 1925. Waziristan & NW Frontier 1921 & 1922. Col, 20 Sep 1925. OiC Records, Shrewsbury, 18 Feb 1926–31 Oct 1927. Brig-Gen, Comd 159 (Welsh Border) Inf Bde (TA), 1 Nov 1927–1931. Retired. D: 28 Feb 1959.

PARKER, Edward Augustus, B: 16 Dec 1868. Enlisted, 1887. 1RWF. Hazara, 1891. RSM 1RWF, 25 Oct 1898. Anglo-Boer War, wounded, DCM & MiD. QM (Hon Lt) 1RWF, 20 April 1904. Hon Capt, 20 Apr 1914 (QM to HOSC when CO 1RWF). Camp Comdt HQ 7 Div (Maj-Gen T. Capper). Graded Staff Capt, 6 May 1915. OBE, MC, MiD. Adjt & QM Staff Coll, 3 Aug 1919. Hon Lt-Col. D: 18 Dec 1939.

PEPPÉ, Cyril Goldney Hawers, B: 30 Mar 1892. 2Lt 1RWF, 3 Sep1913. Lt, 26 Jul 1914. POW Zandvoorde, 30 Oct 1914. Capt & Temp Maj, 3 Mar 1916. Retired, 1922.

POOLE, Bryan Cudworth Halsted (née Davies-Cooke), B: 9 Nov 1892, son of B. Davies-Cooke, JP, of Marbury Hall, Whitchurch, Salop. Assumed name of Poole in 1907 in order to inherit Marbury Hall. Ed: Wellington & RMC. 2Lt 1RWF, 15 May 1913. Lt, 26 Feb1914. Capt, 8 Oct 1915. POW, 30 Oct 1914 at Zandvoorde. MiD, Feb 1915. Retired, May 1919. M: 11 Nov 1925.

REYNOLDS, Alfred Howard, B: 16 Nov 1877, son of Sir A. J. Reynolds, JP, of Ayot Bury, Welwyn, Herts (A Lt of City of London). Ed: Winchester & Magdelen Coll, Oxford. 2Lt 1RWF, 4

Jan 1899. Anglo-Boer War – galloper to Lt-Col Lyle (q.v.) who commanded mounted troops of Col Hicks' column. Then CO 1RWF (Colleton) gave him command of Mounted Inf Coy of 1 RWF. To 2RWF at Chakrata, India, 22 Jun 1903. On 21 Oct 2RWF began march to Agra, but Reynolds died at Meerut, 1 Nov 1904.

RICHARDS, Frank, B: 7 April 1883. An orphan, brought up by uncle and aunt in Monmouthshire. Coal miner 1890. Joined RWF, April 1901. Served 2RWF India and Burma, 1902–09, extended until 1912. Re-joined 2RWF and spent whole of First World War with them on the Western Front. DCM, MM. With the encouragement of Robert Graves he wrote *Old Soldiers Never Die*, 1933. It was an instant success. He then had published in 1936 *Old Soldier Sahib* about his service in India. M: Mary James November 1937, one daughter, Margaret (Holmes) born 1938. D: 26 August 1961.

RICHARDS, Henry Meredyth, B: 30 June 1870, son of R. M. Richards, JP, DL, of Caerynwch, Dolgellau. Ed: Winchester & RMC. 2Lt 2RWF, 11 Dec 1889. Capt, 24 Mar 1897. Crete, 1897–8. Peking, 1900. Retired, 8 Feb 1905. M: 1907. JP, DL & HS Merioneth, 1910. Temp Maj, 1914, with 26 (Service) Bn RWF. OBE, 1919. D: 28 Oct 1942.

RICKMAN, Graham Egerton, B: 10 May 1869, son of Lt-Gen W. Rickman, Barkham Manor, Wokingham and his wife Mary, d of Rt Hon Sir William Hayter Bt, PC, QC, MP, Judge Advocate General. Ed: Winchester & RMC. 2Lt 1RWF, 12 Feb 1890. Capt, 11 Jan 1899. Anglo-Boer War, MiD (twice). Retired, 3 May 1905. With 3 (Militia) Bn RWF in Great War. OBE. D: 19 Jan 1940.

ROBERTS, Sir Frederick S., VC, KG, KP, OM, GCB, GCSI, GCIE, VD, B: 30 Sep 1832. Ed: Eton, RMC & Hon East India Coy's Seminary Addiscombe. 2Lt Bengal Artillery, 1851. Indian Mutiny, 1857–8. VC. Abyssinia, 1868. QMG India, 1875. Maj-Gen, KCB, 1878 for victory over Afghans. Kabul, 1879. Kabul–Khandahar, 1880. GCB. C-in-C India, 1885–93. Baron, 1892. FM, 1895. C-in-C Ireland, 1895–99. Anglo-Boer War 1899–1900, Earl and KG. First Col of Irish Guards. Succeeded Wolseley as C-in-C of British Army, Jun 1901 until post abolished, Feb 1904. D: France, 14 Nov 1914.

ROTHERHAM, Henry, B: 21 Jul 1869, son of John Rotherham, JP, of Keresley Grange, Coventry. 2Lt 3 (Militia) Bn R Warwick R. 2Lt 2RWF, 10 Oct 1891. Crete, 1897–8. Capt, 16 Apr 1900. Peking, 1900. D: Keresley Grange, 28 Nov 1902 from disease contracted in China.

SCINDIA, Madho Roa, Madhavrao II, 5th Maharaja of Gwalior, B: 20 Oct 1876. Reigned 1886–1925 (Hal Cadogan attended his coronation, see letter dated 3 Dec 1894). Regency ended 1894. Served as colonel in China. Awarded China War Medal 1900–01. Provided hospital ship at his own expense. GCSI, 1895. GCVO, 1902. GCSt.J, 1911. GBE, 1917. D: 5 June 1925.

SKAIFE, Eric Ommanney, B: 18 Oct 1884, son of F. Skaife, Chichester (GP). Ed: Winchester & RMC. 2Lt 1RWF, 4 Nov 1903. Russian interpreter, 1908. Adjt 1RWF, 26 July 1911–25 July 1914. Capt, 18 Dec 1912. Probably second capt A Coy in Oct 1914. Wounded and POW on Menin–Roulers road, 19 Oct 1914. MiD. Learned both Welsh and Russian while POW. Maj, 4 Nov 1918. GSO2 WO, 1918–9. OBE. 2RWF Waziristan, 1919–21 &1921–4. MiD. CO 1RWF, 10 Sep 1929–18 May 1933. Brevet Col AAG Eastern Comd. Military Attaché Moscow, 1934–7. Comd 158 (RW) Inf Bde TA, 1937–41. Foreign Office, 1941–4. Hon Col 636(RW) Light Anti-Aircraft Regt RA TA, 1947–55. Col RWF, Feb 1948–Oct 1952. DL Merioneth. CB 1952. Knighted 1956. HS Merioneth, 1956. Member of the Druidic Order of the Gorsedd at National Eisteddfod. D: 2 Oct 1956.

SMITH, William Frank, B: 28 Jan 1870. 2Lt 1RWF, 21 Sep 1889. Hazara, 1891. Transferred to Indian Staff Corps, serving with 33rd Bengal Inf, 1895. Great War Lt-Col Indian Army, 21 Sep 1915. OBE, MiD. Col, 8 Aug 1920.

SMYTH-OSBOURNE, John Greville, B: 27 July 1886, son of J. Smyth-Osbourne, JP, DL, of Ash, Devon. Ed: Clifton & RMC. 2Lt Worcester Regt, 11 Apr 1906. Adjt, 23 Nov 1909–22 Nov 1912. Transferred Capt 1RWF, 28 Nov 1913. POW Broodseinde, 21 Oct 1914. MiD 1920 for escape attempts. Staff Capt then DAAG Western Comd, 14 May 1919–22 Jan 1922. M: 1923. Maj, 12 May 1924. GSO2 43 (Wessex) Div, 1 Apr 1925. Retired, 15 Dec 1927. JP, Kent, lived near Canterbury. D: 6 Aug 1979.

SNEAD-COX, Geoffrey Philip Joseph, B: 20 Feb 1895, son of John Snead-Cox of Boxwood Court, Hereford. Ed: Downside & RMC. 2Lt 1RWF, 17 Sep 1913. Served Malta and UK. French interpreter, 1914. KIA Broodseinde, 20 Oct 1914

SOAMES, Frederick Evelyn, B: 25 Feb 1891, third son of F. W. Soames of Bryn Estyn, Wrexham, and his wife, Julia, dau of H. West, QC of Co Dublin. Ed: Wellington and RMC. 2Lt 2RWF 19 Apr 1911. Lt 14 Nov 1911. Retd. Lived Bangor-on-Dee. In First World War served with 8th (Service) Bn RWF and Capt with 9th (Service) Bn in France. With MGC, Maj 1915. Gas casualty 1917. Invalided out. Took over family brewery which became Border Breweries. Director and Chairman. D: 14 Mar 1967. His sister, Edith, married Maj W. M. Kington, DSO, RWF, *qv*.

STOCKWELL, Clifton Inglis, B: 27 Sep 1879. Ed: Haileybury & RMC. 2Lt 2RWF, 11 Feb 1899. Capt, Jan 1907. Maj, 1 Sep 1915. Brigade-Major France, Aug 1915–Feb 1916. CO 1RWF, 4 Feb 1916–16 Sep 1916. Comd 164 Bde, 18 Sep 1916–31 Mar 1919. CB, CMG, DSO, MiD (9 times). Brig Comd Irish Comd, 1921–2. Comd 11 Bde Armadnagar, 1930–2. Retired. Recalled Second World War, Group Comd Shetlands, 1941–2. D: 4 Dec 1953. Father of Lt-Col N. C. Stockwell and grandfather of Maj M. J. C. Stockwell, both RWF. Cousin of Gen Sir Hugh Stockwell.

THOMAS, George Oliver, B: 19 Jan 1884, second son of G. E. Thomas of Calcutta. 2Lt 3rd (Militia) Bn RWF 19 Sep 1903; 2Lt 2RWF in India 25 Aug 1906; Lt 1 April 1911. Capt when KiA in France with 2RWF 26 Sep 1915.

THOROLD, Charles Cecil Harford, son of Sir John Thorold, 11th Bart, of Marston, Lincs. Ed: Eton. Lt 5 R Lancs Militia Bn, 15 May 1872. Lt RWF, 13 Jun 1874.Adjt 2 RWF, 1882–7. Adjt 29 (Vol) Bn, Sep 1887–Sep 1892. Maj, 16 July 1890. M: Sep 1883, Mary, d of Thomas Browning of Sale, Cheshire. CO 1RWF, 4 Mar 1896. D: KiA Colenso, 24 Feb 1900.

VYVYAN, William Geoffrey, B: 21 Jan 1876, son of Revd Herbert Vyvyan, rector of Withiel, Cornwall. Lt Falmouth Div, Submarine Miners RE (Militia), 26 May 1897. 2Lt 2RWF, 14 Jun 1899. Peking, 1900. M: Nov 1904. Capt, 1 Apr 1909. Adjt 5 (Flintshire) Bn RWF (TF), 2 Oct 1910–20 Oct 1913. To 1RWF, probably OC A Coy. D: (of wounds) 24 Oct 1914 after being captured two days earlier at Zonnebeke. Father of Lt-Col J. G. Vyvyan, Regimental Secretary RWF & grandfather of Capt A. G. Vyvyan, RWF.

WALFORD, John Ashton Henshaw, B: 4 Nov 1864, eldest son of J. H. N. Walford, JP, of Ruyton, Shropshire. 2Lt Welch Regt 9 Sep 1882. Transferred to 1RWF 11 Oct 1882. Burma 1886–87. Wounded, and invalided to UK. Retd 1890. Col British S. Africa Police, commanding southern defences, Mafeking 1900. DSO. D at sea en route home, 3 June 1903.

WALMSLEY, Alan, B: 29 Jan 1896, father barrister. Ed: RMC. 2 Lt 1RWF 12 Aug 1914. Wounded near Zonnebeke, 22 Oct 1914. Returned 1RWF. Fought gallantly at Festubert, at one moment commanding 1 RWF as a Lt. MC. MiD. Wounded again at Loos, Sep 1915. To half-pay because of wounds, Apr 1917. Retired, Dec 1922. D: 25 Nov 1968.

WEBBER, Raymond Sudeley, B: 16 Jun 1865, eldest son of Maj-Gen C. E. Webber, CB, RE, by his first wife, Hon Alice, dau of 2nd Baron Sudeley. Lt 4th (Militia) Bn, SWB 22 Jul 1882; Lt Dorset

Regt 23 May 1885; Lt 1RWF 18 Jul 1885. Burmah 1886–87. Invalided sick to India. With 2RWF in march through north Wales 1892. With Egyptian Army 12 Feb 1894–22 Feb 1898. With 12th Sudanese Bn under Kitchener on Dongola Expedition in 1896. MiD. Capt 1 Nov 1894. To 2RWF in Crete 1897–98. Rejoined 1RWF Nov 1899 in Anglo-Boer War. Wounded. Mi D. Brevet Maj 29 Nov 1900. ADC to Sir Leslie Rundle 1902. M: Geraldine, dau of Charles Magniac, MP, 1903. Retd 26 Aug 1905. During First World War served on Special Res of Irish Guards. Brevet Lt Col 3 June 1917. HM Hon Corps of Gentlemen at Arms 2 May 1914 until he resigned 1935.

WHITE, George Stuart, B. Portstewart, Londonderry, 1835. Ed: King WIlliam's College, Isle of Man and Bromsgrove School and RMC. 2Lt 27 (Inniskilling) Regt. Indian Mutiny. Second Afghan War, 1879 as 2iC of 92nd Regt (later Gordon Highlanders). VC. CiC India, 1893. Commanded garrison at Siege of Ladysmith, 1899–1900. Governor Gibraltar, 1900–04. Field Marshal, 1903. GCB, OM, GCSI, GCMG, GCIE, GCVO. M: Amelia Baly, daughter of Archdeacon of Calcutta. D: 1912.

WILLES, Charles Edward, B: 18 Jul 1870. Ed: Malvern & RMC. 2Lt 1RWF, 23 Apr 1890. Hazara, 1891. Capt, 22 Feb 1899. Adjt 2 (Vol) Bn RWF, Aug 1898–Aug 1903. Res of Officers, May 1905. CO 2 (Vol) Bn RWF, 26 Jul 1905–08. In CO 13 (Service) Bn RWF, Nov 1914–Sep 1915. AA& QMG until 1 Jun 1917. CO 3 (Garrison) Bn RWF till 1919. CMG. MiD twice. D: 4 Nov 1952. Uncle of Col J. E. T. Willes, Col RWF.

WILLIAMS, Shem, B: 29 Sep 1872. Served 23 years with 1RWF. LSGC Medal 1908. Sergeant Maj (RSM) 1RWF 1912–14. Wounded 26 Oct 1914. Commissioned Lt, 31 Jan 1915; Temp Capt 17 May 1915. Rejoined 1RWF, 28 May 1915. Wounded, 25 Sep 1915. Att to 3 (Res) Garrison Bn, then att to 3 Beds. Retd 6 May 1920.

WILLIAMSON, Robert Frederic, B: 29 Apr 1843, son of Lt-Col J. Williamson of Carrokeal, Mallow, Co Cork. 2Lt RWF, 8 Feb 1861. Adjt 2RWF, 12 Jun 1868–2 Sep 1870. Capt, 3 Sep 1870. Ashanti, 1873. Maj, 1 Jul 1881. Lt-Col, 9 Dec 1885. M: d of Gen Sir George Chesney, KCB, MP. Burma, 1885–7, MiD & Brevet Col. CO 2RWF in Galway, 2 Apr 1887 (Hal Cadogan's first CO). Swapped comd of battalions with Lt-Col E. S. Creek (q.v.). CO 1RWF (India), Jan 1890–2 Apr 1891. Comd 1 Bde during Hazara Expedition, 1891. CB, MiD. Retired, 23 Sep 1891. JP & HS Dorset 1911. D: 29 Oct 1938 aged ninety-five.

WODEHOUSE, Edmond, B: 25 Mar 1894, son of Rear-Admiral C. Wodehouse. Ed: Winchester & RMC. 2Lt 1RWF, 17 Sep 1913. Wounded & POW Zandvoorde, 30 Oct 1914. Capt, 1 Aug 1916. Waziristan, 1919–21. Maj, 1929. M: Persis Roper, 22 Aug 1935. CO 2RWF, 11 Aug 1939–14 Mar 1941. Comd Brig in Northumberland, Mar 1941–42. Military Attaché Dublin until 1945. CBE, 1948. Retired. Secretary Stewarts' Hospital, Dublin. D: 31 Dec 1959. Father of Maj A. J. Wodehouse, RWF.

WYNNE-EDWARDS, John Copner, B: 20 Nov 1890, son of Col T. A. Wynne-Edwards, VD, JP, DL, of Plas Nantglyn, Denbigh (CO 1st Vol Bn RWF from 1 Oct 1894 through its conversion to 4 RWF TF in 1908, until 3 Oct 1913). Ed: Cheltenham and Cambridge. 2Lt 2RWF 18 Jul 1911; Lt 16 May 1912; Capt 31 Oct 1914; Adjt 64 Trg Res Bn RWF 1917–18; Adjt 7 RWF (TF) 17 Mar 1920–30 Sep 1921; to Res of Offs 7 Jan 1922. M: 1916 Kathleen, dau of Capt C. J .C. Touzel, 3rd (Militia) Bn RWF. Recalled 1939. Maj 1940; local Lt-Col 1941; Quartering Officer NW Dist; Retd 1946. DL Denbighshire, 1947. D: 1967.

Appendix 2

Composition of an Infantry Battalion
BEF August–September 1914

Total Establishment
30 officers & 977 other ranks (ORs), total 1007.
56 horses, including 13 riding for senior officers.

Battalion Headquarters & HQ Company
5 Officers. CO (lieutenant-colonel), second-in-command (major), adjutant (captain/lieutenant), and two captains/lieutenants for 'general HQ duties'.
76 ORs. These included the regimental sergeant-major, who controlled the specialist sergeants including signals, transport, armourer, drummer, pioneer, cook, shoemaker, orderly-room clerk and quarter-master sergeant.

Signallers:
Corporal & 15 privates with bicycles. These also acted as runners. By 1915, a sergeant and 18 privates. There were 3 privates (sometimes 4) per company, remainder in the battalion HQ.

Machine Gun (MG) Section:
Lieutenant & 17 ORs, with 2 machine guns (Maxims or the new Vickers). Each machine gun section carried 3,500 rounds.

Snipers:
8 privates, or more if CO required them, operating in 2 man teams; one man with telescope/periscope and the other with SMLE rifle with a special sight.

Transport:
11 privates with 43 draught and pack horses.
6 ammo carts carried 32,000 rounds of rifle ammo.
3 wagons carried 2 machine guns and tools, and 8,000 rounds of reserve ammo.

Medical:
RAMC captain in Regimental Aid Post, with 2 orderlies & 16 stretcher bearers. A cart carried supplies and equipment.
RAMC corporal and 4 privates operated 2 water carts.

Rifle Companies:
4 rifle companies, each commanded by a captain, with a second in command (second captain), and 17 OR in coy HQ. Total company establishment: 6 officers and 221 ORs.

Platoons:
4 platoons in each rifle company, with 1 officer (lieutenant/2nd lieutenant) and 3 ORs in each platoon HQ. Total platoon establishment: 1 officer and 51 ORs

Sections:
4 sections in each platoon, each commanded by a corporal or lance corporal, with 11 privates.

Reinforcements:
1 officer and 100 ORs remained at the battalion's base. In France and Belgium, once the battalion was deployed there, these formed the battalion's first reinforcements.

Appendix 3

7 Division Operation Order N⁰· 19

5th Kil. On Ypres–Menin Road, 18th October 1914

Map 2.

1. The enemy occupies entrenched positions at Menin and Wervicq. He has a post with artillery at Gheluwe; aeroplanes located his battery at the 0 of 20 [^{1}/$_2$ mile] S. of Gheluwe with wagons 400 yards to the S.E. He has a second entrenched post at Kleythoek * (3 miles N. of Menin).

Our 3rd Cavalry Division is at Moorslede. One brigade will be at St. Pieter at 7 A.M. to-morrow to protect our left flank. Our III Army Corps is moving East and was about 2^1/$_2$ miles west of the River Deule (N.W. of Lille) this evening.

2. The present intention is to carry out an attack on Menin in three distinct phases as follows:-

> 1st phase an attack by the 22nd Infantry Brigade on the trenches at Kleythoek from the north.
> 2nd phase a combined attack by the 20th and 21st Infantry Brigades against Gheluwe.
> 3rd phase a combined attack by the division from Gheluwe and Kleythoek on Menin.

Orders for the 2nd and 3rd phases will be issued later.

3. 22nd Infantry Brigade and 54th Field Company R.E. will Rendezvous at Strooiboomhoek clearing Becelaere by 6 A.M. The attack on Kleythoek will be supported by the divisional artillery as follows:-

> (a) XIV. Heavy Artillery Brigade (less 1 battery) and 1 Heavy Battery (111th) from Kruiseecke to keep down artillery fire from Wervicq.
> (b) XXXV. Field Artillery Brigade and 1 Heavy Battery (112th) In position near Terhand but S.W. of Becelaere – Terhand – Gheluwe Road to support the attack of the 22nd Infantry Brigade.
> (c) XXII. Field Artillery Brigade in position near Terhand but N.E. of the same road to keep down artillery fire from Gheluwe.

The order for the advance of the 22nd Infantry Brigade will be issued by divisional headquarters.

When the trenches at Kleythoek have been captured the 22nd Infantry Brigade will re-form and reconnoitre for the attack on Menin.

55th Field Company R.E. will be attached to the 20th Infantry Brigade. The Northumberland Hussars will protect the left flank Of the 22nd Infantry Brigade and connect with the 3rd Cavalry Division. The Cyclist Company will be in divisional reserve at Poezelhoek.

4. The 20th and 21st Infantry Brigades will remain in concealment ready to advance near Kruiseecke and Terhand respectively.

5. Orders to the Field Ambulances will be issued by the A.D.M.S.

6. Refilling point for supplies will be at the Railway Station at Ypres. Supply Sections must be clear of their Brigade Areas by daylight. Baggage Sections will accompany Supply Sections as far as Hooge where they will park clear of the road.

6. Divisional headquarters will be at the **H** [³/₄ mile S.W. of Becelaere] of Poezelhoek after 7 A.M.

H. Montgomery, Colonel,
General Staff.

Issued at 8.30 P.M.

Appendix 4

1st Battalion, The Royal Welsh Fusiliers
Awards October–December 1914

DCM

9284   Sjt J. BLACKTIN

For gallant conduct and devotion to duty on 20th and 21st October 1914, in rescuing the wounded and attending on them under heavy shell and rifle fire and for the fine example shown by him to the stretcher-bearers. (1.4.15)

[Probably the captain of the successful battalion soccer XI, 1912–3 in Dorset.]

10582   Sjt Drummer H. CHAPMAN

For gallant conduct on 20th and 21st October 1914, in conveying ammunition to the firing line whilst exposed to heavy shell and rifle fire. (1.4.15)

[At Broodseinde crossroads, Zonnebeke.] Commissioned November 1914. KiA 15 May 1915.

10736 Pte F. JACOBS

For gallantry in assisting to rescue a wounded man. (1.4.15)

6891 Sjt E. J. SMITH

For gallant conduct on 19th October 1914, in assisting to rescue a wounded Officer whilst exposed to heavy rifle and shell fire. (1.4.15)

[Probably rescuing 2nd Lt Naylor, maybe his platoon commander]

MC

Captain (QM) E. A. PARKER, DCM.
(DCM awarded when he was RSM 1RWF in S Africa.)
In first list of MCs, Feb 1915.

MID

Lt-Col H. O. S. CADOGAN (twice)
Maj R. E. P. GABBETT
Capt R. V. BARKER
Capt E. O. SKAIFE
Lt A. E. C. T. DOONER

	Lt B. C. H. POOLE
Capt (QM)	E. A. PARKER, DCM
7975	Cpl R. FARMER
11463	Pte G. BEECH
11773	Pte S. A. BRITTON
9935	Pte J. BUTLER
10767	Pte A. T. DUNN
4418	Pte J. EVANS
11780	Pte A. E. FOREST
4870	Pte P. GOODE
4439	Pte E. A. W. LEWIS
4810	Pte J. O. MORTON
11787	Pte R. J. PHILLIPS
11670	Pte J. WHALIN

DCM Awarded to Sgt Tom Jones

Private Tom Jones, from Henllan, Denbighshire, survived 1st Ypres and was later awarded an excellent DCM while serving with 13th Bn RWF. The details, published in the *London Gazette,* dated 3 September, 1918, were as follows:

> 16960 Cpl (Acting Lance-Sergeant) T. I. Jones Royal Welsh Fusiliers (Henllan)
> For conspicuous gallantry and devotion to duty. During an attack, when his officer was wounded, this NCO took charge of the platoon, and captured a machine gun that was holding up the advance, led the men on and gained the objective. On another occasion, when in charge of a section, he received the surrender of a party of the enemy whom he had isolated in a shell-hole. Some of those who had given themselves up began to throw bombs, but Sergeant Jones promptly dispatched several of them and saved the section from heavy casualties. He then took charge of half the company and arranged his posts with great ability, and was largely instrumental in defeating an enemy counter attack the next morning. Throughout the operations he showed great coolness and presence of mind.

Tom Jones became an RSM, serving with the Royal Norfolk Regiment in the Second World War. In his eighties he was living with his daughter in Wrexham where, in 1979, he recounted his memories of service with the 1st Battalion, Royal Welsh Fusiliers in 1914.

Appendix 5

Roll of 1st Bn, The Royal Welsh Fusiliers Belgium, 10–31 October 1914

Produced from a careful study of all the surviving sources this roll details all the officers, ncos and men who served under the command of H. O. S. Cadogan between 6 and 31 October 1914. Other than decorations awarded during the course of the war or whether individuals died in captivity, no details of events which occurred after 31 October are shown.

PoW – prisoner of war
DoW – died of wounds
KiA – killed in action
n.d. – no date

Decorations
DSO – Distinguished Service Order
DCM – Distinguished Conduct Medal
MC – Military Cross
MM – Military Medal
MiD – Mentioned in Despatches
CdeG – *Croix de Guerre* (France / Belgium)
AVM – *Medaglia d'Argento al Valore Militare* (Italy)

Officers

Ackland-Allen, H.T., Lt, KiA 21.10.14
Alston, Ll.A.A., Lt, DSO, MC, MiD, wounded 21.10.14
Barchard, D.M., Lt, MiD, PoW 21.10.14
Barker, R.V., Capt, MiD, KiA 31.10.14
Barrow, E.E., Capt, from 3DCLI 29.10.14, PoW 30.10.14
Bingham, G.R.B., 2Lt, PoW 21.10.14
Brennan, J.H., Capt, from 3RWF, KiA 19.10.14
Burke, D.J.G., Capt, from 3DCLI 29.10.14, wounded 30.10.14
Cadogan, H.O.S., Lt-Col, MiD, KiA 30.10.14
Chance, G.O.deP., Lt, KiA 19.10.14
Courage, J.H., Lt, wounded PoW 21.10.14
Disney, J.H., Capt, MiD, from 3Essex 29.10.14, wounded n.d.
Dooner, A.E.C.T., A.Capt & Adj, MiD, KiA 30.10.14
Edye, C.V.deG., Lt, from 2DCLI 29.10.14, KiA 30.10.14

Egerton, R. leB., 2Lt, KiA 30.10.14
Evans, A.M.G., 2Lt, PoW 30.10.14
Evans, J.M.J., Lt, MC, MiD, CdeG, wounded 21.10.14
Gabbett, R.E.P., Maj, MiD, wounded 19.10.14
Harris-St John, W., Capt, DSO, wounded 19.10.14
Hindson, R.E., Lt, MiD, PoW 21.10.14
Hoskyns, E.C.L., Lt, KiA 20.10.14
Jones, S., Capt, wounded 19.10.14
Kington, W.M., Capt, DSO, KiA, 20.10.14
Lloyd, M.E., Capt, from 3RWF, KiA 20.10.14
Naylor, R.E., 2Lt, wounded 19.10.14
Parker, E.A., Hon Capt & QM, MC, DCM, MiD*, CdeG
Peppé, C.G.H., Lt, PoW 20.10.14
Poole, B.C.H., Lt, MiD, PoW 30.10.14
Proctor, E., 2Lt, wounded 26.10.14
Pymm, N., 2Lt, from 3DCLI 29.10.14, missing 30.10.14
Robertson, H., Capt, RAMC, PoW 30.10.14

Skaife, E.O., Capt, MiD, wounded and PoW 19.10.14
Smythe-Osbourne, J.G., Capt, PoW 21.10.14
Snead-Cox, G.P.J., 2Lt, KiA 20.10.14
Vincent, W., Capt, from 3DCLI 29.10.14, KiA 30.10.14
Vyvyan, W.G., Capt, wounded PoW 20.10.14 died 24.10.14
Walmsley, A., 2Lt, MC, MiD, wounded 21.10.14
Wodehouse, E., 2Lt, sick 15.10.14 rejoined, wounded PoW 30.10.14

Other ranks

10392, Pte Adderley, J.L., PoW 20.10.14
4219, L.Cpl Ainsworth, H.
10100, L.Cpl Ainsworth, T., PoW 21.10.14
5517, C.Sgt Albutt, W.H., wounded 20.10.14
10959, Pte Alderson, T., wounded 19.10.14
10774, Pte Aldows, F.
9934, Pte Aldridge, P.A, PoW 30.10.14
6703, Pte Alexander, W., sick 20.10.14
10859, Pte Allcock, J.H., wounded 21.10.14
6256, Cpl Allen, E.T., PoW 26.10.14
99691, Pte Allen, I., DCM, missing 20.10.14
10208, Pte Allen, J., wounded 31.10.14
10879, Pte Allen, J., sick 23.10.14
6324, L.Sgt Allen, R.E., PoW 30.10.14
10544, L.Cpl Allen, T., wounded 21.10.14
6170, C.Sgt Allen, W.P., PoW 30.10.14
4402, Sgt Ambrose, H.G. DoW, 29.11.14
4849, Pte Andrews, J.
4893, Pte Ankers, S.
6208, Pte Ansell, C.
6292, Pte Ansell, J.
10816, Pte Arbon, W.
11243, L.Cpl Arbuthnot, C., wounded 31.10.14
11095, L.Cpl Arbuthnot, F., PoW 30.10.14
11124, L.Cpl Arbuthnot, W.H., PoW 13.10.14
5569, Pte Arkell, W.
9884, Pte Arnshaw, G.
10743, L.Cpl Ashford, C., PoW 30.10.14
10030, Pte Ashford, S.
10830, Pte Ashford, S.
4553, Pte Ashley, W., PoW 20.10.14
10251, Pte Askew, J.H.
6151, Pte Astbury, S., wounded 20.10.14
9233, Pte Astill, S.
8060, Sgt Astill, T., PoW 20.10.14
9175, Sgt Aston, L., PoW 30.10.14
5011, Pte Atkins, E.
9919, Pte Attwell, F.R. DoW, 20.10.14
9679, Sgt Austin, E., wounded 19.10.14
6570, Sgt Austin, J.R.
10256, Pte Austin, G., wounded 27.10.14
10546, Dvr, Bacon, J.H.B.
8321, Pte Badams, J., PoW 21.10.14
4704, L.Cpl Bailey, J.W., PoW 19.10.14
7765, Pte Baird, J., PoW 30.10.14
7644, Pte Baker, G.H.
11015, L.Cpl Baker, R.A.C.
10337, Pte Baker, W., KiA 21.10.14

6084, Pte Baldwin, A., wounded 21.10.14
4594, Pte Baldwin, E., DoW 8.11.14
11259, Pte Ballinger, W., wounded 23.10.14
6735, Pte Bancroft, R., PoW 20.10.14
10810, Pte Band, A., wounded 22.10.14
9930, Pte Banner, J., KiA 21.10.14
10421, L.Cpl Banning, A.H., KiA 21.10.14
6535, Pte Barber, S., PoW 30.10.14
9925, Pte Barge, H, wounded 20.10.14
10346, Bndm Barker, J.J., wounded 30.10.14
9990, Pte Barkley, W.
10425, Pte Barlow, E.
9016, Pte Barnett, H., KiA 19.10.14
9018, L.Cpl Barnett, P., PoW 30.10.14, died 25.2.15
9674, Pte Barrett, F.E., wounded 20.10.14
9791, Pte Barter, J.T. KiA 30.10.14
10908, Pte Bartlett, J.
5858, Pte Barton, C.E., PoW 20.10.14
11043, Pte Bastian, A., PoW 20.10.14
9984, Pte Bateman, W.
7788, Pte Bates, F.
7665, L.Sgt Bath, H., PoW 30.10.14
10836, Pte Bayliss, B.J., KiA 30.10.14
8234, Pte Bayliss, W.
10471, L.Sgt Beale, W.E., KiA 30.10.14
9739, Pte Beard, J., sick 23.10.14
8635, Sgt Beardmore, H., PoW 20.10.14
9926, Pte Beasley, R.L., PoW 30.10.14
10779, Pte Beckett, A.
8404, Pte Beckett, H., PoW 20.10.1914
8535, Pte Beddowes, J.
8869, Pte Beddows, C.
8220, L.Cpl Beech, W.
10969, L.Cpl Beeks, J., KiA 30.10.14
8936, Pte Bell, F.
10234, Pte Bell, G., PoW 20.10.14
11049, Pte Bellis, A., PoW 20.10.14
10812, Pte Bench, C., KiA 21.10.14
6776, Pte Bennett, R.H., wounded 19.10.14
10931, Pte Bennett, T.
10291, Pte Berridge, A., KiA 30.10.14
9338, Pte Bessant, T.
10673, Pte Betts, G.A., PoW 20.10.14
10869, Pte Bingham, J.
8134, Pte Black, F.
10675, Cpl Blacktin, G.H., PoW 30.10.14
9284, L.Cpl Blacktin, J.
6479, Cpl Blake, E., KiA 19.10.14
10683, Pte Blake, W., KiA 30.10.14
11201, Pte Blakemore, J., PoW 20.10.14
7829, Pte Bloomfield, W., KiA 30.10.14
9878, Sgt Bloxham, H., wounded 23.10.14
6118, Sgt Bluck, T., wounded 30.10.14
10134, Pte Blythen, C.B., PoW 20.10.14
10394, Pte Boden, R
5920, Pte Bolton, G.H., KiA 21.10.14
10775, L.Cpl Bosley, E.C., wounded 30.10.14
9360, Sgt Boswell, W., PoW 30.10.14
6428, Pte Bott, B., sick 24.10.14

7723, Sgt Boundy, C.E., KiA 20.10.14

3337, Bnm, Bowden, E., PoW 30.10.14

10890, Pte Bowen, W., PoW 30.10.14

5019, Pte Bowen, W.J.

10800, Pte Bowhay, H.H.

7649, Pte Bowler, J., KiA 30.10.14

9334, Pte Bowler, W.

10302, Cpl Box, E., PoW 20.10.14

9182, Pte Brace, F.

9939, Sgt Brackley, T., KiA 30.10.14

10782, Pte Bradley, J., PoW 20.10.14

9905, Pte Bradwick, W.

3820, Pte Bradshaw, F., KiA 22.11.14

10753, Pte Bradshaw, L.R., KiA 20.10.14

9009, Pte Brain, H.

4850, Pte Bramwell, A.

6094, Pte Bramwell, A., DCM, PoW 19.10.14

10714, Pte Brazier, A., wounded 21.10.14

5934, Pte Breeze, R.O., PoW 30.10.14

11008, Pte Brennan, A., wounded 27.10.14

8415, Cpl Brereton, M.

10881, Pte Brett, G., PoW 30.10.14

6802, Cpl Brewster, H.

10363, Pte Bridgeman, W.H., wounded 21.10.14

7736, Pte Bridgewater, A.T.

10499, Pte Bridgewater, W., wounded 21.10.14

7818, Pte Brierley, F.

7199, L.Cpl Broadfield, C.

9790, Pte Broadhurst, E., wounded died as PoW 30.10.14

10814, Pte Bromley, H., PoW 30.10.14

10308, Cpl Brooks, H., PoW 30.10.14

10387, Pte Brooks, W., PoW 30.10.14

9853, Pte Broome, W.F., PoW 30.10.14

9259, Pte Broomhall, R.

10045, Pte Broomhall, W.C., MM

8361, Pte Brophy, J.

10825, Pte Brotherton, S., DoW 19.10.14

5757, Pte Brown, A.

10974, Pte Brown, C., wounded 23.10.14

6438, Pte Brown, G., missing

10804, Cpl Brown, H, wounded 30.10.14

7947, Pte Brown, J.

8160, Pte Brown, J., KiA 30.10.14

9715, Pte Brown, J., PoW 20.10.14

7861, Dvr, Brown, S.

10116, Pte Brown, S., wounded 23.10.14

10004, Pte Brown, T., sick 15.10.14

10759, Pte Bull, W., wounded 24.10.14

8480, Pte Bullivant, G.

11096, Pte Bunce, W., KiA 30.10.14

10542, Pte Bunney, T.J., wounded 20.10.14, DoW 1.11.14

10489, Pte Burke, L., PoW 20.10.14

10899, Pte Burnell J. wounded 22.10.14

8351, Pte Bustin, C., MM

7985, Pte Bustin, R.

Pte Butler, F., unconfirmed

7728, Sgt.Cook, Butler, J., MC, DCM

9935, Pte Butler, J., MiD, wounded 30.10.14

5986, Pte Butterworth, J., wounded 25.10.14

9000, Pte Buxton, A., PoW

8145, L.Cpl Buxton, J.

7293, L.Sgt Byles, W., wounded 19.10.14

9087, Pte Caddick, D.

11063, Pte Cadman, S., wounded 27.10.14

5603, Pte Callaghan, D., 19.10.14

10438, Pte Cambridge, J.H.

10863, Pte Cameron, J., wounded 29.10.14

6359, Pte Candy, W.T.

10318, Pte Cannon, H.

10927, Pte Capelin, M., DCM

10188, Pte Carpenter, F., PoW 10.10.14

10838, Pte Carpenter, R.S., DoW 19.10.14

11339, Pte Carpenter, R.W., PoW 13.10.14

6135, Pte Carroll, F., KiA 30.10.14

11178, Pte Carroll, M.

7146, Pte Carter, E., wounded 29.10.14

5873, Pte Carter, W.

9896, Pte Carvell, J.

9924, Sgt Cashmore, J.W.G.

8347, Pte Cassidy, G., PoW 30.10.14

11430, Cpl Casson, O., wounded 20.10.14

8407, Pte Caulfield, J., wounded 27.10.14

6336, L.Cpl Chantler, T., sick 15.10.14

5879, Pte Chapman, F.W., PoW 21.10.14

10582, Sgt.Drum, Chapman, H.F., DCM

10954, Pte Chapman, J.

9298, L.Cpl Chappell, C.

10561, Pte Chard, P., wounded 27.10.14

10151, Pte Charney, B., wounded 19.10.14

10472, Pte Cheers, S., wounded 20.10.14

8199, Pte Chesters, C.

10724, Pte Chickett (also Checkett), F.E.A., KiA 30.10.14

9763, Pte Chillcott, H., wounded 20.10.14

6707, L.Cpl Christy, A., MiD, MM

5975, Pte Chugg, John

10564, L.Cpl Claffey, B., PoW 30.10.14

10599, Pte Claffey, W., PoW 20.10.14

10322, L.Cpl Clancey, H.G., wounded 30.10.14

10970, Pte Clancy, D., PoW 30.10.14, killed 22.3.16

6253, L.Sgt Clarke, A.H., KiA 30.10.14

9816, Pte Clarke, C.A., KiA 20.10.14

10245, Pte Clarke, C.T.,

9370, L.Cpl Clarke, F.W., KiA, 27.10.14

10799, Pte Clarke, H., PoW 20.10.14, died

4805, Pte Clarke, T.G., PoW 20.10.14

9287, L.Cpl Clarke, W., wounded 25.10.14

10336, Pte Clarke, W., PoW 30.10.14

7686, Pte Clarke, W.G.

10321, Pte Clulow, W., sick 15.10.14

10334, Pte Clewley, A.F., PoW 30.10.14

10435, Pte Coates, J., wounded 21.10.14

5914, Pte Codeman, S.H., sick 15.10.14

10856, Pte Cody, J., wounded 31.10.14

8304, Pte Cole, W., PoW 20.10.14, DoW 23.10.1914

11208, Pte Coles, F.J., KiA 21.10.14

11254, Pte Coley, T., missing 30.10.14
10478, Pte Colledge, P., wounded 21.10.14
7010, Pte Collier, G., KiA 30.10.14
8430, Pte Collins, A., PoW 30.10.14
10444, Pte Collins, A., PoW 30.10.14
6282, Pte Coltman, F.J.
8184, Pte Condrey, C.
8280, Pte Condrey, J.F.
11074, Pte Constance, S., PoW 30.10.14
7043, Pte Cook, F.
9908, Pte Cook, H., PoW 20.10.14
10849, Pte Cook, H.
7756, Pte Cook, J.A., PoW 30.10.14
7762, Pte Cook, R.
10294, Pte Cook, W.M., KiA 20.10.14
10405, Pte Cooper, C.L., DoW 31.10.14
10713, L.Cpl Cooper, E., PoW 20.10.14
6260, Pte Cornes, W.H., KiA 30.10.14
10191, Cpl Cornish, F., PoW 30.10.14, died 26.1.15
8536, Pte Cornwall, R.
8276, Pte Costello, F., KiA 7.11.14
10847, Cpl Cotter, W.J., KiA 21.10.14
10239, Pte Cotterill, W.
2251, RQMS, Cottrill, J., DSO, DCM, MiD
11025, Pte Coulson, T., PoW 30.10.14
10297, Pte Coulson, W.
7163, Pte Coulthard, J., KiA 21.10.14
10978, Pte Cowen, J., wounded 23.10.14
10101, Pte Crabb, W.
10219, Pte Craddock, C., PoW 30.10.14
7184, Pte Craven, F., PoW 30.10.14
8284, CQMS, Craven, S., KiA 30.10.14
10038, Pte Crawford, J., PoW 30.10.14
8808, Pte Craythorne, F.
7857, Sgt Craythorne, L.E., sick 15.10.14
7954, L.Sgt Crockett, M.
9880, Pte Crook, F., PoW 30.10.14
10985, Pte Crooks, F.
3238, Pte Cross, J., PoW 30.10.14
10577, Pte Crossley, J.
5261, Pte Cuel, H.S., KiA 30.10.14
10281, Pte Cullen, J., PoW 21.10.14
3877, Pte Cullen, S.
7911, Pte Curragh, J.H., PoW 30.10.14
9736, Pte Currens, H.H., PoW 30.10.14
7269, Pte Curtis, C.J., PoW 20.10.14
10833, Pte Curtis, C.H., PoW 20.10.14
10469, Pte Dacies, G.H., PoW n.d.
6551, Pte Dakin, H.
8322, Pte Dalley, J.E., KiA 21.10.14
11041, Pte Daniels, A.R.
9753, L.Cpl Daniels, I., PoW 20.10.14
7737, L.Cpl Dann, F., PoW 30.10.14
10315, Pte Dare, A., missing 30.10.14
10913, Pte Darkin, A., sick 28.10.14
10140, Pte Darlington, F., PoW 30.10.14
10669, Pte Darran, G.F., PoW 20.10.14
8409, L.Sgt Davenport, A., KiA 7.11.14
9734, Pte Davey, J.

6045, Cpl Davies, A., wounded 19.10.14
7162, Pte Davies, A.
10488, Pte Davies, A., PoW 30.10.14 died
10798, Pte Davies, A., PoW 19.10.14.
10840, Pte Davies, A., KiA 31.10.14
10936, Pte Davies, A., KiA 30.10.14
5951, Pte Davies, A., PoW 20.10.14
10953, Pte Davies, C., sick 15.10.14
5739, Pte Davies, D., PoW 30.10.14
4632, Pte Davies, D.D.
4675, Pte Davies, E., DoW 6.11.14
5154, Pte Davies, G., unconfirmed
9329, Sgt Davies, G.
10757, Pte Davies, G., PoW 30.10.14
10469, Pte Davies, G.H.
6382, Pte Davies, H., sick 15.10.14
10482, L.Cpl Davies, H., sick 28.10.14
7987, Pte Davies, J., missing 30.10.14 rejoined
9917, Pte Davies, J.
10356, Pte Davies, J.
10507, Pte Davies, J.
10872, Pte Davies, J., KiA 20.10.14
10885, Pte Davies, J., PoW 30.10.14
11134, Pte Davies, J., missing 30.10.14 rejoined
11174, Pte Davies, J., PoW 20.10.14
8608, Pte Davies, J.G.
6698, Pte Davies, J.W.
11139, Pte Davies, J.W., KiA 14.10.14
11099, Pte Davies, L., PoW 20.10.14
3837, Pte Davies, O.E.
7129, L.Sgt Davies, R.H., wounded 30.10.14
4873, Pte Davies, R.
4815, Pte Davies, R.W.
3733, Pte Davies, R.
10758, L.Cpl Davies, S.G.
5750, Pte Davies, T. KiA 30.10.14
6749, Pte Davies, T.
10808, L.Cpl Davies, T., wounded 19.10.14
10903, Pte Davies, T., PoW 20.10.14
9960, Pte Davies, T.C., PoW 20.10.14
4474, Pte Davies, T.J.
4920, L.Cpl Davies, W.
4225, Pte Davies, W.A.
10409, Pte Davies, W.A., missing 30.10.14 rejoined
5804, Pte Davies, W., wounded 25.10.14
6040, Pte Davies, W., KiA 30.10.14
11100, Pte Davison, J., PoW 30.10.14.
5061, Pte Day, A., PoW 30.10.14
9178, Pte Day, F.
10942, Pte Day, R.H
5289, Pte Dean, T.D., KiA 20.10.14
9142, Cpl Dellenty, R.
9311, Sgt Dempsey, J., wounded 19.10.14
10971, Pte Desmond, J., wounded 24.10.14
10395, Pte Deville, T., sick 15.10.14, missing 30.10.14 rejoined
4546, Pte Dexter, E., missing 30.10.14 rejoined
7235, Pte Diamond, F.
10572, Pte Dier, R.S., KiA 19.10.14

11033, L.Cpl Dinning, R.C., PoW 20.10.14
6360, Pte Dobbins, W.F., wounded 30.10.14
4499, Pte Dobson, T., wounded 28.10.14
7110, Pte Dodd, T. D.N,
10393, L.Cpl Dolphin, J., PoW 30.10.14
10987, Pte Donegan, W.
8460, Pte Dooley, W.
6894, Pte Double, A.J.
4379, Pte Doubler, M., wounded 19.10.14
11058, L.Cpl Dowling, W.
7014, Pte Dowling, G.
9866, Pte Dowling, J.
5253, CQMS, Down, A.J., MiD, wounded 25.10.14
8751, Sgt Down, S., unconfirmed
10535, Pte Downes, A., PoW 30.10.14
9274, L.Cpl Downes, H.
10817, Pte Downey, H.
9271, Sgt Downs, H., unconfirmed
10130, Pte Draycott, T., missing 30.10.14 rejoined
6693, Pte Drinkwater, H.
6150, Pte Driver, A., wounded 23.10.14
11109, Pte Duckers, G.
6650, Pte Duckers, T.W.
11017, Pte Duckworth, J, PoW 30.10.14
4466, Pte Dugdale, T.
4325, Pte Dumphy, E., PoW 19.10.14
6334, Pte Dunleavy, J., missing 30.10.14 rejoined
10786, Pte Dunn, A.T., MiD, PoW 30.10.14
10141, Pte Dunne, A., sick 27.10.14
9331, Pte Dyson, G.H., wounded 26.10.14
9729, Pte Dyson, G.
6188, Pte Eaton, C., PoW 30.10.14
6345, Pte Eavers, F.
9004, Pte Eccles, J.W.
8196, Cpl Edge, E., MM, PoW 30.10.14
8370, L.Cpl Edkins, A.V.
9860, Pte Edmunds, J.
9897, Pte Edmunds, W.
4943, Pte Edwards, A., unconfirmed
8408, Pte Edwards, D., KiA 30.10.14
6753, Cpl Edwards, H., MiD, wounded 24.10.14
10614, Pte Edwards, H., PoW 19.10.14
11253, Pte Edwards, H.
5665, Pte Edwards, J, wounded 13.10.14
7717, Pte Edwards, J.
3971, Pte Edwards, R.W., KiA 30.10.14
10820, Pte Edwards, T., PoW 20.10.14
10935, Pte Edwards, T.
5500, Pte Edwards, W., wounded 21.10.14
9980, Pte Elliot, W.T., wounded 30.10.14
6660, Pte Ellis, H., sick 26.10.14
10005, Pte Ellis, J.
8486, Pte Ellis, R.
8421, Pte Ellis, W.
8201, Pte Ellson, F.
6913, Pte Elston, J.
9694, Sgt Evans, A., MiD, CdeG, missing 19.10.14 rejoined
11004, Pte Evans, A., PoW 20.10.14

9986, Pte Evans, C., PoW 30.10.14
7793, Bnds, Evans, F.W., unconfirmed
3696, Pte Evans, G., PoW 30.10.14
6176, Pte Evans, G., PoW 30.10.14
10203, Pte Evans, H.
10375, Sgt Evans, H., PoW 30.10.14
4708, Pte Evans, J.D., PoW 30.10.14
6510, Pte Evans, R., PoW 20.10.14
9071, Sgt Evans, R., DCM, OStG
11227, Pte Evans, W.
9886, Pte Everitt (also Everett), F.
10415, Pte Everitt, H.
10173, Pte Everton, A., PoW 30.10.14
10032, Pte Eyton, J., PoW 20.10.14
8265, Pte Fallon, J. KiA 30.10.14
8311, Pte Fawcett, W., KiA 30.10.14
6145, Cpl Ferguson, G., PoW 30.10.14
5997, L.Cpl Fermalon, W.
7083, Pte Fern, W., KiA 30.10.14
5386, Pte Ferriday, T.
10313, Pte Field, J., PoW 30.10.14
6720, L.Cpl Fieldhouse, S. PoW 20.10.14
10734, Pte Filler, F., PoW 30.10.14
10581, Pte Filsell, A., KiA 30.10.14
2815, Pte Fisher, T.
8718, Pte Fisher, W.O., PoW n.d.
3867, Pte Fitzgerald, D., PoW 20.10.14
10397, Dvr, Fitzgibbons, J.B.C. (also C.J.B.)
10143, Pte Fitzpatrick, F., KiA 20.10.14
10596, Pte Flannaghan, R.
6183, Pte Fletcher, T., KiA 30.10.14
6112, Pte Flynn, P.
4635, Pte Flynn, W., PoW 30.10.14
10609, L.Cpl Fogg, C.
8071, Pte Fogg, J.
10962, Pte Forsyth, J., PoW 20.10.14
5580, L.Cpl Fountains, L., PoW 30.10.14
9668, Pte Fowler, G., wounded 19.10.14
10424, Pte Fox, H., missing 30.10.14 rejoined
4634, Pte Fox, M.A., KiA 19.10.14
10604, Sgt Frampton, H.
10731, Pte Francis, T.
10818, Pte Franklin, F., wounded 30.10.14
10150, Pte Fraser, W., PoW 20.10.14
9964, Pte French, W., PoW 19.10.14
10120, Pte Frett, J.E., PoW 30.10.14
4170, Pte Fry, A., missing 30.10.14 rejoined
9788, Pte Fry, R.E.
6747, Pte Fuller, M., wounded 31.10.14
10742, Pte Furber, J., PoW 30.10.14
7714, L.Cpl Gallagher, J., wounded 21.10.14
10708, L.Cpl Gamsby, J., wounded 21.10.14
6374, Pte Gape, D., KiA 30.10.14
10860, Pte Gardner, R.F., wounded 21.10.14
10385, Pte Garner, G., wounded 30.10.14
9895, Pte Garrett, A., KiA 30.10.14
9404, L.Cpl Garrett, E., unconfirmed
9997, Pte Gee, O.
7023, Cpl George, G.F., KiA 24.10.14

10638, Pte Gerrard, A., wounded 24.10.14
10433, Pte Gibbard, G., KiA 21.10.14
10381, Pte Gibbons, B.
9904, L.Cpl Gilderthorpe, L., PoW 20.10.14
6782, Pte Gill, J., MM
6788, Pte Gilligan, R.
9892, Pte, Gladwyn, G., DCM, AVMil
11241, Pte Glynn, N., PoW 20.10.14
4228, Pte Godwin, W., KiA 20.10.14
11142, Pte Gooding, S., PoW 20.10.14
10310, Cpl Goodman, W.T., PoW 20.10.14
10690, Pte Goodman, W.
10149, Pte Goodyear, F., wounded 20.10.14
7121, Pte Gordon, J.J.B.
8377, Sgt Gorham, W., PoW 20.10.14
9780, Pte Gorman, P.W., PoW 20.10.14
11087, Pte Gough, P.
9959, Pte Gowers, C., PoW 20.10.14
9861, Pte Green, F., wounded 20.10.14
5963, Pte Green, F.E., KiA 21.10.14
10876, Pte Green, J., PoW 30.10.14
5384, Pte Green, J., PoW 30.10.14
6413, L.Cpl Greenway, F.W.F., missing 30.10.14 rejoined
2595, L.Cpl Grey (also Gray), T., PoW 20.10.14
10884, Pte Griffin, A.P., wounded 21.10.14
10699, Pte Griffin, E.P., wounded 26.10.14
9691, L.Cpl Griffin, J., PoW 30.10.14
10464, Pte Griffin, W.
10382, Pte Griffiths, E.
10916, Pte Griffiths, G., wounded 30.10.14
8425, Pte Griffiths, J., wounded 30.10.14
10740, Pte Griffiths, J., wounded 20.10.14
11001, Pte Griffiths, J., PoW 20.10.14
5914, Pte Griffiths, W., KiA 30.10.14
10083, Pte Grinehart, R., wounded 19.10.14
9380, Bd, Grist, S.
8776, Pte Grundy, F.
8946, Dvr, Gueran, W.
10941, Pte Gurney, C., PoW 30.10.14
9918, Pte Gwenhall, P., died PoW 30.10.14 died 15.12.14
6334, Pte Habberley, T.H.
9898, Pte Hall, G.
11180, Pte Hall, T., missing 30.10.14 rejoined
9772, Pte Hanks, R., PoW 30.10.14
8413, Sgt, Hannon, T., MC, DCM, MiD*, CdeG
9988, Pte Harding, J., wounded 19.10.14
5892, Pte Harnes, T., KiA 30.10.14
9868, Pte Harris, G., wounded 21.10.14
9967, Pte Harris, W., missing 30.10.14 rejoined
6213, Sgt Harrod, R., KiA 21.10.14
11003, Pte Harwood, A., PoW 21.10.14
6393, Pte Hasprey, T., wounded 24.10.14
10087, L.Cpl Hawkins, T., KiA 21.10.14
8169, Pte Haynes, H.
3993, Pte Hayward, S., wounded 30.10.14
6553, Pte Haywood (also Hayward), C.
4483, Pte Hazell, G., unverified

5870, Pte Headington, J.T.
10651, Pte Heafield, F.
8046, Pte Healey, T.
10633, Pte Healey, W., wounded 30.10.14
6721, Sgt Healy, D.J., KiA 21.10.14
9835, Pte Heard, J., wounded, PoW 30.10.14
8062, Pte Hearne, J., PoW 30.10.14
7200, Pte Heath, J.
10868, Pte Hemming, T., KiA 30.10.14
11000, Pte Henderson, D.
10160, Cpl Henderson, W.A., MC, AVMil
10485, Dvr, Henebury (also Henebery), J., PoW 20.10.14
10940, Pte Hennessey (also Hennessy), C., KiA 30.10.14
5919, Pte Henry, R., KiA 30.10.14
10526, Pte Hewer, A.
9212, Cpl Hewer, P., PoW 30.10.14
9771, Pte Hewitt, T.
10745, Pte Higgins, T.
6078, Pte Higginson, F., missing 30.10.14
9906, Pte Hill, R., PoW 30.10.14
10218, Pte Hill, E.S., wounded 19.10.14
8357, Pte Hill, T.
10423, Pte Hill, T., KiA 30.10.14
10643, Pte Hill, T., wounded 19.10.14
5861, Pte Hill, W., KiA 20.10.14
9745, Pte Hillett, W.F., KiA 30.10.14
9414, Pte Hillier, W.
10342, Cpl Hinton, W.A., wounded 30.10.14
10417, Pte Hiscock, C., KiA 30.10.14
8296, Pte Hitchen (also Hitchin), F.
6014, L.Cpl Hobson, A., KiA 30.10.14
9815, Pte Hodgette, F., PoW 30.10.14
10327, L.Cpl Hodgkinson, W., PoW 20.10.14
10630, L.Sgt Hodson, W., wounded 30.10.14
10676, Pte Hogan, J., wounded 23.10.14
6424, Pte Hogan, W., KiA 27.11.14
6761, Cpl Holden, C., wounded 14.10.14
7923, Sgt Holden, W.S., KiA 21.10.14
10598, Pte Holder, P., PoW 30.10.14
10257, Pte Holderness, H., PoW 30.10.14
5505, Pte Holland, T., wounded 30.10.14
5985, Pte Holmes, H., MM, wounded 30.10.14
6143, Pte Honeybourne, H., KiA 30.10.14
10357, Pte Hook, N.C., PoW 20.10.14
10351, Pte Hooper, G., missing 20.10.14 rejoined
11036, Pte Hooper, H.J., KiA 19.10.14
4905, Pte Hooson, D., KiA 20.10.14
10994, Pte Hopkins, I., wounded 28.10.14
7775, Pte Hopkins, J.
8208, Pte Hopkins, W., sick 15.10.14 rejoined, missing 21.10.14 rejoined
10866, Pte Horn, F.J., wounded 19.10.14
11023, L.Cpl Horn, W., wounded 23.10.14
8671, Pte Horton, A.
9744, Pte Horton, T., PoW 30.10.14
9696, Pte Horton, T.
10965, Pte Hoskins, A., wounded 19.10.14

6080, Pte Hoskins, J., KiA 28.10.14
10504, Sgt Howell, A.E., PoW 20.10.14
10205, Sgt Howell, H., wounded 20.10.14
10339, Pte Howells, G.F.
10103, Pte Hughes, E., wounded 30.10.14
10253, Pte Hughes, E.G., wounded 21.10.14
10575, Pte Hughes, F., PoW 30.10.14
7130, Pte Hughes, H., wounded 30.10.14
7288, Pte Hughes, J.
11128, Pte Hughes, J.
10027, Pte Hughes, M.H., KiA 19.10.14
3555, Pte Hughes, P., PoW 30.10.14
6981, Pte Hughes, R.
5819, Pte Hughes, R.
4414, Pte Hughes, W., sick 15.10.14
6773, Pte Hulbert, T.
9973, Pte Humphries, A.T., CdeG
7880, Pte Humphries (also Humphreys), H.
10735, Pte Humphries, T., PoW 30.10.14
10832, Pte Humphries, T., PoW 20.10.14
10252, Sgt Hunt, A., PoW 30.10.14
10763, Pte Hunt, A., KiA 20.10.14
8736, Dvr, Hutchins, W., wounded 27.10.14
10483, Dvr, Hutchinson, J., missing 20.10.14
6783, Pte Hutchinson, T.
10679, Pte Hyde, W.
9923, Pte Inston, W., PoW 30.10.14
9103, Pte Jackson, J., wounded PoW 30.10.14
9817, Pte Jackson, J., wounded missing 19.10.14
10354, L.Cpl Jackson, J.J., PoW 30.10.14
11215, Pte Jackson, J., wounded 19.10.14
10736, Pte Jacobs, F., DCM, wounded 21.10.14
6292, Pte James, E.G., DCM, MStG, wounded 30.10.14
10190, Pte James, J.
6751, Pte James, T.
8128, Pte James, W.
5093, Pte James, W.
10703, Pte Jankinson, J., wounded 19.10.14
9891, Pte Jays, J.
10304, Pte Jeal, R.D., KiA 20.10.14
4980, Pte Jeffries, T., missing 30.10.14 rejoined
6892, Pte Jeffreys, T.
11007, Pte Jenkins, J., PoW 30.10.14
6465, Pte Jenkins, W., wounded 30.10.14
4280, L.Cpl Jennings, W.
8126, L.Cpl Joesbury, S.
6571, C.Sgt Johns, S.B., commissioned 16.10.14 SWB
10413, Pte Johnson, A.
10431, Pte Johnson, H.
5966, Pte Johnson, P., KiA 30.10.14
4802, Pte Jones, A., wounded 21.10.14
7122, Pte Jones, A.W., PoW 30.10.14
10015, Pte Jones, C., PoW 20.10.14
11175, Pte Jones, C., PoW 30.10.14
10761, Pte Jones, C.H., PoW 20.10.14
10960, Pte Jones, D., KiA 30.10.14
5875, Pte Jones, D.M.
10410, Pte Jones, D.P.
10110, Pte Jones, D.R., wounded 21.10.14

11027, Pte Jones, E.
5915, Pte Jones, E., KiA 30.10.14
6830, Pte Jones, E.
8483, Pte Jones, E.
10434, Pte Jones, E., KiA 21.10.14
10487, Pte Jones, E., sick 15.10.14 rejoined, missing 30.10.14 rejoined
11136, Pte Jones, E., missing 13.10.14 rejoined
10924, Pte Jones, E.G., wounded 31.10.14
7180, L.Cpl Jones, F., wounded 30.10.14
6591, Cpl Jones, G.
7049, Pte Jones, G., KiA 30.10.14
6024, Pte Jones, G.R.
6365, Pte Jones, H.
6764, Pte Jones, H.
9928, Pte Jones, H.
10168, Pte Jones, H.
10283, Cpl Jones, H.
10003, Pte Jones, I., wounded 21.10.14
11126, Pte Jones, I., KiA 30.10.14
7959, Pte Jones, J
5648, Pte Jones, J.
7893, Pte Jones, J.
7959, Pte Jones, J., missing 13.10.14 rejoined
9250, Pte Jones, J.
8580, Pte Jones, J.C.
10287, Pte Jones, J., PoW 21.10.14
10479, Pte Jones, J.R., PoW 30.10.14
10878, Pte Jones, J., PoW 30.10.14
5097, Pte Jones, J.
5915, Pte Jones, J., KiA 30.10.14
6258, Pte Jones, J., PoW 21.10.14
4345, Pte Jones, J.D., KiA 19.10.14
4142, Pte Jones, L.
9527, Pte Jones, O.T., PoW 30.10.14
2737, Pte Jones, R.
8986, Pte Jones, R.
10494, Pte Jones, R., PoW 21.10.14
4522, Pte Jones, R., KiA 30.10.14
5825, Pte Jones, R., wounded 30.10.14
5152, Pte Jones, R.
10040, Pte Jones, R.E., PoW 21.10.14
10467, Pte Jones, R.E., PoW 30.10.14
11050, Pte Jones, R.J., PoW 20.10.14
8489, Pte Jones, T.
9498, Pte Jones, T.
5268, Pte Jones, T.
6487, Pte Jones, W.
7988, Pte Jones, W.
9827, Pte Jones, W.
9833, Pte Jones, W.
9945, Pte Jones, W.
10039, Pte Jones, W.
10174, Pte Jones, W.
10553, Pte Jones, W., PoW 20.10.14
4569, Pte Jones, W., wounded 30.10.14
6766, L.Cpl Jones, W.G., KiA 19.10.14
8340, Pte Jones, W.H.
5869, Pte Jones, W.J., wounded 20.10.14

5826, Pte Joyce, M.

8316, Cpl Jukes, A.G.S. Died, 2.11.14

11002, Pte Kane, J., KiA 30.10.14

6263, Cpl Katherine (also Katherines), G., PoW 19.10.14

10819, Pte Keating, P., wounded 30.10.14

10246, Pte Keefe, A., KiA 20.10.14

10973, Pte Kellaway, G.H., KiA 20.10.14

4301, Pte Kelly, F., KiA 19.10.14

10928, Pte Kelly (also Cutts), G.E., KiA 20.10.14

5611, Pte Kelly, J., wounded 19.10.14

10781, Pte Kelly, J.F., wounded 21.10.14

10069, Pte Keneally, J., wounded 27.10.14

7878, Pte Kenny, A.P., PoW n.d.

11219, L.Cpl Kensitt, J., PoW 30.10.14

10379, Sgt Kerry, A.E., PoW 30.10.14

6034, Pte Kilminster, W.

10380, Pte Kinchin, F., PoW 20.10.14

10851, Pte King, F.E., PoW 30.10.14

9789, CQMS, Kirby, J., MiD

7759, L.Cpl Knight, A.P., PoW n.d.

10883, Pte Knight, J., PoW 20.10.14

9697, Pte Knowles, J.

7940, Pte Kyte, T.

10508, Pte Laing, D.J.

6232, Pte Lakin, J.F., PoW 30.10.14

10640, Pte Lambourne, C., KiA 30.10.14

9785, Pte Lampitt, C., PoW 21.10.14

10792, Pte Lane, C.W.P., PoW 21.10.14

7871, Cpl Lane, G

10727, Pte Lane, J., KiA 20.10.14

10770, Pte Large, S., KiA 30.10.14

10841, Pte Larner, E.F., KiA 20.10.14

8106, Pte Latham, W.

10189, Pte Lavender, A., wounded 19.10.14

4691, Pte Law, A.J., KiA 20.10.14

9359, Dvr, Lawes, F., PoW 30.10.14

10795, Pte Lawrence, G.

9947, Pte Lawton, J.

10909, Pte Leach, G.H., PoW 30.10.14

8444, Pte Leader, J.

4288, Pte Leaver, W.

11371, Pte Leaves, J.

10760, Pte Lediard, C, missing 30.10.14 rejoined

8905, Pte Lee, A.

3876, Pte Lee, D.

4119, Pte Lee, F.

7261, Pte Lee, J.

10746, L.Cpl Lee, L.P., KiA 19.10.14

10449, Pte Lee, M.

10929, Pte Leeke, E.

9995, Pte Leishman, A., wounded 31.10.14

7050, Pte Lekman, J.

6089, Pte Lennon, S., wounded 19.10.14

5015, Pte Lenton, J.

7849, L.Cpl Lester, S.

4288, Pte Lever, W.

11117, L.Cpl Lewis, A., PoW 20.10.14

10702, L.Cpl Lewis, A.W., KiA 30.10.14

9348, Pte Lewis, C.

10938, Pte Lewis, C.V., PoW n.d.

6162, Pte Lewis, D.

10719, Pte Lewis, E., PoW 30.10.14

8257, Pte Lewis, G.

10805, Pte Lewis, G., PoW 30.10.14

10064, Pte Lewis, H., PoW n.d.

5972, Pte Lewis, J., wounded 24.10.14

10369, Pte Lewis, P.L., PoW 30.10.14

5606, Pte Lewis, R.

10715, Pte Lewis, R.S., KiA 30.10.14

10266, Pte Lewis, T., PoW 30.10.14

4439, Pte Lewis, T.W.

10066, Pte Lewis, W.J.

3944, Pte Lewis, W.H.

4091, Pte Lilley, H.

4710, Pte Lily-Green, J., PoW 30.10.14

5576, Pte Limbrick, J.

6746, Pte Lindon, E.

4462, Pte Linegar, H.

7900, Pte Little, W.

6820, Pte Littler, A.E.

9017, Bd, Llewellyn, H., PoW 30.10.14

10752, Pte Llewellyn, W.T., PoW 30.10.14

3960, Pte Lloyd, A.J., PoW n.d.

9444, L.Cpl Lloyd, D.O.

10451, Pte Lloyd, E., KiA 20.10.14

11072, Pte Lloyd, G.N., wounded 21.10.14

5777, Pte Lloyd, H., KiA 30.10.14

4530, Pte Lloyd, R.

8899, Pte Lockley, W.

10476, Pte Loftus, A.E.

5332, Pte Long, A.

10730, Pte Long, J., KiA 19.10.14

8283, Sgt Lord, S.B., MSM, MiD

6429, Pte Lovatt, J.

8431, Pte Lovatt, J.

5213, Pte Lovell, A.

8875, Pte Lowe, G.

11135, Pte Lowe, W.

6332, Pte Lowndes, W., wounded 31.10.14

3952, Pte Lucas, P., PoW

7134, Pte Lucas, W.

8365, Pte Luke, R., PoW 30.10.14

11170, Pte Lyle, B.G., wounded 30.10.14

5207, Pte Lyle, F.

6541, Cpl Lynch, C., PoW 30.10.14

10988, Pte Lynch, M., PoW 20.10.14

7609, Pte Lyth, E.

5075, Pte Macey, J.

4894, Pte Madden, J.

10605, Pte Madden, J.

9748, L.Cpl, Maddocks, W.H.

10963, Pte Maddox, D., KiA 30.10.14

9985, Pte Madeley, R., PoW 30.10.14

11059, Pte Madine, W.

2637, Pte Mahoney, W.

10332, Pte Malins, T.W.

10803, Pte Maloney, J., PoW 30.10.14

4434, Pte Manley, W.

6437, Pte Manning, E., PoW 30.10.14

10870, Pte Manning, W.R.

5600, Pte Mannion, W

5188, L.Cpl Marchant, W.H., wounded 19.10.14

5379, Pte Marsden, G.

4509, Pte Marsh, J., KiA 30.10.14

9989, Pte Marston, C., KiA 19.10.14

10576, Pte Martell, H.W, PoW 30.10.14 died

5169, Sgt Martin, A., KiA 19.10.14

10979, Cpl Martin, E., PoW 21.10.14

6019, Pte Martin, H.J.

5255, Pte Martin, J.

10907, Pte Martin, R.

11094, L.Cpl Maskell, A.

11447, Pte Mason, J.

8217, Pte Mason, N., PoW 21.10.14

4342, Pte Mason, T.

5862, Pte Masters, H.

4082, Pte Masters, J.H.

6691, Pte Matthews, E.

5002, Pte Matthews, F.

11183, Pte Matthews, J.

11193, Pte Matthews, J.R.

7732, L.Cpl Matthews, L.

6709, Pte Matthews, S.

6563, Pte Matthews, T., KiA 30.10.14

4285, Pte Maxfield, J., sick 20.10.14

9693, L.Sgt Maycock, H.

10671, L.Cpl Mayne, C., missing 21.10.14

3832, Pte McCarthy, J.

6844, Pte McCarthy, W., PoW 30.10.14

6220, Pte McCarthy, W.

10420, Pte McDade, C., sick 23.10.14

5254, Pte McDermott, J.

10934, Pte McDermott, J., PoW 30.10.14

4496, Pte McDermott, T.

6229, Pte McDonald, S.S.

8307, Pte McElroy, W.

10660, Pte McGarth, J., KiA 20.10.14

6620, Pte McIndoe, J., PoW 30.10.14

10487, L.Cpl McInstry, H.

10694, Pte McKenzie, A., PoW n.d.

6547, L.Sgt McKinley, C.

5536, Sgt McKinley, W., wounded 19.10.14

4743, Pte McLeary, A.

5117, Pte McLeod, R.

10250, Pte McLoughlin, T., PoW 19.10.14

7198, Sgt McNamara, G.

6100, Pte McQuilliam, G.

5025, Pte McSherry, F.

6874, Pte Meakin (also Meaking), T., PoW 30.10.14

8941, Pte Medhurst, A., PoW 30.10.14

5194, Pte Medway, W.

10725, Pte Meehan, T, missing 30.10.14 rejoined

6075, Pte Melia, A.

4444, Pte Melia, A., KiA 27.8.14

11143, Pte Merchant, T.G., DoW 27.10.14

6288, Pte Meredith, E., KiA 30.10.14

12394, Pte Merriman, E.

4356, Bd, Meston, F, PoW 30.10.14

6848, Pte Middleton, F.

10412, Pte Miles, G.

5482, Pte Miles, N., KiA 20.10.14

10360, Bd Sgt Millard, J., KiA 30.10.14

4451, L.Cpl Miller, T.

11184, Pte Mills, W.C., PoW 20.10.14

3407, Pte Millward, D.

9912, Pte Millward, E., KiA 20.10.14

10932, Pte Milner, S.

6000, Pte Minogue, S., wounded 24.10.14

4293, L.Cpl Mitchell, E.

6157, A.Cpl Mitchell, J.H., KiA 30.10.14

6194, Pte Mitchell, W.

4549, Pte Moon, G.

10317, Pte Moore, A., wounded 20.10.14

4081, Pte Moore, H.

7190, Pte Moore, P.

4376, Pte Moran, J.

10682, Pte Moran, T., KiA 20.10.14

9295, Bd, Moreland, G., PoW 30.10.14

8968, Pte Moreton, F., wounded 19.10.14

10744, Pte Morgan, A., PoW 20.10.14

6508, Pte Morgan, B.

5582, Pte Morgan, D.

9961, Pte Morgan, D.

10180, Pte Morgan, D.O., KiA 20.10.14

6286, Pte Morgan, E. KiA, 30.10.14

10776, Pte Morgan, G., KiA 20.10.14

10158, Pte Morgan, R., KiA 20.10.14

6726, Pte Morgan, T., wounded 21.10.14

8176, Pte Morgan, T.

10862, Pte Morgan, T., PoW 21.10.14

11162, Pte Morgan, T.

6372, Pte Morgan, W., PoW 21.10.14

6072, Pte Morris, C.

6082, Pte Morris, E., PoW 30.10.14

5736, Pte Morris, E.J.

5946, Pte Morris, E.

10801, Pte Morris, E., KiA 30.10.14

7885, Pte Morris, F.

8516, Pte Morris, H.

6933, Pte Morris, J.

4672, Pte Morris, J.

5970, Pte Morris, J., wounded 23.10.14

10374, L.Cpl Morris, S., wounded 21.10.14

10925, Pte Morris, S.T., missing 30.10.14 rejoined

8306, Pte Morris, W.

10748, Pte Morris, W., sick 15.10.14

4013, Pte Morrison, C.D.

11223, Pte Morrison, E., PoW 30.10.14

4810, Pte Morton, J.O. MiD

9783, L.Cpl Mosedale, J.T., wounded 19.10.14

10278, Bd, Moysey, A.E., PoW 20.10.14

11176, Pte Mullard, S., PoW 30.10.14

10492, Pte Mullins, H., PoW 20.10.14

4692, Pte Mullock, F.

10326, Dvr Mulvaney, A.W.

10298, Pte Munday, R., PoW 30.10.14

5232, Cpl Munions, J.

11344, Pte Murphy, A.

8139, L.Cpl Murphy, J.

4653, Pte Murphy, M.

4426, Pte Murray, J.

9818, Pte Musson, E., missing 20.10.14 rejoined

11052, Pte Myddleton, T.

10895, L.Cpl Nabbs, F.G., PoW 20.10.14

4638, Pte Nash, E.H.

6005, Pte Nash, J., KiA 30.10.14

7824, Pte NcCann, N.

4644, Pte Neagle, J., PoW 30.10.14

6644, Sgt Neal, E.

10068, Pte Neal, H.

9322, Dvr Neal, J.H., wounded 31.10.14

8753, Dvr Neal, W.

10865, Pte Neil, W. MiD

10854, Pte Newbold, F., PoW 30.10.14

10501, Pte Newing, R.H., PoW 30.10.14

10815, Pte Newland, H., PoW 30.10.14

11216, Pte Newland, J., KiA 30.10.14

6181, Pte Newman, J.

8637, Sgt Newman, W.

10547, Pte Newton, J., missing 30.10.14 rejoined

10113, Pte Nicholls, G.A., PoW 20.10.14

10723, Pte Nicholas, H.

10223, Pte Nicholas, T., missing 20.10.14 rejoined

4984, Pte Nield, A.

4515, Pte Nind, W.J.

11157, Pte Noble, J., PoW 19.10.14

7144, Cpl Nolan, T.

10446, Sgt Norman, F.

11252, Pte Norris, E.A., PoW n.d.

10200, Pte O'Brien, D., missing 30.10.14 rejoined

11242, Pte O'Brien, R., sick 15.10.14 rejoined

10698, Pte O'Brien, T., PoW 30.10.14

8438, Pte O'Gara, G.

11203, Pte O'Grady, D.

6230, Pte Oakwell, W., PoW 30.10.14

9728, Pte Oliver, G.

10490, Pte Oliver, G., wounded 19.10.14

10784, Pte Olley, J., missing 20.10.14

10096, L.Cpl Onions, F., wounded 25.10.14

5986, Cpl Orton, J.

10468, Pte Osborne, A., wounded 19.10.14

10944, Pte Osborne, F., sick 15.10.14 rejoined missing 30.10.14

10187, Sgt Osborne, W., wounded 19.10.14

10192, Pte Osborne, W., wounded 19.10.14 rejoined, PoW 30.10.14

10946, Pte Osborne, W., wounded 19.10.14

4463, Pte O'Shea, J., wounded 19.10.14

7822, Pte Ostle, W., wounded 21.10.14

6147, Pte Otterson, F., missing 30.10.14 rejoined

7202, Pte Owen, T.

7865, Pte Owens, R.

10377, Pte Page, A.O., PoW 30.10.14

10268, Pte Page, G., PoW 21.10.14

6328, L.Cpl Page, S.T., PoW 30.10.14

10737, Pte Page, W., wounded 20.10.14

9008, A.Sgt Paget, J.

9684, Pte Painter, B., wounded 30.10.14

8157, Pte Palmer, A., PoW 30.10.14

6713, Pte Palmer, E., PoW 30.10.14

11103, Pte Palmer, L.C., KiA 20.10.14

5358, Pte Palmer, W.G., sick 15.10.14

10693, Pte Parfitt, W., PoW 30.10.14

9367, Pte, Parker, E., wounded 21.10.14

2762, Pte Parker, J., KiA 20.10.14

10399, Pte Parkes, E.

6710, Pte Parkes, G.

10538, L.Cpl Parkhouse, W., wounded 19.10.14

10904, Pte Parkman, G., PoW 20.10.14

10741, Pte Parnell, H., wounded 24.10.14

8896, Sgt Parry, A.E., wounded 20.10.14

11195, Pte Parry, E.

10590, Pte Parry, H., PoW 20.10.14

4916, Pte Parry, J., PoW 30.10.14

9808, Pte Parry, J.

2012, Pte Parry, J.M.

9700, Pte Parry, R.

11137, Pte Parry, R., missing 30.10.14 rejoined

11030, Pte Parry, W., KiA 30.10.14

10551, L.Cpl Parson, F.H.

8741, Pte Parsons, E.

8203, Pte Parsons, F

11245, Pte Parsons, W., PoW 20.10.14

9819, Pte Passmore, F., PoW 20.10.14

10007, Pte Patrick, A.

10615, Pte Paul, W.J., KiA 20.10.14

11119, Pte Payne, E., PoW 20.10.14

4746, Pte Pearce, E., wounded 19.10.14

10777, Pte Pearce, F., DCM

10235, Pte Pearce, T., wounded 20.10.14

10918, Pte Penlington, B.

10871, Pte Penn, J., wounded 19.10.14

10958, Pte Penn, M., deserter, executed 22.4.15

10131, Pte Penney, W.J., KiA 19.10.14

6003, Pte Peploe, W., KiA 30.10.14

10289, Pte Pepper, C., wounded 24.10.14

9774, Pte Percival, T., PoW 20.10.14

7742, Pte Perry, S.

10891, Pte Perry, W., PoW 30.10.14

7233, Pte Peters, E.T.

10183, Pte Peters, E.A., PoW 20.10.14

7038, Pte Peters, J.H.

9769, Pte Peters, W.H.

10241, L.Cpl Pettifer, T.B., KiA 21.10.14

6078, Pte Phillips, R., unconfirmed

8469, Pte Pickering, F.

8491, Pte Pickering, F.

10105, Pte Pickering, J., missing 30.10.14 rejoined

4645, Pte Pike, J.H., PoW 30.10.14

5144, Pte Piller, P., unverified

4422, Pte Plaine (also P.H. Jackson), A., wounded 20.10.14

10721, Pte Platt, A., sick 15.10.14 rejoined, missing

30.10.14 rejoined
10709, Pte Pointon, S, PoW 30.10.14
7179, Pte Pope, W.H.C., KiA 30.10.14
10277, Bd Poulton, W., PoW 30.10.14
10813, Pte Powell, E., wounded 19.10.14
10923, Pte Powell, J., PoW n.d.
6225, L.Cpl Powell, R., PoW 20.10.14
8147, Cpl Poyner, G.
6447, Pte Poynton, A.
6885, Pte Prean, C., unverified
9742, Pte Preston, C.
10427, Pte Price, J., PoW 30.10.14
8057, Cpl Price, T.
10048, L.Cpl Price, T.
10440, Pte Price, T.J., PoW 20.10.14
5520, Pte Price, W., PoW 30.10.14
10439, Pte Priday, F.H., PoW 30.10.14
10080, Pte Pritchard, A., wounded 21.10.14
7093, L.Cpl Pritchard, C., KiA 30.10.14
6700, Sgt Pritchard, G.
4391, Pte Pritchard, H., KiA 21.10.14
10290, Pte Pritchard, J.
10534, Pte Pritchard, R.
10063, L.Cpl Prodger, J., KiA 21.10.14
6629, L.Sgt Provin, A., PoW 30.10.14
4969, Pte Pugh, R., MM, unverified
10793, L.Cpl Pullen, E.G., KiA 19.10.14
8251, Pte Pullinger, A.
7187, Pte Purcell, W.
8352, Pte Purcell, W.H., PoW 30.10.14
7840, Pte Quayle, W.H., PoW 20.10.14 died
8527, Cpl Quick, B., missing 20.10.14
10889, Pte Quill, D.J., KiA 21.10.14
10756, Pte Quiney, H., wounded 30.10.14
8744, Sgt Quinn, A., PoW 20.10.14
10773, Pte Quinn, J., KiA 21.10.14
10707, Pte Rail, D.S., wounded 24.10.14
9473, Sgt Randalls, W., PoW 30.10.14
10098, Pte Randalls, J., PoW 30.10.14
4521, Pte Rathbone, R., PoW 30.10.14 died
9682, Pte Ravenhill, E., wounded 20.10.14
8317, Pte Rea, M.
9954, Pte Redford, J., wounded 19.10.14
10331, Pte Redman, F., sick 15.10.14
8247, Pte Redmond, J.
9660, Pte Redrup, J., PoW 30.10.14
10000, Pte Rees, D.J., KiA 19.10.14
4930, Pte Rees, R., KiA 30.10.14
4548, Pte Rees, R.J., PoW 19.10.14
6775, Sgt Reeves, J., wounded 30.10.14
6326, Pte Reid, F.W.
3860, Pte Reid, R., wounded 20.10.14
5947, Pte Reynolds, F., unverified
10827, Pte Reynolds, H.G., PoW 30.10.14
10862, Pte Reynolds, J., PoW 19.10.14
7888, Cpl Reynolds, W., KiA 30.10.14
7700, Pte Rice, E.E.
7944, Pte Rice, G.
5334, Pte Richards, D., PoW 20.10.14

9302, Pte Richards, D.J., KiA 21.10.14
10371, Pte Richards, J., PoW 30.10.14
6093, Pte Richards, W.C.T.F., PoW 30.10.14
9364, Pte Richards, T.
10554, Pte Richardson, A., KiA 20.10.14
10338, Pte Richens, E., PoW 30.10.14
5158, Pte Riches, C., KiA 30.10.14
9758, L.Cpl Ricketts, H.J.
9843, Pte Ricketts, W., PoW 13.10.14
10852, Pte Rigby, A.T.
4699, Pte Rigby, H., PoW 19.10.14
7192, Pte Rigby, L, KiA 21.10.14
3839, Pte Riley, E.
5112, Pte Riley, E., unverified
6012, Pte Riley, G., PoW 30.10.14
6845, Pte Riley, J., unverified
8332, Pte Riley, T., PoW 20.10.14
10260, Pte Ritchings, F.W., wounded 19.10.14
7197, Pte Rivington, T.
9062, Pte Roberts, C.V., KiA 30.10.14
10028, Pte Roberts, E., wounded 19.10.14
11262, Pte Roberts, T., wounded 30.10.14
4676, Pte Roberts, G.R., KiA 30.10.14
6597, Cpl Roberts, H., wounded 24.10.14
10915, Pte Roberts, H., PoW 30.10.14
4996, Pte Roberts, J., unverified
10910, Pte Roberts, J.E.
10531, Pte Roberts, O., PoW 20.10.14
6787, Pte Roberts, W.
3965, Pte Roberts, W.M., unverified
5331, Sgt Roberts, W.O., PoW 20.10.14
4368, L.Cpl Roberts, W.O.
11196, Pte Robinson, H., wounded 30.10.14
10809, Pte Roblett, E.
7034, Pte Rogers, B.J.
9315, Cpl Rogers, C.F., KiA 30.10.14
9949, Cpl Rogers, E, PoW 19.10.14
10867, Pte Rogers, F.M.
8648, Pte Rogers, G., unconfirmed
11151, Pte Rogers, J., missing 30.10.14 rejoined
10930, Pte Rogers, W.E., PoW 20.10.14
7882, Pte Rohrer, R., DCM, MM
9764, Pte Rolph, E., PoW 21.10.14
10751, Pte Rose, D., KiA 21.10.14
8174, Pte Rose, H.W., KiA 30.10.14
10629, Pte Rose, J., PoW 20.10.14
8229, Pte Rose, S., wounded 19.10.14
8874, Pte Rowe, C., PoW 20.10.14
9501, Pte Rowe, C.
10536, Pte Rowlands, H, PoW 30.10.14 died
9373, Pte Rowley, G, PoW 21.10.14
10670, Pte Rumsey, C., wounded 21.10.14
9692, Pte Rushton, C.E.
10716, Pte Russell, E., PoW 30.10.14
5087, Pte Russell, G., unverified
10732, Pte Russell, H., PoW 20.10.14
6742, Pte Ryder, A.E.
8182, Pte Sadler, J.W.
10952, Pte Sainsbury, N., PoW 20.10.14

10128, Pte Sandford, G., PoW 30.10.14
10135, Pte Sanford, G.F., KiA 30.10.14
6583, Pte Sant, J., KiA 10.10.14
9845, Pte Satterthwaite, J., KiA 30.10.14
10875, Pte Saunders, C., PoW 30.10.14
10837, Pte Saunders, L.
10641, Pte Saxon, J., wounded 21.10.14
10505, Pte Saxon, R., PoW 20.10.14
10519, Pte Scott, E.
10787, Pte Scott, W.J., KiA 30.10.14
9636, Pte Scragg, W., KiA 30.10.14
10861, Pte Seldon, J., KiA 20.10.14
5541, L.Cpl Selley, A.V.
11020, Pte Sennar, R., KiA 21.10.14
5260, CSM, Shea, C.J., PoW 20.10.14
10583, Pte Shea, W., PoW 20.10.14
6811, Pte Sheldon, A.E., wounded 19.10.14
10984, Pte Shepherd, W.H., sick 23.10.14
6392, Cpl Sheppard, T., PoW 30.10.14
10043, Pte Sherlock, L., wounded 23.10.14
11163, Pte Simcocks, E.H.
11029, Pte Simmons, E., unverified
10920, Pte Simmons, G., wounded 19.10.14
4941, L.Cpl Simmons, V.
10119, Pte Simons (also Simmons), W., wounded 30.10.14
5322, Pte Skelly, W., MM
9870, Pte Slawson, G.
5905, L.Cpl Smale, F.
7651, Pte Smalley, T.
8301, Pte Smallwood, A.
9702, Pte Smallwood, E.W.
10178, L.Cpl Smith, A., KiA 21.10.14
6891, Sgt Smith, E.J., DCM, wounded 21.10.14
10989, Pte Smith, E., PoW 20.10.14
7224, CSM, Smith, F., DCM
8766, L.Cpl Smith, F.J., PoW 20.10.14
9841, Pte Smith, G.L., MM, wounded 26.10.14
10353, Pte Smith, H., PoW 30.10.14
11068, Pte Smith, J.C.
6745, L.Sgt Smith, R.G., PoW 20.10.14
9078, Pte Smith, R., PoW 30.10.14
6379, Pte Smith, T.
11346, Pte Smith, T.C., unverified
7827, Pte Smith, W.
8517, Pte Smith, W.T.
10269, Pte Smith, W.H., PoW 30.10.14
9841, Pte Smith, G.L.
10092, Pte Snape, B., wounded 21.10.14
10193, Sgt Snape, F., wounded 19.10.14
9942, Pte Snell, E., KiA 30.10.14
11070, Bn Soanes, A.E., missing 30.10.14 rejoined
9977, Cpl Sorg, F.
9184, Sgt Soughton, C.V., sick 20.10.14
10210, Sgt Spalding, H., DCM, AVM, wounded 19.10.14
9362, Pte Spalding, J.
8334, Pte Speakman, C.
8738, Dvr, Spear, G., wounded 24.10.14

9982, Pte Speed, J.E., KiA 21.10.14
10822, Pte Spellman, T., PoW 20.10.14
9914, Pte Spencer, L.
10474, Pte Spiers, B.
8261, Pte Spiers, J., wounded 30.10.14
5956, Pte Spilsbury, S.G., KiA 29.10.14
8474, Cpl Spooner, J., DCM, missing 20.10.14 rejoined
8055, Pte Spragg, F
10511, Pte Sprudd, J.T., PoW 20.10.14
6952, Pte Stanton, E.J., missing 30.10.14 rejoined
10229, Pte Stanton, G., wounded 21.10.14
11164, Pte Stanton, W.G.
9902, Pte Starkey, J.
7168, Pte Statham, W.
9883, Pte Steane, W., PoW 20.10.14
10391, Pte Stenner, A., PoW 20.10.14
9456, Sgt Stephens, A.J., MiD, wounded 22.10.14
6455, Cpl Stephens, J.
11439, Pte Stephens, W., PoW 30.10.14
6957, Pte Stephenson, W.
6853, L.Cpl Stevens, E
10484, Pte Stevenson, S., wounded 27.10.14
10280, Pte Stewart, C., KiA 21.10.14
10388, Pte Stokes, S.H., wounded 19.10.14
11026, Pte Stokes, W.
4715, Pte Stonehouse, T.
7731, Pte Stovold, W.M.
10207, Pte Stratford, F.
10607, Dvr, Stretch, E., wounded 20.10.14
8148, Pte Stubley, G.
10422, Pte Sturdy, J., wounded 24.10.14
8262, Pte Stych, T.
10704, Pte Sullivan, P., PoW 30.10.14
4016, CQMS, Sullivan, W., KiA 30.10.14
11047, Pte Sullock, W., PoW 30.10.14
8742, Pte Sussemilch, H., KIA 30.10.14
9707, L.Cpl Sutton, H.J., wounded and PoW 30.10.14
10352, Pte Sutton, J.
11589, L.Cpl Tabor, W.
9179, L.Cpl Tanner, H. unverified
6308, Pte Tay, W.H., PoW 30.10.14
6431, Cpl Taylor, A., sick 15.10.14 rejoined, missing 30.10.14 rejoined
6974, Pte Taylor, A., PoW 30.10.14
10897, Pte Taylor, E., wounded 28.10.14
9813, Pte Taylor, G., PoW 30.10.14
10072, Pte Taylor, G., wounded 19.10.14
6566, Pte Taylor, H.
5911, Pte Taylor, I., PoW 30.10.14
6816, Pte Taylor, J.
10212, Pte Taylor, R., wounded 19.10.14
10611, Pte Taylor, R.A., KiA 30.10.14
10749, Pte Taylor, S.
6895, Pte Taylor, W.
10198, Pte Taylor, W., wounded 21.10.14
10642, Pte Taylor, W., wounded 24.10.14
5989, Pte Tetley, C.H., PoW 21.01.14
10718, Pte Thomas, A.

10842, Pte Thomas, A.J., PoW 30.10.14

9483, Pte Thomas, A.S., KiA 30.10.14

7172, Pte Thomas, C.

5493, Pte Thomas, E.

10011, Bd, Thomas, E., wounded 21.10.14

10047, Pte Thomas, E., wounded 19.10.14

10017, Pte Thomas, G.

6369, Cpl Thomas, H, PoW 20.10.14

7132, Pte Thomas, H.

11166, Pte Thomas, H., KiA 30.10.14

6284, Pte Thomas, H.

10902, Pte Thomas, J., PoW 21.10.14

11138, Pte Thomas, J.A.J., missing 13.10.14 rejoined, missing 20.10.14 rejoined

11112, Pte Thomas, J.P., KiA 21.10.14

6340, Pte Thomas, O.

6893, Pte Thomas, W.

10056, Pte Thomas, W., PoW 20.10.14

10626, Pte Thomas, W., KiA 30.10.14

11108, Pte Thomas, W., PoW 30.10.14

10086, Pte Thomas, W.E.

6345, Pte Thomas, W.J., unverified

10684, Pte Tomlinson, J.S., wounded 29.10.14

5898, Pte Thompson, S.R., KiA 30.10.14

1029, A.Sgt Thorpe, A.

11194, Pte Thorpe, A., wounded 31.10.14, unverified

6983, Pte Thorpe, J.A.

6728, Pte Timbrell, E., PoW 20.10.14

10982, Pte Timms, T., KiA 21.10.14

7123, L.Sgt Tompson, A.A., Md'H

11009, Pte Tooey, E., PoW 20.10.14

5373, Pte Toohey, M.

5958, Pte Tracey, E.

9981, Pte Trimnell, J.A., wounded 15.10.14

10147, Pte Trott, G., PoW 30.10.14

10853, Pte Troughton, A., missing 30.10.14 rejoined; deserter executed 22.4.15

9716, Pte Trueman, W.

9978, Pte Tuckey, A.

6126, Pte Tuckwell, J.T., PoW 30.10.14

10964, Pte Tudor, R., wounded 25.10.14

6920, Pte Tunney, T., missing 30.10.14

6406, Pte Turner, H., MC, MM, MiD, wounded 30.10.14

10272, Pte Twist, F., wounded 19.10.14

9946, Pte Tyler, A.C., KiA 21.10.14

6009, Pte Tyrrell, W.J., PoW 20.10.14

4829, CQMS, Underwood, A., wounded 19.10.14

10495, Pte Urch, W., MM, PoW 20.10.14

11158, Pte Usher, W., PoW 30.10.14

6175, Pte Vaughan, A.

6463, Pte Vaughan, C., PoW 30.10.14

11055, Pte Vaughan, L.

10864, Pte Vaughan, T., wounded 19.10.14 rejoined

10284, L.Cpl Vernals, J., KiA 25.10.14

9737, Pte Vernals, L., PoW 19.10.14

5064, Pte Vickers, H., PoW 30.10.14

10341, L.Cpl Viles, A.F.

8095, Pte Waight, E., missing 10.10.14 rejoined, DoW 24.10.14

7661, Pte Waldon, H.

10055, Pte Waldron, W.

10992, Pte Walkden, J.

10951, Pte Walker, G., KiA 24.10.14

9351, Pte Walker, H.

9784, L.Cpl Walker, H.

10532, Pte Walker, H.J., PoW 20.10.14

9975, Pte Walker, J., PoW 20.10.14

10486, Pte Walker, L., PoW 30.10.14

10050, Pte Walton, G., wounded 22.10.14

9150, L.Cpl Warburton, S.

10733, Cpl Ward, A., commissioned King's Liverpool Regt 16.10.14, killed 20.10.14

11066, Pte Ward, C.

9095, Pte Ward, G.W.

4375, Pte , T.

10432, Pte Ware, J., KiA 21.10.14

8435, Sgt Waring, J.

9937, Pte Warner, F., wounded 20.10.14 rejoined, PoW 30.10.14

10163, Dvr, Warner, L., PoW n.d.

10403, L.Cpl Warren, F.L., KiA 30.10.14

10695, Pte Warry, F.B., PoW 20.10.14

11075, Pte Waters, E., PoW 20.10.14

4806, Pte Watkins, J., PoW 20.10.14

11005, Pte Watkins, S., DCM, wounded 19.10.14

6708, Cpl Watson, E., wounded 23.10.14

10204, Pte Watson, E., wounded 20.10.14

10701, Pte Watson, J., PoW 30.10.14

4073, Pte Watson, J.E.

10844, Pte Watson, W., PoW 30.10.14

9998, Pte Webb, J.

8520, Pte Webb, W.

10009, Pte Webb, W.

7611, Pte Webber, J., KiA 30.10.14

5422, Pte Webber, W., unverified

10980, Pte Webster, C.L.

4688, Pte Webster, F., wounded 20.10.14

5960, Pte Webster, J.A., unverified

11231, Pte Webster., J.

6823, Pte Wells, W., KiA 30.10.14

7259, Pte Wells, W.

6699, Pte Welsh, M., KiA 21.10.14

10049, Pte Welton, H.C., wounded 21.10.14

10807, Pte Weston, H.

6718, Pte Westwood, J.T., KiA 27.10.14

6101, Pte Wharred, T., unverified

5551, Pte Wheeler, F.R., PoW 20.10.14

10790, Pte Wheeler, H.H.

9915, Pte Wheldon, W., wounded 30.10.14

10677, Pte Whitbread, W., wounded 21.10.14

6502, Pte White, J.

8192, Pte White, R., PoW 20.10.14

9800, Pte White, T., PoW 20.10.14

7754, Pte Whittaker, D., unverified

8200, Pte Whittaker, J.S., wounded 23.10.14

10540, Cpl Whitters, J.T., wounded 20.10.14

10998, Pte Whitty, D.

6562, Pte Whyatt, A.W., PoW 21.10.14

6388, Pte Whyatt, H.

10791, Pte Wickett, J., wounded 29.10.14

7807, Pte Wilde, L., PoW 20.10.14

6239, Pte Wilkes, H.

6770, Pte Wilkins, W.E., sick 15.10.14

10122, Pte Wilkinson, G., wounded 20.10.14

11207, Pte Wilks, H., PoW 20.10.14

10378, Pte Willey, C.E., PoW 30.10.14

8252, Pte Williams, C., unverified

3980, Pte Williams, C., PoW 30.10.14

6381, Pte Williams, D., wounded 21.10.14

10191, Pte Williams, E.T., PoW 20.10.14

3500, Pte Williams, E.W., missing 30.10.14 rejoined

4474, Pte Williams, F.

3804, Pte Williams, G., unverified

6110, Pte Williams, H., unverified

6962, Pte Williams, H., PoW 13.10.14

7719, Pte Williams, H., missing 30.10.14 rejoined

6075, Pte Williams, H., PoW 30.10.14

10177, Pte Williams, H.H.

11228, Pte Williams, I., wounded 21.10.14

6905, Pte Williams, J., unverified

10661, Pte Williams, J.

10755, Pte Williams, J. , wounded 20.10.14

11048, Pte Williams, J., wounded 20.10.14

11121, Pte Williams, J., wounded 20.10.14

11295, Pte Williams, J., unverified

10072 (also 10972), Pte Williams, N., wounded 30.10.14

4742, Pte Williams, R., unverified

8238, Pte Williams, R., PoW 30.10.14

10570, Pte Williams, R., sick 15.10.14

11097, Pte Williams, R., wounded 20.10.14

11161, Pte Williams, R., PoW 13.10.14

6186, Pte Williams, R., PoW 30.10.14

3358, RSM Williams, S., commissioned 10.10.14, wounded 26.10.14

6164, Pte Williams, T.

5164, Pte Williams, T.W.

11786, Pte Williams, W.

5658, Pte Williams, W., sick 11.10.14

5040, Pte Williams, W.H.

10631, Pte Willis, S., PoW 30.10.14

10129, L.Cpl Wilshaw, T.

7721, Pte Wilson, D., PoW 30.10.14

9795, Pte Wilson, F.

4575, Pte Wilson, J.D., MM, wounded 20.10.14

10692, Pte Wilson, R., missing 20.10.14 rejoined

10525, L.Cpl Wilson, T.

7262, Pte Wilson, W. D.N., PoW 20.10.14

9001, Cpl Wiltshire, S., wounded 19.10.14

9607, Pte Winslow, E., PoW 30.10.14

10739, L.Cpl Winstanley, T.

10295, Pte Wood, H., PoW 20.10.14

8373, CSM, Wood, M., PoW 20.10.14

10821, Pte Wood, R., wounded 21.10.14

11212, Pte Woodcock, C., PoW 20.10.14

9956, Pte Woodford, J., KiA 30.10.14

10112, Pte Woodman, W.

11197, Pte Woods, J., PoW 30.10.14

10138, Pte Woodworth, G., PoW 20.10.14

8204, Pte Woolrich, W.

6557, Pte Worsford, W., KiA 19.10.14

10877, Pte Wrench, E., PoW n.d.

9056, Pte Wright, B.

10600, Cpl Wright, G., PoW 20.10.14

10070, Pte Wright, J.

10900, Pte Wyman, C., PoW 30.10.14

10892, Pte Wynne, P., PoW 20.10.14 died

9767, Pte Wyton, H.

9839, Pte Yapp, A., PoW n.d.

10164, Pte Yates, A., PoW 30.10.14

5889, Pte Yates, C., KiA 30.10.14

11152, Pte Yates, T., wounded 29.10.14

9907, Pte Yorath, W.H., wounded 19.10.14

9591, Pte Yorke, F., PoW n.d.

Bibliography

Published Works

BAYNES, John, *The Forgotten Victor*, Brassey's (UK) Ltd, 1989.

BECKETT, Ian F.W., 'Sir Thompson Capper', *Dictionary of National Biography*.

EDMONDS, Brig-Gen Sir James, *History of the Great War, Military Operations France and Belgium*, vol 1 (1933) and II (1925).

FRENCH, David, *Military Identities, the Regimental System, the British Army, and the British People, 1870–2000*, Oxford Univesity Press, 2005.

GRAVES, Robert, *Goodbye to All That*, Jonathan Cape, London, 1929.

HAMILTON, Lord Ernest, *The First Seven Divisions* (18th Edition), Hurst and Blackett, London, 1916.

HOLMES, Richard, *Sahib, The British Soldier in India*, Harper Collins, London, 2005.

HOWELL, Georgina, *Daughter of the Desert. The Remarkable Life of Gertrude Bell*, Macmillan, London, 2006.

JAMES, Lawrence, *Raj*, Little Brown Book Group Ltd, 1997 and Abacus 1998.

KEEGAN, J. and HOLMES, R., *A History of Men in Battle*, Hamish Hamilton, London, 1985.

KIPLING, Rudyard, *Kim*, Macmillan, 1901.

LEHMAN, J.H., *All Sir Garnet, a Life of Field-Marshall Lord Wolseley 1833–1913*, Cape, 1964.

PETRE, Loraine F., EWART, Wilfred & LOWTHER, Maj-Gen Sir Cecil, *Scots Guards in the Great War*, 1925.

POLLOCK, John, *Kitchener*, Robinsons UK, 1998.

RAMSBOTTOM, Roy, *Marching as to War*, Privately Printed, copyright Roy F. Ramsbottom, 2000.

RICHARDS, Frank, *Old Soldiers Never Die*, Krijnen & Langley, 2004.

RICHARDS, Frank, *Old Soldier Sahib*, The Naval & Military Press, 2003.

ROYAL FUSILIERS CHRONICLE, May 1953. Obituary of Lt-Gen Sir S. Lawford, KCB.

SIMPSON, K., Capper and the Offensive Spirit, RUSI *Journal*, vol. 118, No 2, 1973

SIXSMITH, E.K.G., *Douglas Haig*, Weidenfeld & Nicolson, London, 1976.

SKAIFE, E.O., *A Short History of the Royal Welch Fusiliers*, Gale and Pol Aldershot, 1913.

TOUCHMAN, Barbara W., *A Distant Mirror*, Macmillan, London, 1979.

WARD, C.H. Dudley, *Regimental Records of the Royal Welch Fusiliers,* vols II, III & IV, Cary & McCance, London, 1928.

Papers, etc

India Office Library

      H 725 393 (our page 14)

King's College, London

      Kerrich, Brig W. A. F., Papers in Liddell Hart Centre for Military Archives, National Archives

      WO95/709, Official History of the War, IV Corps Report, 14 November 1914

      22 Infantry Brigade War Diaries, October 1914

      1 RWF War Diaries, October 1914

Index